Western Rivermen, 1763–1861

MICHAEL ALLEN

Western Rivermen, 1763–1861

Ohio and Mississippi Boatmen and the Myth of the Alligator Horse

LOUISIANA STATE UNIVERSITY PRESS
Baton Rouge and London

Designer: Laura Roubique Gleason
Typeface: Bembo
Typesetter: G&S Typesetters, Inc.
Printer and binder: Thomson-Shore, Inc.

Library of Congress Cataloging-in-Publication Data

Allen, Michael, 1950–
    Western rivermen, 1763–1861 : Ohio and Mississippi boatmen and the
myth of the alligator horse / Michael Allen.
        p.   cm.
    Includes bibliographical references.
    ISBN 0-8071-1561-4 (alk. paper)
        1. River life—Ohio River—History.   2. River life—Mississippi
River—History.   3. Boatmen—Ohio River—History.   4. Boatmen—
Mississippi River—History.   5. Ohio River—Social life and customs.
6. Mississippi River—Social life and customs.   7. Folklore—Ohio
River.   8. Folklore—Mississippi River.   I. Title.
F517.A39   1990
977'.02—dc20   90-5860
                                                                                      CIP

The author is grateful to the editors of the following publications for permission to
use material that originally appeared in these articles: "The Lower Mississippi in 1803:
The Travelers' View," *Missouri Historical Review,* LXXVIII (April, 1983), 253–71;
"Reminiscences of a Common Boatman," *Gateway Heritage: Quarterly Journal of the
Missouri Historical Society,* V (Fall, 1984), 36–49; and "Sired by a Hurricane: Mike
Fink, Western Boatmen, and the Myth of the Alligator Horse," *Arizona and the West,*
XXVII (Autumn, 1985), 237–52.

Louisiana Paperback Edition, 1994
03 02 01 00 99 98 97 96 95 94   5 4 3 2 1

For my family

Contents

Illustrations

Acknowledgments

I would like to thank the many people who have contributed to this book or have in other ways assisted me in my career. If I omit a name or two, which I probably will, I ask the forgiveness of those I have neglected.

At Central Washington State College in Ellensburg, Zolton Kramar and Gordon Warren offered encouragement and support far outweighing my abilities, and Larry Lowther was especially generous with his time and counsel. At the University of Montana in Missoula, Paul Gordon Lauren, Robert O. Lindsay, H. Duane Hampton, the late K. Ross Toole, Robert Dozier, Dave Emmons, and the redoubtable Harry Fritz demonstrated to me that sound scholarship and exciting teaching go hand in hand. Dr. Dan Adams and Joan Adams generously provided me a spacious and friendly place to live and work. Greg and Mary Lenihan, Chris Huck, and John Westenberg became close friends during my four years in the northern Rockies.

During my stint working on towboats, from 1978 to 1981, I met many rivermen for whom I will always feel great respect and friendship: Captain Dave Miller, with whom I spent many fine hours talking river lore in the wheelhouse on the Lower Mississippi; Captain Roy Pharr, who helped me get my first cooking job on a line boat; and all my friends at Valley Towing in Memphis and National Marine in St. Louis still on the river. If you read this, fellows, please know that although I am on the bank now, a little bit of me will always be out there with you.

At the University of Washington in Seattle, Alfred Runte, Lewis O. Saum, Richard Johnson, Jon Bridgman, John Griffith, David Pinkney, John Findlay, Aldon Bell, and Robert E. Burke offered much help and encouragement. Terrence and Marjorie Cole and Frank and Lisa Mighetto all became good friends, and Gary Lawrence, Pat Totten, Lloyd Nickel, Dave and Teresa Forbes, and Bob Burke helped bring a bit of eastern Washington State to that rusty megalopolis. So did my friend and patron Dr. Bob Dunnington.

Scholars in related fields throughout America have read chapters and offered advice and encouragement. I especially thank Robert C. Carriker, Erik F. Haites, Bruce J. Dinges, Mary K. Dains, Donald F. Carmony, John Harkins, Wanda Corn, Walter Blair, John Jakle, Gary M. Walton, Richard E. Oglesby, Sir Jack D. L. Holmes, Ray Swick, and Herbert L. Roush, Sr.

During the course of my research I worked in more than forty libraries and archival depositories in sixteen states. I can never fully acknowledge the generous assistance and counsel given me by the scholars affiliated with these institutions, and regret that I can mention only a few of them here. Many thanks to the staffs of the following: Suzzalo Library, University of Washington, Seattle—especially Ruth Kirk and Anna McCausland; Central Washington University Library; Fort Union National Historic Site, Williston, North Dakota (Paul Hedren); Joint Collection, State Historical Society of Missouri, Columbia (Randy Roberts); Campus Martius, the Museum of the Northwest Territory, Ohio Historical Society, Marietta; Blennerhassett Island Historical Commission, Parkersburg, West Virginia; Old Courthouse Museum, Vicksburg, Mississippi (Gordon Cotton and Mrs. Blanche Terry); Special Collections, Loyola University, New Orleans (Mark Flynn); Indiana Historical Society; and the Indiana Division, Indiana State Library (Mary Belle Birch).

Several institutions provided financial support during the course of my education. The G.I. Bill, the Washington State Vietnam Veterans Bonus, and the Washington State tuition freeze for Vietnam veterans enabled me to pursue scholarly endeavors for eleven years, and I am very grateful to the taxpayers for this. The Washington Pioneer Daughters, Seattle Chapter No. 1, awarded me their annual scholarship in 1983, and the Newberry Library granted a fellowship in the summer of 1984. The Institute for Humane Studies awarded a Claude R. Lambe Graduate Fellowship in 1984–1985, and I received an Arthur A. Denny Graduate Fellowship from the University of Washington in 1985. I revised this manuscript for publication as a Huntington Library Fellow during the summer of 1986, and with a Tennessee Technological University release-time grant the following year. Throughout my academic career the Phi Alpha Theta International History Honorary Society has encouraged my work with prize awards for papers and, most recently, with the John Pine Memorial Award.

The editors of the *Missouri Historical Review, Arizona and the West* (now *Journal of the Southwest*), and *Gateway Heritage: Quarterly Journal of the Missouri Historical Society,* allowed me to use portions of copyrighted materials that originally appeared in their publications. Louise Scott typed the manuscript of this book, and I thank her for her friendly, professional assistance. Larry Whiteaker, Calvin Dickinson, George Webb, B. F. Jones, and my colleagues at Tennessee Technological University were very supportive of my work. Margaret Dalrymple and John Easterly of the Louisiana State University Press and Gerry Anders, my editor, have expended great efforts to bring the book to publication, and it is far better thanks to them.

I especially acknowledge and thank two men who have been instrumental in my education as a historian and writer. At the University of Montana, Harry W. Fritz first introduced me to the craft of the professional historian and helped to form in me an abiding love for the history of the early American republic. At the University of Washington, W. J. Rorabaugh paid me the respect of treating me as a fellow historian from the first day we met. His knowledge of the Jacksonian era in particular and of eighteenth- and nineteenth-century Americana in general, his keen analytical bent, and his love of a good story have proved invaluable in the writing of this book.

Throughout all of this my sister, Theresa, my parents, Betty and Stewart Allen, and my wife, Mary Hanneman, have borne up admirably under the burden of having a professional student and river rat for a brother, a son, and a husband. They have assisted me in many, many ways—not the least of which was Mary's proofreading of the manuscript for this book. To Mom, Dad, Theresa, Mary, and our boy, Jim, to all of whom I am forever loyal and grateful, this work is dedicated with love.

Western Rivermen, 1763–1861

Preface

In this trade, the riverman was the fundamental factor. Only by means of his brawn and his genius for navigation could these innumerable tons of flour, tobacco, and bacon have been kept from rotting on the shores. Yet the man himself remains a legend grotesque and mysterious, one of the shadowy figures of a time when history was being made too rapidly to be written. . . . It is therefore only dimly, as through a mist, that we can see the two lines of polemen pass from prow to stern on the narrow running-board of a keel boat, lifting and setting their poles to the cry of steersman or captain.
—Archer B. Hulbert

It is a long way from the semiarid foothills of eastern Washington State, where I was born and raised, to the green and humid valleys of the Ohio and Mississippi rivers. Yet historians are drawn to certain regions and topics of research for strong personal reasons, and my interest in the trans-Appalachian West is no exception. I have always been deeply interested in whatever I could find to read and learn about that region. As a child I was fascinated by Walt Disney's stories of Davy Crockett and Mike Fink. By my high school and college years, this fascination had expanded to include the Mississippi Valley frontier in general and had taken on an academic bent. A parallel interest in revolutionary-era politics led to an M.A. thesis on the Federalists and the West. During this time, I made three cross-country tours and spent many months wandering up and down the Ohio and Mississippi valleys on foot, by bus, and in automobiles. Even so, many portions of the Lower Mississippi remained inaccessible, and I decided one day that the only way to really learn about the river was to work on it. In 1977 I moved to Greenville, Mississippi, and began three years as a towboat cook, deckhand, and tankerman on the Upper and Lower Mississippi, Illinois, St. Croix, Ouachita, and Arkansas rivers and the Gulf of Mexico. With a firmer grasp on the ecology, geography, and climate of the Ohio and Mississippi valleys, I returned to graduate school at the University of Washington in Seattle in September, 1981.

For about five years, I had wanted to write a social history of non-steam rivermen—flatboatmen, keelboatmen, and raftsmen—but no one had given me much encouragement. The usual comment was that there simply were not enough firsthand sources to support such a history. This objection reflects a longstanding problem in researching the early boatmen: most of them were illiterate and left no direct recollections of their experiences. For this reason, the few secondary works written about boatmen have always relied heavily on a small number of firsthand accounts that exist in printed form, combining these with folkloric and literary materials, of which there is an abundance. Unfortunately, although folklore tells us many things, it does not always reveal much about the flesh-and-blood boatmen who worked on the Ohio and Mississippi during the late eighteenth and early nineteenth centuries. As a result, those historians who have tried to write about boatmen have met with limited success.[1]

It was Richard E. Oglesby who first touched upon the manner in which a history of the western boatmen should be written. In his article "The Western Boatman: Half Horse, Half Myth," he argued that although the boatmen were early American folk heroes, their actual lifestyle could not possibly have been that which is depicted in folklore and literature. On the other hand, the myth itself, accurate or not, was vitally important to nineteenth-century Americans. Therefore, a definitive history of the western boatmen must contain separate but parallel discussions of both the mythological boatmen and the real ones. This type of approach has been pioneered in studies of other American topics by Henry Nash Smith and John William Ward.[2]

I have attempted just such a juxtaposition of reality and myth. This book presents a social and cultural portrait of the western boatmen: a social history of the actual rivermen, based on traditional historical sources, and a complementary treatment of the mythological boatmen, based on American literary, cultural, and folkloric sources. I had no problem in finding the latter: hundreds of literary and folkloric sources

1. Leland D. Baldwin, *The Keelboat Age on Western Waters* (Pittsburgh, 1941); Archer B. Hulbert, *Waterways of Westward Expansion: The Ohio River and Its Tributaries* (Cleveland, 1903); Hulbert, *The Paths of Inland Commerce* (New Haven, 1921).

2. Richard E. Oglesby, "The Western Boatman: Half Horse, Half Myth," in John Francis McDermott (ed.), *Travelers on the Western Waters* (Urbana, 1970), 252–66; Henry Nash Smith, *Virgin Land: The American West as Symbol and Myth* (New York, 1950); John William Ward, *Andrew Jackson, Symbol for an Age* (New York, 1953).

document the mythical, "half-horse, half-alligator" boatmen. But what of the anticipated paucity of firsthand accounts by actual boatmen? I found more than *eighty* such accounts, ranging from a short letter to a four-volume memoir. All were written by men who actually worked on flatboats, keels, and rafts during the late eighteenth and early nineteenth centuries. Although most of these accounts are the work of articulate—and therefore "atypical"—rivermen, they nevertheless provide a view of the boatmen's lifestyle never before uncovered. In addition to these firsthand accounts, I have relied on sources such as travelers' journals, autobiographies of river-town residents, newspaper reports, court records, wharf and customs lists, government documents, and Spanish colonial records.

This book focuses almost entirely on Ohio and Mississippi river flatboatmen, keelboatmen, and raftsmen. The reader will find little or nothing about steamboatmen, canal boatmen, ferryboatmen, woodboatmen, falls pilots, or soldier-boatmen. Further, although tens of thousands of pioneer settlers navigated flatboats down the Ohio and Mississippi, I have been concerned mainly with professional rivermen who navigated boats for a wage. And since nearly 90 percent of the nonsteam river commerce was carried by flatboats—not keelboats or rafts—this book is largely about flatboatmen.

Many tributary streams figured importantly in American boating, but I have concentrated on the Ohio–Lower Mississippi trunk line because that was the major artery of commerce. Although the Upper Mississippi, Allegheny, Monongahela, Scioto, Miami, Cumberland, Tennessee, Wabash, St. Croix, Minnesota, Illinois, Arkansas, Yazoo, Red, and many other rivers are inherently part of this subject, I have found it necessary to treat them in a somewhat cursory manner. This is also the case with the Missouri River, the upper portions of which I have purposely neglected except in discussing Mike Fink's death in the Montana country in 1823. As any riverman—even today—would attest, the Missouri is a very special river. I avoided the fur-trading boatmen of the Upper Missouri partly because they were not at all like their Ohio-Mississippi counterparts and partly because so much already has been written about them.

This book is divided chronologically. The first four chapters center on the years from 1763 to 1823, the era of what I call the "preindustrial" (*i.e.,* presteamboat) boatmen. The later chapters deal largely with the heyday of the flatboatmen of the Steamboat Age—roughly, 1823 to 1861. One of the two major theses of this work is that the rivermen of these different eras were themselves strikingly different— that the rise of the steamboat and the advent of "civilized" society in the Ohio and Mississippi valleys brought about great changes in the lifestyle and character of the western boatmen. I chose the year 1823 as a division point for several reasons, one of which is that Mike Fink died in a shooting fray at the mouth of the Yellowstone River in that year, and his death provides a symbolic conclusion for the first era of riverboating. Less symbolically, by 1823 steamboats were regularly plying the western rivers and had begun to change forever the world of the presteam rivermen. Any such division has an arbitrary element, of course, and overlaps inevitably occur: rivermen did not magically transform themselves in one brief moment. But I am satisfied that 1823 can serve usefully as a boundary marker between widely divergent eras on the river.

The second principal thesis of this work does not relate to the real boatmen of the 1763–1861 period at all, but to the mythical, "half-horse, half-alligator" boatmen of folklore and literature. The Alligator Horse was a key figure in the mythology of Jacksonian and pre–Civil War America, but Americans' fantasies about the romantic existence of the hard-drinking, gambling, fighting, promiscuous Ohio and Mississippi boatmen tell us a good deal more about the mythologizers than the mythologized. Although the early, presteam rivermen were undeniably pretty rough characters, there was absolutely nothing romantic about their lonely, dangerous lives. The civilized boatmen of the steamboat era had even less in common with the wild, mythical Alligator Horse. What is important in all this, it seems to me, is that it was during the turbulent Jacksonian era that Americans first began to romanticize frontier boatmen into Alligator Horses. The Alligator Horse was a Jacksonian wish-fulfillment—the yearning of an industrializing people for what they perceived to be a simpler frontier past. The Alligator Horse is thus an important key in studying the complex psyche of pre–Civil War America.

More than eighty years ago, Archer B. Hulbert of Marietta College wrote that a scarcity of sources precluded a study of the western boatmen. It would be extremely difficult, Hulbert wrote, for anyone to write "an authentic history" of these men: "The traditions on the subject are, even at this recent period, so vague and contradictory that it would be difficult to procure anything like reliable or authentic data in regard to them. No story in which the bargemen figured is too improbable to be narrated, nor can one determine what particular person is the hero of an incident which is in turn laid at the door of each distinguished member of the whole fraternity."[3]

When Hulbert wrote this passage he was absolutely correct. The historical societies and libraries of the Ohio and Mississippi valleys had not yet progressed to the point where a researcher could successfully pursue the lost, inarticulate breed of the western boatmen, and so the real boatmen remained hidden behind the mask of the Alligator Horse. Today this is no longer the case. Many sources exist that provide a good view of the common boatmen who worked the western rivers from 1763 to 1861. At the same time, this improved understanding of the actual boatmen makes it possible to see the symbolic importance of the mythical Alligator Horse in a clearer light. In the pages that follow, I will examine both the common boatman and his alter ego, the Alligator Horse. I hope that the reader will enjoy puzzling over the paradox presented by these two Americans as much as I have enjoyed trying to put the pieces together.

3. Hulbert, *Waterways of Westward Expansion,* 162–63.

ONE

Alligator Horses

Whoo-oop! I'm the old original iron-jawed, brass-mounted, copper-bellied corpse-maker from the wilds of Arkansaw! Look at me! I'm the man they call Sudden Death and General Desolation! Sired by a hurricane, dam'd by an earthquake, half-brother to the cholera, nearly related to the smallpox on the mother's side! . . . Cast your eye on me gentlemen! And lay low and hold your breath, for I'm 'bout to turn myself loose!

—The raftsman's challenge
Mark Twain, *Life on the Mississippi*

In 1956, millions of American children met the keelboatman Mike Fink in the Walt Disney television series and movie *Davy Crockett and the River Pirates*. Starring Fess Parker as Davy and Jeff York as Mike, *River Pirates* revolved around the protagonists' keelboat race down the Ohio and Mississippi and their battle with the eponymous river pirates of Cave-In Rock. This was standard Disney: two competing, rugged-individualist frontiersmen and lots of swashbuckling adventures, all with the mighty Mississippi as a background. The addition of several "bad guys" and a couple of Hollywood Indians gave the audience pure grade B fare of the 1950s. Although not exactly great film art, *Davy Crockett and the River Pirates* did possess considerable importance for students of American folklore and literature: Disney reintroduced Americans to Mike Fink, the king of the western boatmen.[1]

Mike Fink and his "half-horse, half-alligator" brethren of the Ohio and Mississippi rivers had evolved earlier, in a nineteenth-century folklore and literature that was rich and powerful. Jacksonian Americans found in Mike Fink and the Alligator Horse a mythological figure through whom they could live out their fantasies and dreams. Their

1. Leonard Maltin, *The Disney Films* (New York, 1973), 134–37; Richard Schickel, *The Disney Version: The Life, Times, Art, and Commerce of Walt Disney* (New York, 1969); Margaret J. King, "The Davy Crockett Craze: A Case Study in Popular Culture" (Ph.D. dissertation, University of Hawaii, 1976).

choice of folk heroes is most interesting. In a complicated, volatile, industrial age, Americans began to celebrate their simpler frontier past, and Mike Fink and the Alligator Horse came to symbolize that vanishing America. Thus, this literature of the Alligator Horse tells us a great deal about the Jacksonian society in which it arose and flourished.

The printed Mike Fink stories were rooted in the folk tales of the frontiersmen of the Ohio and Mississippi valleys and the Old Southwest. Tall tales were a favorite entertainment for the pioneer folk of the trans-Appalachian West. Whenever frontiersmen met—in taverns, inns, or general stores, around campfires, or in their cabins at night—they entertained one another with these stories. In the mid-nineteenth century, western newspaper and magazine journalists began to use these folk tales as the basis for humorous articles. The newspaper humorists relied heavily on frontier settings, local color, and the slang of the Old Southwest. Their pieces were always short, anecdotal, and not really suited for sustained development as in a novel. Like the frontiersmen who originally had told them, the stories were a little rough around the edges.[2]

These journalists depicted the western boatmen as "half horse, half alligator"—a folk phrase commonly used to describe the wild and woolly frontiersman of the trans-Appalachian West. Although the exact origins of the phrases "half horse, half alligator" and "Alligator Horse" are obscure, by the early nineteenth century westerners were using them to denote the great strength and amphibious attributes of the Mississippi Valley hunters, Indian fighters, soldiers, rivermen, and

2. For oral anecdotes and frontier humor, see Bernard DeVoto, *Mark Twain's America* (Boston, 1967), 91–93, 240–68, and Constance Rourke, *American Humor: A Study of the National Character* (New York, 1959), 48, 66, *passim*. For newspaper humor, see DeVoto, *Mark Twain's America*, Appendix A, "Newspaper Humor of the Southwestern Frontier." Note that I refer to this literature as "folk-based" and not as folklore per se. Although some of the newspaper and magazine stories I will discuss qualify as folklore, not all can be traced accurately to the "folk." The methodology for separating folklore from "fakelore" is discussed fully in Richard M. Dorson, *American Folklore and the Historian* (Chicago, 1971), 25, 189–99. Dorson considers the Mike Fink stories to be *based* on authentic folkloric sources—see his *America in Legend: Folklore from the Colonial Period to the Present* (New York, 1973), 80–81—but not all of the Fink stories or other stories about boatmen qualify as folklore. In general, I have not been as concerned in finding a pure folklore about boatmen as in finding one that has folkloric *origins* and that was popular among the "folk" who read it in nineteenth-century newspapers and journals.

squatters. As early as 1808, Christian Schultz, Thomas Bolling Robertson, and other travelers used this language in describing boatmen on the Lower Mississippi. In "The Hunters of Kentucky" (*ca.* 1820), songwriter Samuel Woodworth described Andrew Jackson's western militiamen at the Battle of New Orleans, saying "ev'ry man was half a horse, and half an alligator." Soon the newspaper humorists enshrined the Alligator Horse in tales of Davy Crockett (alias "Nimrod Wildfire") and other "Kentuckians." These characters were hard-drinking, straight-shooting, lawless, crude, and ferocious fighters, but, in some mysterious way, compelling and romantic. Yet some Alligator Horses were even more compelling than others. Caste distinctions existed, it seems, even among westerners. At the top of the heap were the western boatmen.[3]

Jacksonian Americans were fascinated by the western boatmen. The Ohio and Mississippi flatboatmen, keelboatmen, and lumber raftsmen enjoyed a status and mystique in pre–Civil War America very comparable to that possessed today by truck drivers, loggers, railroadmen, and rodeo cowboys. They became folk heroes to frontier squatters and Eastern shopkeepers alike. Their lifestyle lent itself easily to romanticization: nostalgic Americans conjured up images of a brawny, red-shirted, sun-browned, rough-and-ready race of super-frontiersmen plying the western waters. Whether they were poling their keels against the rushing current of the Mississippi, fighting Indians and river pirates, playing outrageous practical jokes on one another, or drinking, gambling, and fighting in Natchez and New Orleans beer sties, the western boatmen grew larger than life in popular literature.[4]

3. Christian Schultz, *Travels on an Inland Voyage . . . in the Years 1807 and 1808* (2 vols.; 1810; rpr. Ridgewood, N.J., 1968), II, 145–46; Thomas Bolling Robertson, "Journal of a Tour Down the Ohio and Mississippi," (MS in Thomas Bolling Robertson Papers, Louisiana and Lower Mississippi Valley Collections, Louisiana State University Libraries, Baton Rouge); Mitford Mathews, *A Dictionary of Americanisms: On Historical Principles* (Chicago, 1951), 767; John William Ward, *Andrew Jackson, Symbol for an Age* (New York, 1968), 13–16, 216–18; Rourke, *American Humor,* 35, 53–55; Stuart W. Hyde, "The Ring-Tailed Roarer in American Drama," *Southern Folklore Quarterly,* XIX (September, 1955), 171–78; Dickson A. Bruce, *Violence and Culture in the Antebellum South* (Austin, Tex., 1979), 212–32; Michael A. Lofaro (ed.), *Davy Crockett: The Man, the Legend, the Legacy, 1786–1986* (Knoxville, 1985), *passim.*

4. DeVoto, *Mark Twain's America,* 58–60; Rourke, *American Humor,* 42; Kent L. Steckmesser, *The Western Hero in History and Legend* (Norman, Okla., 1965), 3–12.

The king of the mythical boatmen was a real frontiersman named Mike Fink. Born near Fort Pitt around 1770, Mike grew up in the forests of western Pennsylvania, where he was known as a fine marksman and scout. When Pittsburgh became a bit too "civilized," Mike Fink took his first trip on a keelboat. He worked on the Ohio and Mississippi as a keelboatman for about twenty years and eventually became a patroon and captain of his own boats. Mike acquired a reputation as a mighty boatman, drinker, fighter, lover, and all-round "ring-tailed roarer," and throughout the Ohio and Mississippi valleys settlers told stories about him. Having helped in conquering two frontiers, Mike eventually moved on to a third—the fur-trapping ground of the Upper Missouri, where he was to die a violent death in 1823.[5]

Fink's reputation continued to grow after his death. He remained a popular subject for folk tales that circulated among frontiersmen and settlers throughout the trans-Appalachian West. These stories began to find their way into print as early as the 1820s, as humorists capitalized on a growing fascination with the vanishing Mississippi Valley frontier. By the middle of the nineteenth century, it was impossible to find the real Mike Fink through the mist of folklore and mythology that enshrouded him, and a considerable body of folk-based literature had evolved from his legend.[6]

During the Jacksonian era, scores of stories about Mike appeared in newspapers and magazines. One full-length novel, a play, and a newspaper serial further recounted the feats of the King of the Keelboatmen. Morgan Neville, Thomas Bangs Thorpe, Ben Casseday, Timothy Flint, John S. Robb, Joseph M. Field, Charles Cist, Menra Hopewell, and the editors of the popular Davy Crockett almanacs all achieved some notoriety as purveyors of the Fink tales. The first published

---

5. Walter Blair and Franklin J. Meine, *Mike Fink, King of the Mississippi Keelboatmen* (1933; rpr. Westport, Conn., 1971). There is no biography of Mike Fink based on non-literary sources because there are only a few such sources. Blair and Meine's biography is a groundbreaking and thoroughly readable book but is by no means a purely historical work. The "real" Mike Fink is discussed again in Chapter 4.

6. Dorson, *America in Legend*, 80–81. The classic collection of Mike Fink tales, Walter Blair and Franklin J. Meine (eds.), *Half Horse, Half Alligator: The Growth of the Mike Fink Legend* (Chicago, 1956), contains every important tale in the Fink genre and a complete bibliography of all the existing printed Fink stories. In my discussion of the Mike Fink stories I have used the original sources whenever possible and otherwise relied on the reprinted versions in Blair and Meine.

story—Neville's "The Last of the Boatmen"—appeared in the *Western Souvenir* in 1828 and established patterns adhered to by Flint in 1829 and the many other writers who followed. Between 1841 and 1861— the exact period of time during which the flatboat was being driven slowly out of existence by the steamboat—nearly fifty of these nostalgic tales appeared in a variety of sources. They began to fade after the Civil War, but Mike Fink stories have persisted in one form or another to the present day.[7]

With the exception of the novel and the newspaper serial, the Mike Fink stories were all short and anecdotal, much in keeping with the oral tradition from which they evolved. In these tales Mike left reality far behind him and took on a stature of heroic proportions. He became a "Mississippi River–god" or, as DeVoto observed, "the boatman apotheosized." Throughout the Jacksonian era authors embellished the tales of this "Western lion"—tales that most often revolved around Mike's rough tricks and practical jokes, his marksmanship, and his drinking and fighting.[8]

Mike Fink loved a good joke, or so his early "biographers" would have us believe. Ben Casseday, in his *History of Louisville,* reported that Mike always warned listeners that he "told his jokes on purpose to be laughed at, and no man should 'make light' of them!" According to Casseday, Mike was especially adept at practical jokes. When summoned to appear in court in Louisville, for instance, he refused to leave his boat. Instead, Mike loaded the keel onto a wagon and ordered his crew to pole it up Third Street to the courthouse, for "he felt at home nowhere but in his boat and among his men." In another Casseday tale, Mike devises a clever means of obtaining a mutton dinner for his crew. Spying a healthy band of sheep, he forces "scotch snuff" up their noses. Summoning the concerned farmer, he informs him gravely that his wheezing sheep have the "black murrain" and will

7. Blair and Meine (eds.), *Half Horse, Half Alligator,* 14–20; John T. Flanagan, "Morgan Neville, Early Western Chronicler," *Western Pennsylvania Historical Magazine,* XXI (December, 1938), 255–266. Catherine Albanese argues that the Crockett almanacs were read by a huge national audience: "Davy Crockett and the Wild Man; or, The Metaphysics of the Long Durée," in Lofaro (ed.), *Davy Crockett,* 82 n. 6.

8. Blair and Meine (eds.), *Half Horse, Half Alligator,* 30, 48; Emerson Bennett, *Mike Fink: A Legend of the Ohio* (1852; rpr. Upper Saddle River, N.J., 1970); Joseph M. Field, "Mike Fink: The Last of the Boatmen," in Blair and Meine (eds.), *Half Horse, Half Alligator,* 93–142; Rourke, *American Humor,* 54; DeVoto, *Mark Twain's America,* 60.

have to be shot and disposed of immediately. Mike not only filches the sheep but is paid "a couple gallons of old Peach brandy" for services rendered. But Mike's recreations sometimes backfired on him. While taking a peaceful swim, he was attacked by Deacon Smith's bull. Mounting the back of the bull to confound the beast, Mike upset a hornets' nest and found himself hanging on for dear life to the bull's tail. "He drug me over every brier and stump in the field, until I war sweatin' and bleedin' like a fat bear with a pack o' hounds at his heels. And my name ain't Mike Fink if that old critter's tail and I didn't blow out sometimes at a dead level with the varmint's back!"[9]

Like his fellow Alligator Horse Davy Crockett, Mike Fink was a crack shot.[10] Back home at Fort Pitt, he supposedly was forbidden to enter shooting competitions because his superior skill "spoilt" the fun. In return for not competing, he received the hide and tallow of the prize beef, which he then sold for whiskey to "treat the crowd." In "The Last of the Boatmen," Morgan Neville tells of Mike's shooting an Indian just as the native fells a deer with his own rifle. As only one shot has sounded, Fink claims both the slain Indian and the venison. In Thomas Bangs Thorpe's "The Disgraced Scalp-Lock," Mike shoots the Indian Proud Joe's sacred ponytail from his head on a dare, only to become the object of Joe's hatred and revenge. But Mike's shooting prowess and racism were not vented only on Indians. John S. Robb's "Trimming a Darky's Heel" tells the story (perhaps true) of how Fink severed "the hinder part of [a] nigger's heel . . . so he kin wear a decent boot!" Arrested and brought to trial for his "prank," Mike demands the judge compensate him "fur trimmin' the heel of one of your town niggers." In the end, he sends "a handful of silver to the darky to extract the pain from his shortened heel."[11]

9. Ben Casseday, *The History of Louisville, from Its Earliest Settlement to the Year 1852* (Louisville, 1852), 73–75, 77–79; Scroggins [pseud.], "Deacon Smith's Bull; or, Mike Fink in a Tight Place," *Spirit of the Times*, March 22, 1851, p. 52. See D. M. McKeithan, "Bull Rides Described by 'Scroggins,' G. W. Harris, and Mark Twain," *Southern Folklore Quarterly*, XVII (December, 1953), 241–43.

10. Mike Fink and David Crockett lived at approximately the same time, but probably never met. Nevertheless, the two have been linked together in fiction from the time of the Crockett almanacs to the 1956 Walt Disney movie.

11. Casseday, *History of Louisville*, 73, 76–77; Thomas Bangs Thorpe, "The Disgraced Scalp-Lock; or, Incidents on Western Waters," *Spirit of the Times*, July 16, 1842, p. 230; John S. Robb ["Solitaire"], "Trimming a Darky's Heel," *Spirit of the Times*, February 13, 1837, p. 605.

The "shooting of the cup," however, was Mike's signature piece. In this Americanized version of William Tell's apple feat, Mike demonstrated his prowess as a marksman by shooting a whiskey cup off the head of a fellow boatman. Morgan Neville introduced the tale and it was retold literally hundreds of times. In Neville's story, Mike makes a bet as his younger brother paces off thirty yards, places a tin whiskey cup on his head, and shouts: "Blaze away, Mike! And let's have the quart." Fink draws a bead and the "sharp crack of the rifle" resounds. The cup is sent flying amid the cheers of the crowd and a round of toasts. Mike once again has proved his skill and loyalty. This story was told in a variety of ways, often with Mike having the cup shot off his own head. Purveyors of Daniel Boone and Davy Crockett stories attributed the feat to their own heroes. Eventually, the "shooting of the cup" served as a melodramatic plot line to explain Mike's death at the mouth of the Yellowstone in 1823.[12]

When Mike was not stealing sheep or shooting the heels off Negroes' feet or cups from the heads of his fellow Alligator Horses, he usually could be found drinking and fighting. Fink's capacity as a drinker was enormous, and one storyteller recounted that "he could drink a gallon [of whiskey] in twenty-four hours without its effect being perceptible in his language or demeanour." A newspaper humorist who wrote under the pseudonym of "Lige Shattuck" noted that Mike once "eat a whole buffalo robe" in order to "dress his insides up in suthin' that 'ud stand the cussed pizen." Having drunk a gallon or two of "flem-cutter" or "anti-fogmatic," Mike felt he "must fight something, or . . . catch the dry rot." Finding an opponent was no problem in the Wild West, but Mike Fink's fights had to be conducted with a certain frontier decorum. Like all the boatmen, Mike prefaced his battles with a boast, establishing the fact (in case anyone doubted it) that he was indeed half-horse, half-alligator. In Emerson Bennett's 1848 novel *Mike Fink: A Legend of the Ohio,* Mike announces: "Hurray for me, you scapegoats! I'm a land-screamer—I'm a water-dog—I'm a snapping tur[t]le—I can lick five times my own weight in wild-cats. I can use up Injens by the cord. I can swallow niggers whole, raw, or cooked. I can out-run, out-dance, out-jump, out-dive, out-drink,

12. I used Morgan Neville's original version of the "shooting of the cup" in Blair and Meine (eds.), *Half Horse, Half Alligator,* 48–49. See also Casseday, *History of Louisville,* 80, and Bennett, *Mike Fink, a Legend of the Ohio,* 21–22.

out-holler, and out-lick any white thing in the shape o' human that's ever put foot within two thousand miles o' the big Massassip." [13]

In Bennett's novel, the King of the Keelboatmen fights his way from one end of the Ohio to the other, eventually thrashing the dreaded river pirates at Cave-In Rock. In other sketches, Mike defeats black, red, and white men alike. Yet interestingly, his most famous fights were the ones he lost. Mike Fink's virility seems to have suffered a decline in the later nineteenth century. Victorianism triumphed briefly as a series of authors had their heroes thrash the toughest of the Alligator Horses. The Reverend Peter Cartwright whipped Mike, as did the "kicking sheriff of Westport" in 1883. But Mike's most devastating defeat came in 1874 at the hands of the flatboatman Jack Pierce. Pierce, a champion "ram butter," butted his forehead against Mike's "three times in quick succession, the blows sounding like a maul upon timber." Fink eventually recovered from the beating, but Jack Pierce "had gained the victory." [14]

Rough jokes, drinking, fighting, and shooting the cup, then, were the hallmarks of the Fink stories. In telling the story of Mike's mysterious death at the mouth of the Yellowstone River, authors drew upon all of these characteristics. Aside from the fact that Fink shot a man named Carpenter and was then shot by a man named Talbot, historians have no solid documentation of the facts surrounding Mike's actual death. The Fink stories provide a score of different versions, many of them widely disparate. Most are set at the confluence of the Missouri and Yellowstone rivers and depict Mike quarreling with Carpenter, for various reasons. To "make up" and prove his friendship,

13. Casseday, *History of Louisville,* 73; Lige Shattuck [pseud.], "Lige Shattuck's Reminiscences," *Spirit of the Times,* April 15, 1848, p. 89; "Crockett Almanack Stories," in Blair and Meine (eds.), *Half Horse, Half Alligator,* 66; Thorpe, "Disgraced Scalp-Lock," 230; Bennett, *Mike Fink: A Legend of the Ohio,* 28. For the supposedly "heroic" origins of Alligator Horse's boast, see Dorothy Dondore, "Big Talk! The Flyting, the Gabe, and the Frontier Boast," *American Speech,* VI (October, 1930), 44–55. I believe Americans took the intensely serious boasts of a Thor or a Roland, turned them upside down, and made them a big joke.

14. Bennett, *Mike Fink: A Legend of the Ohio,* 95–100; "Rev. Peter Cartwright, Jocose Preacher," in Blair and Meine (eds.), *Half Horse, Half Alligator,* 216–219; Frank Triplett, "Mike Fink—Last of the Flatboatmen," in Blair and Meine (eds.), *Half Horse, Half Alligator,* 238–40; Menra Hopewell, *Legends of the Missouri and the Mississippi* (1862–63; rpr. London, 1874), 396–97. Many of Hopewell's tales originally appeared in the St. Louis *Missouri Republican.*

Mike decides to shoot the cup. Carpenter is suspicious, but agrees. Mike puts a bullet in his head. Talbot, seeking revenge, shoots Fink and soon after accidentally drowns.[15]

Joseph M. Field, a St. Louis newspaperman and humorist, was the first author to create a consistent plot line leading to Mike's death. In "Mike Fink: The Last of the Boatmen," an 1847 serial in the St. Louis *Reveille,* Field spins a farfetched yet interesting tale. Young Mike, it seems, is disappointed in love when his sweetheart, Mary Benson, is forced by her father to marry the villainous Taggart. Heartbroken, Mike takes to keelboating to try to forget. Taggart becomes a river pirate and is defeated (but not captured) by Mike, who finds Mary dying, holding her and Taggart's newborn son in her arms. Mike raises the boy. After twenty years, the two head west together to trap beaver on the Upper Missouri. They have a falling out at Fort William Henry, but agree to make up by shooting the cup. Both men have been drinking heavily, and the boy's shot grazes Mike's skull. Enraged, Fink shouts "I taught you to shoot better than that!" and kills the young man. The crowd is stunned, and Mike is filled with remorse. Before long he is shot by Talbot—who, it is revealed, is really Taggart. Mike's final words are: "I didn't mean to kill my boy!"[16]

As the Fink genre flourished in the mid-nineteenth century, it spawned other Alligator Horse boatmen in a variety of printed forms. Newspapers and magazines published tales by writers who continued to rely upon the Alligator Horse in their tales. For example, Thomas Bangs Thorpe's *The Mysteries of the Backwoods, The Hive of the Bee-Hunter,* and a quasi-historical article of 1855, "Remembrances of the Mississippi," all feature flatboatmen and raftsmen. During this same time, Big Jim Girty emerged as a potential literary rival to Mike Fink and even borrowed some of Mike's tricks. In "Jim Girty's Beef Story," Jim and his flatboat crew steal a fat beef cow from a farmer by use of trickery, just as Mike and his crew had stolen sheep a few years earlier.[17]

15. For varying accounts of Mike Fink's death, see Blair and Meine (eds.), *Half Horse, Half Alligator,* 257–77.

16. Field, "Mike Fink: The Last of the Boatmen," *ibid.,* 93–142. Field's story is actually much more complicated: After losing Mary Benson, Mike takes up with a woman named Mira Hodgkiss, whom he eventually jilts. Mira then marries Talbot (who is really Taggart), and the couple have a daughter. The quarrel between Mike and his "boy" erupts when the boy (who is Taggart's son) falls in love with his own half-sister.

17. Thomas Bangs Thorpe, *The Mysteries of the Backwoods* (Philadelphia, 1846); *The*

Many other printed tales evince popular perceptions of boatmen as clever, democratic, swashbuckling Alligator Horses. For example, a journalist for the *Western Citizen* wrote in 1846 of a Kentucky flatboat captain caught "tearing up" Donaldsonville, Louisiana. Arrested and fined heavily on the basis of the testimony of a humorless Frenchman, the Kentuckian reluctantly pays the judge the last of his pocket money. Then, although insolvent except for his cargo, the boatman asks how much the fine would be for beating up the Frenchman who had "squealed" on him. When the magistrate informs him the fine for assault is fifty dollars, the Alligator Horse matter-of-factly asks him if the court will accept payment in corn.[18]

In the Huntsville, Alabama, *Southern Advocate,* there appeared another tale of a "first rate 'Mississippi snag' from Kentucky." Spying a "powdered French dandy" riding horseback in New Orleans, the boatman feigns deference, sarcastically pulling off his hat and swinging it so low that the Frenchman's horse bolts and throws its rider into a monstrous mud puddle. Rising and returning the boatman's salute, the mud-soaked dandy opines, "Saire, you are a little too d——nd polite, saire." Ohioan James Hall told a story of a group of equally democratic boatmen who went ashore to explore an abandoned village and discovered a whipping post, long out of use. According to Hall, the rivermen were so appalled at the vile object and thoughts of its former function that they pulled it up from the ground and threw it into the river, remarking "them that wanted to be whipped *mought* go after it."[19]

One recurrent published tale concerns an incident that supposedly took place in the 1790s. A keelboat captain named Thomas Carter takes a job carrying Louis Philippe (the dispossessed French Bourbon), his brothers, and their entourage down the Ohio and Mississippi

---

Hive of the Bee-Hunter (New York, 1854), 126–34, 266–70; "Remembrances of the Mississippi," *Harper's New Monthly Magazine,* XII (December, 1855), 25–41; Milton Rickels, *Thomas Bangs Thorpe: Humorist of the Old Southwest* (Baton Rouge, 1962). "Jim Girty's Beef Story" is in Thomas D. Clark, *The Rampaging Frontier: Manners and Humors of Pioneer Days in the South and Middle West* (Indianapolis, 1939), 95–97. For an Upper Cumberland version, see William Lynwood Montell, *Don't Go Up Kettle Creek: Verbal Legacy of the Upper Cumberland* (Knoxville, 1983), 110 n. 88.

18. Clark, *Rampaging Frontier,* 79–80.

19. Huntsville *Southern Advocate* quoted in Arthur K. Moore, *The Frontier Mind* (New York, 1963), 117; James Hall, *Letters from the West* (1828; rpr. Gainesville, Fla., 1967), 89–90.

to New Orleans. The trip begins smoothly enough, but because of low water their keelboat begins to run aground regularly. Undeterred, Captain Carter acts in a most democratic fashion. Upon running aground, he simply yells down into the cabin hold: "You Kings down there! Show yourselves, and help us three-spots pull off this bar!" The French royal family—so this apocryphal story goes—bounds up the stairs, jumps into the river, and sets to work. Royal birth, it seems, was of no relevance whatsoever to the Alligator Horse.[20]

While the printed page provided an important stage for the Alligator Horse, it was not his only cultural outlet. He appeared upon the real stage as well, in a number of dramas and theatrical productions. Mike Fink was portrayed as a minor character in Alphonso Wetmore's St. Louis production of *The Pedlar* in 1821—while the real Mike Fink was still alive. The most successful portrayal of an Alligator Horse was James Hackett's turn as Nimrod Wildfire (a thinly disguised Davy Crockett) in J. Kirk Paulding's 1831 production of *The Lion of the West*. James Rees capitalized upon this popularity when he wrote and starred in his own drama, *Mike Fink, the Last Boatman of the Mississippi*.[21]

Popular songsters proved equally enthusiastic in celebrating the Alligator Horse. Blackfaced minstrels often included boatmen's folk songs and other tunes about rivermen in their traveling shows. Minstrel Dan Emmett composed the most famous of all river songs, "The Boatmen's Dance," in 1843 (see Appendix) at the height of the Alligator Horse craze, and the lyrics of the song reflect the mythology of rivermen that had become so popular.

> De boatmen dance, de boatmen sing,
> De boatmen up to ebry ting,
> An when de boatman gets on shore,
> He spends his cash an works for more.
>
> Den dance de boatmen dance,
> O dance de boatmen dance,
> O dance all night till broad daylight,
> An go home wid de gals in de morning.

---

20. The version of this story quoted here can be found in Leland D. Baldwin, *The Keelboat Age on Western Waters* (Pittsburgh, 1941), 72.

21. Dorson, *America in Legend*, 91; Walter Blair to Michael Allen, June 20, 1986, in possession of Michael Allen; Walter J. Meserve, *Heralds of Promise: The Drama of the*

Other minstrels copied Emmett's themes in "Down the River" and "Jolly Raftsman's Life for Me." E. P. Christy, one of America's greatest minstrels, included several river songs in his 1851 collection, *Plantation Melodies*. A typical example is "The Moon Is Up—Row, Boatmen Row!" In it, Christy's Minstrels sang:

> The moon is up, the hour is late,
> And down the stream, the black girls wait
> Our tardy coming, to prolong
> The dance, the revel, and the song
> Row, boatmen row![22]

Painters and illustrators did not delay in tapping the powerful imagery of the western boatmen. The rivermen proved perfect subjects for the new school of "local color" painters that flourished during the Jacksonian era. Charles Wimar, William Baldwin, George Catlin, Karl Bodmer, Thomas Doney, Henry Lewis, and, later, the Currier and Ives lithograph artists all painted river scenes for a large national audience. Nearly all of them painted the western boatmen in a characteristic pose, lounging aboard a southbound flat, lazily enjoying the spring weather and the fiddling and dancing of their fellow rivermen. Such paintings tend to be strikingly similar, and for good reason: the artists all borrowed from a contemporary painter, the greatest river portraitist of all, George Caleb Bingham of Missouri.[23]

Raised on the Lower Missouri frontier in the 1820s and 1830s, George Caleb Bingham rose from obscurity to become one of the greatest American local-color painters. While earning a reputation as the Missouri Artist, he simultaneously cultivated a clientele and following among more urbane Easterners hungry for rural color and

American People During the Age of Jackson, 1829–1849 (Westport, Conn., 1986), 109–11, 146.

22. Robert C. Toll, *Blacking Up: The Minstrel Show in Nineteenth-Century America* (New York, 1984), 8–9, 40–41; "De Boatmen's Dance: An Original Banjo Melody by Old Dan D. Emmett," in Bessie Mae Stanchfield Papers, Minnesota Historical Society, St. Paul; A. W. Mason, "Down the River," in Carl Carmer, *Songs of the Rivers of America* (New York, 1942), 157; "Jolly Raftsman's Life for Me," in H. Dichter, *Handbook of American Sheet Music* (Philadelphia, 1951), no. 1614; E. P. Christy, *Christy's Plantation Melodies, Number 4* (Philadelphia, 1851), 37.

23. Joshua C. Taylor, *America as Art* (Washington, D.C., 1976), 37–95; John Francis McDermott, "Jolly Flatboatmen: Bingham and His Imitators," *Antiques,* LXXIII (March, 1958), 267–69.

scenes from the Wild West. Bingham painted landscapes, fur trappers, Indians, soldiers, common folk, and politicians (he was himself a prominent Whig leader) in his genre works. Among his most beloved paintings are his river series. Bingham painted over a dozen significant works using boatmen and riverboating as a motif, including *Boatmen on the Missouri* (1846), *Raftsmen Playing Cards* (1847), *The Wood Boat* (1850), *Mississippi Boatmen* (1850), *In a Quandary* (1851), and *Raftsmen By Night* (1854). The most famous and enduring (and romanticized) of these works are those in his *Jolly Flatboatmen* series.[24]

Bingham painted *The Jolly Flatboatmen* in 1846. He enjoyed so much success from the work that he eventually painted three other versions, in 1848, 1857, and 1878. The last has been lost, but the three extant *Jolly Flatboatmen* paintings are all similar in content, depicting a flatboat crew during a relaxed moment on a clear, beautiful day: the men are making music with a fiddle and a frying pan while one of them dances a merry jig atop the flatboat's deck. The *Jolly Flatboatmen in Port,* the most spectacular of the series, adds a supporting cast of landsmen to admire the jaunty Alligator Horses. The effect is striking, the colors are bold, and the flatboatmen emerge as working-class folk heroes.[25]

Bingham (and a score of imitators) complemented the efforts of newspaper and journal humorists, playwrights, and minstrel song-writers in pushing the Alligator Horse to the center stage of American popular culture. Bingham's nostalgic paintings of the frontier struck a responsive chord in the bustling, modernizing America of the 1840s. The Missouri Artist depicted a vanishing way of life that appeared simple and good. In this sense, his popular works tell us much more about the antebellum Americans who embraced his depiction of *The Jolly Flatboatmen* than about the boatmen themselves.[26]

Meanwhile, on the literary front, the waning of the Jacksonian era brought a slow decline in the popularity of the Alligator Horse boat-

24. John Francis McDermott, *George Caleb Bingham: River Portraitist* (Norman, Okla., 1959); E. Maurice Bloch, *George Caleb Bingham: The Evolution of an Artist* (Berkeley, 1967); Albert Christ-Janier, *George Caleb Bingham: Frontier Painter of Missouri* (New York, 1975).

25. McDermott, *Bingham: River Portraitist,* 55–57, 92, 124–25; Bloch, *Bingham: The Evolution of an Artist,* 86–88, 92.

26. McDermott, *Bingham: River Portraitist,* 193.

man. During the Civil War and postbellum years, many American authors began to embrace the new frontier folk heroes of the trans-Mississippi West: cowboys, trappers, frontier soldiers, and scouts. There were some important exceptions to this rule, however. John Henton Carter of St. Louis worked as a riverman for twenty years before launching a postbellum journalistic career and authoring a number of novels, poems, and collected works that centered on river life. Using the *nom de plume* "Commodore Rollingpin" (a reference to his steamboat galley experiences), Carter painted exciting descriptions of Ohio and Mississippi steamboatmen, flatboatmen, and raftsmen in *The Log of Commodore Rollingpin* (1874), *The Man at the Wheel* (1898), *Mississippi Argonauts* (1903), and the autobiographical novel *Thomas Rutherton* (1890).[27]

A more famous steamboatman-turned-writer was Samuel Langhorne Clemens, better known as Mark Twain. Like Carter, Twain was very interested in Alligator Horses. Flatboatmen and lumber raftsmen often visited his hometown of Hannibal, Missouri, when he was growing up in the 1840s and early 1850s, and the newspapers for which he apprenticed featured numerous tall tales that starred the western boatmen. This anecdotal style of storytelling became Twain's trademark, and raftsmen played an important role in a projected chapter of *The Adventures of Huckleberry Finn* that appeared in *Life on the Mississippi*. In this scene, Huck secretly hitches a ride on a lumber raft and witnesses the boatmen in their mythical pose. They are drunk, and two are preparing to fight. But first comes the boast: "Whoo-oop! bow your neck and spread, for the kingdom of sorrow's a-coming! Hold me down to earth, for I feel my powers a-working! whoo-oop! I'm a child of sin, *don't* let me get a start! . . . I'm the man with a petrified heart and biler-iron bowels! The massacre of isolated communities is the pastime of my idle moments, the destruction of nationalities the serious business of my life! . . . Whoo-oop! bow your neck and spread, for the Pet Child of Calamity's a-coming!" Twain, how-

27. James V. Swift, "From Pantry to Pen: The Saga of Commodore Rollingpin," *Missouri Historical Society Bulletin,* XXIV (1968), 113–21; John Henton Carter, *The Log of Commodore Rollingpin: His Adventures Afloat and Ashore* (New York, 1874); *The Man at the Wheel* (St. Louis, 1898); *Mississippi Argonauts* (New York, 1903); *Thomas Rutherton* (New York, 1890). *Thomas Rutherton* is Carter's fictionalized account of his first flatboat trip to New Orleans. He made the journey as a teenager in the 1840s.

ever, puts an interesting twist on his battle of the boatmen. As it turns out, both are craven cowards. They exchange boasts in order to stall for time, until "a little black-whiskered chap" thrashes them both and forces them to confess that "they was sneaks and cowards and not fit to eat with a dog or drink with a nigger." Then the Alligator Horses become fast friends again as their raft continues on its course down the mighty Mississippi.[28]

The printed folktale flowered in the work of Mark Twain. As DeVoto has shown, Twain was a frontier storyteller who stayed true to the folklore from which his writing evolved. His work was also a farewell performance for the Alligator Horse, for in the late nineteenth century Mike Fink and his fellow boatmen fell on hard times. A good example of the decline is a story mentioned earlier—"Jack Pierce, the Hunter, the Flatboatman, and the Ram Butter," in Menra Hopewell's *Legends of the Missouri and the Mississippi*. Hopewell portrays the western boatmen as ignorant, depraved, and vicious men, all too fond of "vulgarity, swearing, carousing," and fighting. Jack Pierce's "one angel-virtue which lent a somewhat redeeming grace to his character," the writer declares, "was his love of his mother." Pierce already has licked Mike Fink and Negro Jim (a tough New Orleans boatman) when he meets his match in St. Louis: his head is crushed in a butting contest with a huge ram, and he dies a horrible death. Although Fink and Negro Jim happen to be in town at the time, they do not even have the decency to mourn for their fallen adversary. Instead, they declare "their gratification of the catastrophe which was so mourned by the others" and give "full license to their depraved appetites." The whole story is odd, the ram included: it seems the beast belonged to Auguste Chouteau, the founder of St. Louis.[29]

The mythical boatmen rebounded eventually from their treatment by Hopewell and others, but they never regained quite the same stature and veneration they had enjoyed during Mike Fink's heyday in the nostalgic Jacksonian era. Boatmen appear occasionally in the Beadle "Dime Novels" and in the works of a few late-nineteenth-century and

---

28. Samuel Clemens [Mark Twain], *Life on the Mississippi* (1874; rpr. New York, 1960), 12–13. The "missing" raftsmen chapter has been reinserted in the new edition of *Adventures of Huckleberry Finn* (Berkeley, 1985), 119–38.

29. DeVoto, *Mark Twain's America*, 94; Hopewell, *Legends of the Missouri*, 376, 379, 394–95, 401–402.

twentieth-century writers. In John G. Neihardt's splendidly peculiar *The Song of Three Friends* (1919), the story of Fink, Carpenter, and Talbot is told in epic poetry, and Mike's death at the hands of Talbot takes on ancient and heroic proportions. Mike and his fellow Alligator Horses appear again in Julian Rayford's solid 1951 novel, *Child of the Snapping Turtle: Mike Fink.* Based upon considerable research in folkloric and historical sources, Rayford's work is the most successful treatment of the Mike Fink legends in sustained fiction. Yet Mike Fink's great moment in the twentieth century came on celluloid, not on the printed page. It was Walt Disney who made Mike Fink once again a viable figure in American folk culture.[30]

In 1955, Disney's *Davy Crockett, King of the Wild Frontier* played to huge television and movie audiences. This success surprised the Disney writers themselves: unwittingly, they had killed off their hero at the Alamo after only one movie. Undaunted by his untimely death, Davy found himself resurrected the following year in *Davy Crockett and the River Pirates.* New words to his then-famous theme song introduced Mike Fink, "King of the River." In the movie, Mike is Davy's perfect nemesis. "What a small world," says Fink to Davy, adding, "You're about a foot shorter than you ought to be." Retorts Davy's buddy, Georgie Russell (Buddy Ebsen), "He's still growing." The first half of the movie portrays Mike as a villain. In a keelboat race against Crockett's boat, the *Gullywhumper,* Fink and his crew cheat shamelessly. The rival crews' battle reaches slapstick proportions. By winning, Davy gains Mike's respect. The two men become fast friends and team up to lick the Ohio River pirates at Cave-In Rock. Thus, Disney's portrayal of Fink is classic Alligator Horse: Mike is a rascal, yet in the end he is worthy of respect and adulation. Even as second fiddle to Davy Crockett, Mike Fink had returned triumphantly to the American scene.[31]

In all of the stories of Mike Fink and the western boatmen, from

30. Metta Victoria Victor, *Alice Wilde, the Raftsman's Daughter: A Forest Romance* (New York, 1861); H. K. Shackleford, *Flat Boat Fred; or, The Young Swamp Hunter of Louisiana* (New York, 1890); George Cary Eggleston, *The Last of the Flatboats* (Boston, 1900); John G. Niehardt, *The Song of Three Friends* (New York, 1919); Julian Lee Rayford, *Child of the Snapping Turtle: Mike Fink* (New York, 1951).

31. Schickel, *The Disney Version,* viii; Margaret J. King, "The Recycled Hero: Walt Disney's Davy Crockett," in Lofaro (ed.), *Davy Crockett,* 137–58; Maltin, *Disney Films,* 122–24, 134–36.

Morgan Neville's tale of 1828 to Walt Disney's movie of 1956, the myth of the Alligator Horse shows a certain consistency. The western boatman of literature was a hard-working, hard-drinking, fighting, promiscuous, romantic drifter, sailing the Ohio and Mississippi in search of adventure. Using the Alligator Horse as a leading character, early American writers took frontier folk tales and transferred them from an oral tradition to the written page. From this beginning a crude native literature emerged, eventually maturing in the earthy prose of Mark Twain. The Mike Fink stories never really transcended the folk idiom, however, and those writers who attempted to do so (such as Field and Bennett) found themselves in foreign territory. Yet the chroniclers of the western boatmen did make one great contribution to the refinement of American literature. Through their use of frontier violence, local dialect and setting, and indigenous humor, they built one of the first vehicles for realism in American literature.[32]

On the other hand, just how real *were* the western boatmen of literature? Surely the story of Mike Fink's crew poling its keel up Third Street in Louisville does not tell us much about the actual lives of the rivermen. Ordinarily, one would turn to the works of historians for answers. But the historiography of the boatmen is especially ambiguous, for the simple reason that most flatboatmen, keelboatmen, and raftsmen were illiterate and left no diaries or letters. Confronted with a paucity of evidence, historians have plowed ahead and written about the boatmen anyway. The results have been interesting: like the humorists, painters, songwriters, and film makers, historians in general have adopted the legends surrounding the Alligator Horse.

Amateur historians in the mid-nineteenth century embraced the Alligator Horse and used his antics to enliven their portrayals of life in the trans-Appalachian West. Ben Casseday, in his *History of Louisville,* expressed a few reservations yet went on to use the Mike Fink stories as "the only example here given to illustrate the character of the western bargemen." Mark Twain, in a widely read, quasi-historical *Atlantic Monthly* article, "Old Times on the Mississippi," did not bat an eye as he depicted the "rough and hardy . . . brave . . . elephantinely jolly, foul-witted, profane" Alligator Horses as actual historical figures in Mississippi Valley society. Earlier, Thomas Bangs Thorpe had

---

32. DeVoto, *Mark Twain's America,* 93–94, 98–99, *passim;* DeVoto, "Bully Boy," *Saturday Review of Literature,* April 8, 1933, p. 523; Blair and Meine (eds.), *Half Horse, Half Alligator,* 31–34.

pursued an identical theme in his "historical" *Harper's Magazine* article "Remembrances of the Mississippi."[33]

Similar portrayals appeared in more scholarly works. In *The Winning of the West,* Theodore Roosevelt described the Ohio and Mississippi river flatboatmen as "rude, powerful, and lawless" men, famous for their drinking bouts and fighting sprees. America's most famous early professional historian, Frederick Jackson Turner, concurred. Turner was too good a prose stylist to leave untapped the romantic potential of the Alligator Horse. In *The Rise of the New West,* he dramatically concluded: "Flatboatmen, raftsmen, and deck-hands constituted a turbulent and reckless population, living on the country through which they passed, fighting and drinking in true 'half-horse, half-alligator' style."[34]

More recent historians have offered less flamboyant but still romanticized views of the boatmen. Solon and Elizabeth Buck, in *The Planting of Civilization in Western Pennsylvania,* qualified their portrayal of these "unruly, hard-drinking . . . exemplars of frontier hardihood," as did R. Carlyle Buley in *The Old Northwest.* Relying heavily on literary and folkloric sources, Thomas D. Clark concluded in *The Rampaging Frontier* that "underneath their uncouth habits and their eternal drinking and fighting," the boatmen "were endowed with a spirit of defiance which made them noble pioneers." In *The Paths of Inland Commerce,* Archer B. Hulbert stressed the lack of dependable sources with which to assess the boatmen but could not resist the temptation to wax romantic in discussing them. Leland D. Baldwin, in his groundbreaking *Keelboat Age on Western Waters,* attempted to rise above the mythology and base his account entirely upon traditional historical sources. And yet, in a book devoted entirely to flatboating and keelboating, Baldwin could gather only enough material for one chapter on the boatmen themselves.[35]

33. Casseday, *History of Louisville,* 73; Samuel Clemens [Mark Twain], "Old Times on the Mississippi," *Atlantic Monthly,* LV (January–June, 1875); Thorpe, "Remembrances of the Mississippi," 29–30. Twain's *Atlantic Monthly* pieces later were used as the first twenty chapters of *Life on the Mississippi.* The quotation given here is on p. 10 of that book.

34. Theodore Roosevelt, *The Winning of the West* (6 vols.; New York, 1906), VI, 147, 149; Frederick Jackson Turner, *The Rise of the New West, 1819–1829* (New York, 1906), 102–103.

35. Solon J. Buck and Elizabeth H. Buck, *The Planting of Civilization in Western Pennsylvania* (Pittsburgh, 1939), 246; Roscoe Carlyle Buley, *The Old Northwest: Pioneer Period, 1815–1840* (Indianapolis, 1950), 437–44; Clark, *Rampaging Frontier,* 95, 81;

Since the publication of Baldwin's book, historians have made more progress in their quest for the western boatmen. Economic historians Louis C. Hunter, Harry N. Scheiber, James Mak, Erik F. Haites, and Gary M. Walton have compiled vital data concerning the economics of antebellum river commerce and flatboating. Their work is complemented by Richard E. Oglesby's excellent essay measuring the extent to which boatmen lived up to their reputations as heavy-drinking, hard-fighting, river rowdies. Not surprisingly, Oglesby finds that although some may have fitted the Alligator Horse mold, "the boatmen as a class were a more or less normal frontier group . . . generally just normal, rough human beings going through a difficult and dangerous business." Yet in the long run, Oglesby concludes, the "real" boatman is not nearly so important in American history as his mythical Alligator Horse counterpart. It is the romanticized boatman who has captured the imagination of Americans and become an integral part of our folklore. Therefore, a study of the boatmen in literature may tell us more about the mythologizers than the mythologized.[36]

Thus, the question of why Jacksonian Americans idealized the boatmen becomes important. If Richard M. Dorson is correct in arguing that the vital folklore and legends of a given period in American history reflect the main concerns, values, and tensions of that period, then what conclusions can be drawn from the reign of the Alligator Horse? Several come to mind. The Mike Fink stories peaked in the years from 1828 to 1861, an exuberant and unsettling epoch that saw the rise of industrialism, Jacksonian democracy, and sectional discord. Americans were excited about the future, but they often cast nostalgic—and sometimes troubled—glances over their shoulders at the vanishing agricultural society of their youth. Politically, this nostalgia manifested itself in the election and deification of western patriots like

---

Archer B. Hulbert, *The Paths of Inland Commerce* (New Haven, 1921), 70–71, 211–16; Baldwin, *Keelboat Age,* 85–115. Baldwin's chapter on the boatmen is actually based on literary and folkloric as well as traditional historical sources.

36. Louis C. Hunter, *Steamboats on Western Rivers: An Economic and Technological History* (Cambridge, Mass., 1949); Harry N. Scheiber, "The Ohio-Mississippi Flatboat Trade: Some Reconsiderations," in David M. Ellis (ed.), *The Frontier in American Development: Essays in Honor of Paul Wallace Gates* (Ithaca, 1970), 277–98; Erik F. Haites, James Mak, and Gary M. Walton, *Western River Transportation* (Baltimore, 1975); Richard E. Oglesby, "The Western Boatman: Half Horse, Half Myth," in John Francis McDermott (ed.), *Travelers on the Western Waters* (Urbana, 1970), 252–66.

Jackson and Harrison—Old Hickory and Old Tip. Culturally, the nostalgia focused on the frontier exploits of Daniel Boone, Davy Crockett, Leatherstocking, and the Alligator Horse. Keelboats still moved up the tributaries, and flatboats plied the main rivers in great numbers well into the 1850s, but in this Steamboat Age the flat-boatmen, keelboatmen, and raftsmen represented a vanishing frontier society. The western boatman—sailing his flat serenely down the Mississippi, drifting with the current, raising hell in Natchez, and then floating on to the glamorous Crescent City of New Orleans—seemed to be a free spirit. In an increasingly complicated era, the rugged boat-man stood apart: independent, uncomplicated, and unconquerable.[37]

Jacksonian shopkeepers, mechanics, and farmers reveled in the antics of the Alligator Horse, and Alligator Horse boatmen proliferated in American popular culture. Boatmen's songs were sung on stage and in minstrel shows. George Caleb Bingham's fanciful portraits of *The Jolly Flatboatmen* swept the nation and were imitated by scores of art-ists. Mike Fink gained fame in more than fifty newspaper and maga-zine stories. Significantly, nearly all of these tales portrayed Mike as "The Last of the Boatmen"—the last of a vanishing race of frontiers-men. In Thorpe's "Disgraced Scalp-Lock," Mike laments: "What's the use of improvements? When did cutting down trees make deer more plenty? . . . Who ever found wild buffalo or a brave Indian in a city? Where's the fun, the frolicking, the fighting? Gone! Gone!" Like Leatherstocking, Mike stands alone in the face of civilization's "improvements" and refuses to budge. In a gripping scene in Field's "Mike Fink: The Last of the Boatmen," Mike challenges the symbol of the progress he so despises. Spying a steamboat moving upstream, Mike refuses to steer his keel out of the center of the channel. The steamboat approaches, loudly blowing its horn while

> a thousand orders, cries, and execrations arose. . . . Fink, the enor-mous sweep firm within his grasp, stood erect at the stern of the keel, and came terribly down upon them! A crash that hurled the chimneys overboard, that tore the larboard guard and bow to pieces, and sent

37. Dorson, *America in Legend,* xiv; Marvin Meyers, *The Jacksonian Persuasion: Politics and Belief* (Stanford, 1957); Henry Nash Smith, *Virgin Land: The American West as Symbol and Myth* (New York, 1950); Ward, *Andrew Jackson.* The best contemporary ac-count of the Jacksonian epoch is Alexis de Tocqueville, *Democracy in America* (2 vols.; 1835; rpr. New York, 1945).

water pouring through an hundred gaping seams, told the weight and force of the collision. . . . "Keel's sinking, Mike!" roared a dozen throats around that grim steersman. With a savage smile, he was directing the bow towards the bank, but a great portion of the freight was lead, and another moment would complete the disaster.[38]

Jacksonian Americans idolized the Alligator Horse and mourned the passing of "The Last of the Boatmen." Later generations have joined in the adulation, but in so doing they have ignored completely the Alligator Horse's real-life counterpart, the western boatman. It is true that the fictional boatman is more important to the American self-image and national consciousness than the fellows who actually steered the Ohio and Mississippi flatboats of the late eighteenth and early nineteenth centuries—but the fact that these rivermen's historical lives were not as romantic as their folkloric life does not render them unworthy of investigation. Indeed, the history of the Ohio and Mississippi flatboatmen, keelboatmen, and raftsmen is a missing link in the history of the early American frontier. Who were the real western boatmen? To begin to answer this difficult question, the historian must turn his attention to the Ohio and Mississippi valleys during America's first surge westward.

38. Thorpe, "Disgraced Scalp-Lock," 230; Field, "Mike Fink: The Last of the Boatmen," in Blair and Meine (eds.), *Half Horse, Half Alligator,* 127–28.

TWO

1803: The World the Boatmen Knew

The first time I descended the Ohio and Mississippi rivers I left Cincinnati in December 1808 with five flat boats, all loaded with produce. At that time there were but few settlers on the Ohio River, below the present city of Louisville. The cabins on the river below Louisville were few and far between. . . . The Banks of the Mississippi river from the mouth of the Ohio river to Natches were still more sparsely settled . . . [and] might be regarded as an unbroken wilderness.

—Joseph Hough

The world the early boatmen knew was the world of the Ohio and Mississippi valleys. It was a world of environmental extremes—from the mountains of western Pennsylvania and Virginia to the sweltering bayous of lower Louisiana. It was a humid, lush, green world inhabited by a myriad of wild animals, fish, fowl, and insects. And it was a world inhabited by a great variety of humankind: Indians, Frenchmen, Britons, Americans, African slaves and freemen, Spaniards, Acadians, and Creoles. The boatmen complemented this diverse group of natives, adventurers, and frontiersmen. By 1803—the year the French briefly reassumed formal control of Louisiana from the Spanish, then sold it to the Americans—the western boatmen had become fully integrated into the rough society of the early Ohio and Mississippi valleys. To understand these men, we first must try to envision and understand this world they knew.[1]

1. Arthur Preston Whitaker, *The Spanish-American Frontier, 1783–1795* (1927; rpr. Lincoln, Neb., 1969); Whitaker, *The Mississippi Question, 1795–1803: A Study of Trade, Politics, and Diplomacy* (1934; rpr. Gloucester, Mass., 1962); Malcolm J. Rohrbough, *The Trans-Appalachian Frontier: People, Societies, and Institutions, 1775–1850* (New York, 1978). The Ohio and Mississippi valleys changed so dramatically during the early years of boating that it is pointless to try to write a general essay describing the region during the entire late eighteenth and early nineteenth centuries. I have chosen the year 1803 because it was historically pivotal and because it lies well within what I consider the age of "preindustrial" boatmen, *ca.* 1763–1823. In writing this chapter, I have used the first-

Boatmen called the Ohio River *la belle rivière,* and wrote about "the extraordinary fertility, extent, and beauty of the river bottoms . . . and the superior excellence of its navigation." The riverbed of the Upper Ohio was covered with boulders and stones; the water was clean and clear, in marked contrast to the Lower Ohio, and certainly to the muddy Mississippi 1,100 miles to the southwest. Keelboatmen found it much easier to set poles on the rocky bottom of the Ohio, but traveler François André Michaux complained that the Upper Ohio "runs so extremely serpentine, that in going down it, you appear following a track directly opposite to the one you mean to take." Navigation of the Ohio required a good amount of knowledge and preparation. The water of the Upper Ohio, near Pittsburgh, was very low. Captain Meriwether Lewis, heading southwest in 1803 with a crew of soldiers and professional rivermen bound for the Upper Missouri, ran aground continually. Boatmen also had to contend with Letart's Falls and the Great Falls of the Ohio at Louisville. Actually, both were rapids—and particularly hazardous during low water. Zadok Cramer, whose *Ohio and Mississippi Navigator* served as a bible for many fledgling rivermen, wrote naively in 1802 that "as the navigation is so very good below Limestone, there is little need on entering into minute detail" concerning it. That was wishful thinking. Like most Americans at the time, Cramer knew so little of the floodplains and lower reaches of the Ohio that "minute detail" was out of the question.[2]

Geography, climate, plants, and wildlife underwent a gradual but marked transition as the Ohio flowed from Pittsburgh to its juncture with the Mississippi. Travelers and boatmen on the Upper Ohio commented on the beauty of the heavily forested mountains that bordered the river, especially on the Virginia and eastern Kentucky shores. These "high banks, covered with stately forests" were the foothills

---

hand accounts of actual boatmen whenever possible, and otherwise those of travelers who engaged the services of boatmen. Nearly all of the accounts were written in or near the year 1803. The best secondary work describing the Ohio Valley is John A. Jakle's *Images of the Ohio Valley: A Historical Geography of Travel to 1860* (New York, 1977).

2. Zadok Cramer, *The Ohio and Mississippi Navigator* (Pittsburgh, 1802), 5, 33; F. A. Michaux, *Travels to the West of the Allegheny Mountains by François André Michaux,* in Reuben Gold Thwaites (ed.), *Early Western Travels, 1748–1846* (32 vols.; Cleveland, 1904–1907), III, 163–64; "The Journals of Captain Meriwether Lewis and Sergeant John Ordway Kept on an Expedition of Western Exploration, 1803–1806," *Publications of the State Historical Society of Wisconsin Collections,* XXII (1916), 31–32.

of the Allegheny, or northern Appalachian, range. Westerners called them the Endless Mountains, but the terrain gradually flattened out to the west. On the northern, "Indian" side of the Ohio and in Kentucky, rolling hills turned into rich bottom land that extended past Louisville. Here, Cramer noted, "the low lands commence. The hills which higher up the river are uniformly to be met with either on one side or the other, now entirely disappear." The French scientist Constance F. Volney observed that throughout these lowlands the earth was "overshadowed by deep woods, or drowned in swamps."[3]

Hard winters were common on the Upper Ohio. A Cincinnati physician, Daniel Drake, wrote that in the winter of 1796–1797, "the thermometer was 18 degrees below 0" and the "Ohio, that winter, was shut up with ice four weeks, and frost occured as late as May." The winters ushered in by 1798, 1803, 1804, 1806, and 1808 were all severely cold, making navigation and life on the river extremely difficult. To the southwest the winter temperatures warmed a bit, with perhaps freezing rains and sleet instead of snow on the ground. Spring and summer brought great change, for then the humid Ohio Valley was characterized by intense heat. These weather patterns combined with wind, fog, and rain to the detriment of river navigation. The missionary John Peter Kluge complained of "a terrible windstorm" that "made our rowing very hard" and filled his boats with water. Meriwether Lewis' pilot recommended tying up to the bank because "there was so thick a fogg on the face of the water that no object was visible 40 paces," and many rivermen complained about violent thunderstorms and rain that "pour'd in sheets & torrents." John May, a 1780s Ohio River merchant flatboatman, wrote a vivid account of one such storm:

> [A]bout 8 o'clock [we] committed ourselves to the waters of this beau-
> tiful river—it is true the prospect before us was gloomy, a heavy cloud
> right ahead from whence darted flashes of lightening and the grumbling
> of thunder roar'd at a distance/it was so dark we could but just discern
> the black mountains on each side of us, except when the flashes came/
> then we star'd with all our eyes . . . the scene was so grand, so many
> different noises, that I staid up 6 hours and kept the helm chief of the

3. Lewis H. Garrard (ed.), *Memoirs of Charlotte Chambers* (Philadelphia, 1856), 31; C. F. Volney, *A View of the Soil and the Climate of the United States,* trans. C. B. Brown (1804; rpr. New York, 1968), 24–25, 31–32; Cramer, *Ohio and Mississippi Navigator,* 37.

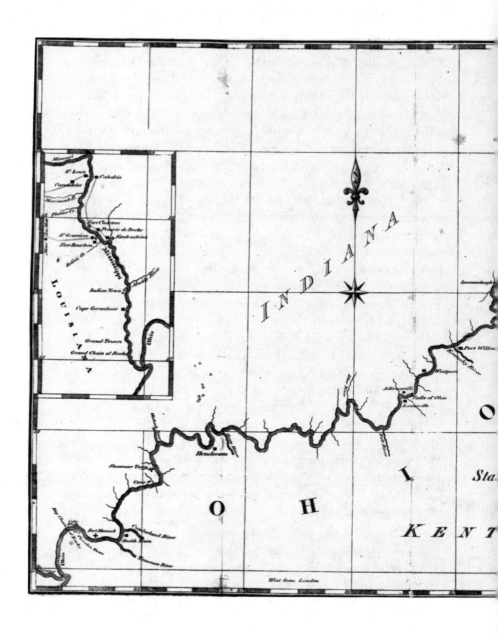

Courtesy Newberry Library, Chicago. Reprinted from Christian Schultz, *Travels on an Inland Voyage . . . in the Years 1807 and 1808* (2 vols.; 1810).

time, with one to look out and four to rowe, the rest slept sound and we mov'd on still as night—in the thick forests on either hand was the howling of wild beasts—the Owl hoop'd his dismal sound, and the Screech Owl scream'd the altus and a burst of thunder, all these things and many more kept my imagination awake—I must confess it was the grandest night I ever beheld—about two o'clock the sky was serene and clear, the moon about 2 hours high.[4]

Screech owls were just one contingent of an array of wild animals inhabiting the Ohio Valley frontier in 1803. May complained that the "Catfish and Perch, make such noise under my boat, that they frequently keep me awake half the night." Christian Schultz, traveling to New Orleans on a keelboat with a crew of four, observed hundreds of geese on the Lower Ohio in 1807, and Dr. Drake wrote of doves, redheaded woodpeckers, and nighthawks. Captain Samuel Newman saw bears and deer, and Meriwether Lewis recorded a rather bizarre sight—hundreds of squirrels "swimming the Ohio and universally passing from the W. to the East shore they appear to be making to the south." Both sides of the river were covered with a lush growth of forest, brush, and grasses. Boatmen passed "poplars . . . beech . . . hickories and walnuts . . . 2 or 3 oaks . . . grapevines . . . red maple" and, to the southwest, the prolific willows and cottonwoods. At narrow places the Ohio must have seemed a green, meandering tunnel.[5]

Civic boosters like Dr. Drake and Zadok Cramer talked a great deal about the "thriving" and "prosperous" Ohio Valley civilization, yet "promising" was perhaps a more realistic adjective for the scattered

4. Daniel Drake, *Notices Concerning Cincinnati* (Cincinnati, 1810), 12; Michaux, *West of the Allegheny Mountains*, in Thwaites (ed.), *Early Western Travels*, III, 187; John Peter Kluge, "Diary from Goshen on the Muskingum to White River, March 24 to May 25, 1801," ed. Lawrence Henry Gipson, *Indiana Historical Collections*, XXIII (1938), 78; "Journals of Captain Meriwether Lewis," 32; [?] Lawrence to Catherine Lawrence, May 25, 1805, in Catherine Lawrence Collection, Indiana Historical Society, Indianapolis; Samuel Newman, "A Picture of the First United States Army: The Journal of Captain Samuel Newman," *Wisconsin Magazine of History*, II (September, 1918), 64; Dwight L. Smith (ed.), *The Western Journals of John May, Ohio Company Agent and Business Adventurer* (Cincinnati, 1961), 46.

5. Smith (ed.), *Journals of John May*, 53; Christian Schultz, *Travels on an Inland Voyage . . . in the Years 1807 and 1808* (2 vols.; 1810; rpr. Ridgewood, New Jersey, 1968), II, 19; Drake, *Notices Concerning Cincinnati*, 6, 26–28; Newman, "First United States Army," 59; "Journals of Captain Meriwether Lewis," 42; Thaddeus Mason Harris, *The Journal of a Tour into the Territory Northwest of the Allegheny Mountains . . . 1803*, in Thwaites (ed.), *Early Western Travels*, III, 350.

towns and villages along the banks of the Ohio in 1803. Anthony Wayne's victory over the Indians at Fallen Timbers was only nine years past, but already Pittsburgh, Wheeling, Marietta, Gallipolis, Limestone, Cincinnati, and Louisville had begun to grow. In between lay a number of smaller villages and forts; the rural population exceeded 100,000. Few people lived southwest of Louisville, however: that low country could boast only Shawneetown, Fort Massac, a few tiny frontier posts, and a great wilderness as evidence of its "thriving" society. Altogether, the early Ohio Valley evinced the first awkward stages of a burgeoning frontier civilization.

Ensconced at the confluence of the Monongahela and Allegheny rivers, residents of Pittsburgh accurately described their town as the "key to the Western Territory." The French first recognized the crucial importance of this juncture of great rivers when they built Fort Duquesne in 1754. During the French and Indian War, the victorious British renamed the place Fort Pitt—a name that endured through four tumultuous decades that witnessed the Revolution, Indian warfare, and the Whiskey Rebellion. By 1803 Fort Pitt, no longer an armed camp, had become Pittsburgh, a growing frontier community of nearly two thousand inhabitants.[6]

Early Pittsburgh presented the rivermen with a scene of constant activity. Penn Street, facing the Allegheny, formed the heart of the business district of a town that boasted two newspapers, a public market, two glass factories, cabinet shops, nail and tobacco manufactories, and "near 40 retail stores, all of which seem continually busy." Local shipwrights built the Caribbean-bound brigs whose short and fascinating history was to be dashed at the Falls of the Ohio. But the thousands of pioneers and adventurers who passed through the area in the early 1800s on their way to the Ohio country and points south were more interested in the flatboats and keels for which Pittsburgh was famous. "*Boat building, boat buying,* and *boat selling* seem to be part of the business of at least one-half of the town," wrote Christian Schultz while shopping for a boat and a crew in 1807. Both were plentiful, and he purchased a keelboat and hired two hands, with a pas-

6. Michaux, *West of the Allegheny Mountains,* in Thwaites (ed.), *Early Western Travels,* III, 156–57. The best secondary account of early Pittsburgh as well as other western cities is Richard C. Wade, *The Urban Frontier: Pioneer Life in Early Pittsburgh, Cincinnati, Lexington, Louisville, and St. Louis* (Chicago, 1964). For early Pittsburgh, see pp. 7–13.

senger volunteering to pilot. Had Schultz shopped around a bit more, he might have hired an experienced Pittsburgh boatman named Mike Fink, who at the time still made his headquarters in the area.[7]

The fifty-mile stretch of the Upper Ohio running northwest from Pittsburgh was shallow and dangerous enough to induce many travelers and boatmen to cross overland to Wheeling, in what was then Virginia, to begin their journey. Those who made the trip by river found a well-settled farming region whose inhabitants supplemented their incomes by hitching up their teams and pulling stranded flatboats off sandbars. The boats passed Logtown, old Fort McIntosh, and Georgetown before arriving at the Pennsylvania-Virginia-Ohio border. Here the Ohio turned south and then southwest as it meandered toward the Mississippi, more than a thousand miles away.[8]

By 1803, Wheeling already had become an important transportation center. Here the great post roads from Philadelphia, Baltimore, and Virginia converged and crossed the Ohio en route to Kentucky and the Northwest Territory. Wheeling's location, combined with the growing river trade, made this village of about fifty houses a hub of commercial activity. Situated on a high bank and surrounded by forested mountains, the town consisted mainly of one long street containing numerous shops, warehouses, and boatbuilding establishments. It was an active and interesting place, but not everyone found it pleasing. "We had but poor society in Wheeling," complained the devoutly religious traveler Lewis Condict. "The inhabitants lead very loose lives; Drinking & gambling are the principal employments."[9]

South of Wheeling, boatmen passed through a sparsely settled country known chiefly for its Indian mounds and good bear hunting.

7. Harris, *Northwest of the Allegheny*, in Thwaites (ed.), *Early Western Travels*, III, 342–43, 346; Wade, *Urban Frontier*, 7–11; Cramer, *Ohio and Mississippi Navigator*, 19–21; Michaux, *West of the Allegheny Mountains*, in Thwaites (ed.), *Early Western Travels*, III, 157–60; Lewis Condict, "Journal of a Trip to Kentucky in 1795," *New Jersey Historical Society Proceedings*, n.s., IV (1919), 114; Leland D. Baldwin, *The Keelboat Age on Western Waters* (Pittsburgh, 1941), 159–74; Schultz, *Travels on an Inland Voyage*, I, 126; Henry Howe, "A Talk with a Veteran Boatman," *Historical Collections of Ohio* (2 vols.; Columbus, 1888), I, 322. Fink headquartered between Pittsburgh and Wheeling.

8. "Journals of Captain Meriwether Lewis," 33–36; Cramer, *Ohio and Mississippi Navigator*, 22.

9. Condict, "Trip to Kentucky," 115; Francis Bailey, *Journal of a Tour in Unsettled Parts of America in 1796 and 1797*, ed. Sir Jack D. L. Holmes (London, 1969), 60.

Cramer's *Ohio and Mississippi Navigator* cites no villages or towns until Marietta, Ohio, at the mouth of the Muskingum River. In the fledgling society of the Northwest Territory, fifteen-year-old Marietta was, in 1803, the granddaddy of them all. Founded by New England army officers of the Ohio Company in 1788, Marietta had become a substantial village of "more than two hundred houses, some of which are built of brick . . . nearly all of them . . . in front of the Ohio." Its location at the mouth of the navigable Muskingum made the village an entrepôt and transshipment center for southbound agricultural goods; by 1803 Marietta already had developed an important flatboat economy, and many of its citizens worked as flatboatmen and boatbuilders. Like their counterparts in Pittsburgh, many Mariettans had invested in shipbuilding. André Michaux noted that the transplanted New Englanders, enamored with "the idea of exporting directly to the Carribbee Islands . . . were building three brigs, one of which was two hundred and twenty tons burthen."[10]

Continuing south, rivermen passed "various large islands on which the finest farms and large houses are located." One of these was Harman Blennerhassett's island, but no one in 1803 made note of that eccentric Irishman and confidant of Vice-President Aaron Burr. Three years later, Cincinnatian Charlotte Chambers wrote of a report "that Aaron Burr, in conjunction with others, is forming schemes inimical to the peace of his country; and that an armament and fleet of boats are now in motion on the Ohio." Burr subsequently was arrested, tried for treason, and acquitted, whereupon he retired to New York to ponder, among other things, his brief but memorable riverboating days.[11]

Besides Blennerhassett Island, boatmen in 1803 passed a myriad of

10. "Journals of Captain Meriwether Lewis," 41; Daniel Drake, *Natural and Statistical View or Picture of Cincinnati and the Miami Country* (Cincinnati, 1815), 200–218; Cramer, *Ohio and Mississippi Navigator,* 24–25; Michaux, *West of the Allegheny Mountains,* in Thwaites (ed.), *Early Western Travels,* III, 177; Josiah Espy, *Memorandums of a Tour Made by Josiah Espy in the States of Ohio, Kentucky, and Indiana Territory in 1805* (Cincinnati, 1870); Kluge, "Diary from Goshen on the Muskingum," 74.

11. Garrard (ed.), *Memoirs of Charlotte Chambers,* 63. Cramer calls the island "Backus Island," but by 1802 Blennerhassett had moved onto the island and built his house. There are a number of accounts of the Burr "conspiracy," but Marshall Smelser, *The Democratic Republic, 1801–1815* (New York, 1968), 111–24, handles this rather complicated affair ably and succinctly.

small farms, orchards, and tiny villages: Vienna, Belpre (on the Ohio shore), and Belleville (just downstream from the mouth of Ohio's Big Hockhocking River). Point Pleasant, at the mouth of the Great Kanawha River, was reportedly "a handsome little town, well situated, commanding an extensive view of the Ohio." By way of contrast, the region's most famous village, Gallipolis, could tell a short and rather sorrowful tale. Lured by promises of Scioto Company land agents, hundreds of ill-prepared emigrés from revolutionary France founded Gallipolis in 1790. The hardships of climate, Indian warfare, frontier living, and unscrupulous land agents quickly ended their venture. A few did remain, achieving success as orchardists, farmers, and innkeepers. But even these determined few stood in marked contrast to hardy, Americanized Frenchmen like those Fortescue Cuming observed aboard a keelboat docked at Gallipolis in 1807: "We found at the landing a keel loaded with lead from Kaskaskias on the Mississippi. It was worked by eight stout Canadians, all naked except a breech [cloth]. They are the descendents of the original French settlers, and they resemble the Indians both in their manners and customs. . . . They are preferred to any other description of people for navigating the craft on the rivers in this country being patient, steady, and trustworthy, and never deserting their boats until their engagement is fulfilled, which the American boatmen frequently do."[12]

The Big Sandy River, forming part of what was then the Virginia-Kentucky boundary, entered the Ohio fifty-five miles below Gallipolis, and about one-third of the way down the Ohio. Forty miles farther downstream lay the mouth of the Great Scioto River, flanked by two little Ohio villages, Alexandria and Portsmouth. Most Kentucky-bound settlers headed for Limestone, a village touted as "the oldest

12. Cramer, *Ohio and Mississippi Navigator*, 27, 29; Volney, *A View*, 322–30; Michaux, *West of the Allegheny Mountains*, in Thwaites (ed.), *Early Western Travels*, III, 182–85; F. Cuming, *Sketches of a Tour to the Western Country Through the States of Ohio and Kentucky*, in Thwaites (ed.), *Early Western Travels*, IV, 147. Cuming traveled no farther south on the Ohio and Mississippi than Natchez. To complete the description of the Mississippi Valley, the original editor of his manuscript appended a travel account by an unidentified Pittsburgh flatboat merchant who traveled to New Orleans in 1799 and then sailed back to Philadelphia via the Gulf of Mexico and Atlantic. All references to Cuming's *Tour to the Western Country* dealing with the Mississippi south of Natchez will be taken from that unidentified merchant flatboatman's account.

and most accustomed landing place in the whole state of Kentucky."
Limestone (later renamed Maysville) was one of the most important
boating towns on the western waters in 1803. Cramer described "a
small harbor for boats . . . accommodation for the storage of goods,"
and a number of boatmen milling about looking for work. United
States Army captain Samuel Newman was one of several travelers
who found the village "abominably filthy and dirty."[13]

Sitting opposite the mouth of Kentucky's Licking River, Cincinnati
was not yet the Queen City of the West in 1803, but it would gain that
distinction with the passage of a few years. Founded by land speculators in the early 1790s, the town already was experiencing the growth
that naturally accompanied its location and status as a military center
and territorial and state capital. Its 750 residents lived either in "the
bottom" or on "the hill," sandwiched between heavily forested hills
and the Ohio. Cincinnati in 1803 housed an army garrison at Fort
Washington, accommodated a swarm of Ohio and Mississippi river
traders and boatmen, bristled with state and local politicians, and was
the home of the influential newspaper *Centinel of the Northwest Territory*. Dr. Daniel Drake proudly noted that "the town contains two
cemeteries"—one for the Methodists and one, presumably, for everyone else. Cincinnati was not a highly sophisticated town, but even urbane travelers might well have luxuriated in its amenities: the cultural
and social pickings would become considerably slimmer down the
Ohio to the southwest.[14]

After passing North Bend and the mouth of the Great Miami
River, the boatmen entered a thinly settled region important mainly
for its connection with the navigable Kentucky River. Passing through
this country on his way to Louisville in 1796, Constance Volney
"scarcely met with five infant villages and eight farms." Madison, Indiana, did not yet exist, but boatmen could go ashore nearby and view
the "Big Bone Lick," where, according to the *Ohio and Mississippi
Navigator*, "remarkable large bones have been found . . . which must
have belonged to some monstrous animal whose race is now tho't to

---

13. Cramer, *Ohio and Mississippi Navigator*, 30, 33; Kluge, "Diary from Goshen on
the Muskingum," 77–78; Newman, "First United States Army," 60.

14. Wade, *Urban Frontier*, 22–27; Drake, *Notices Concerning Cincinnati*, 5, 29–30,
passim.

be entirely extinct." Their sightseeing finished, the rivermen tensed as they approached Louisville. Soon their skills would be pitted against the fury of the Great Falls of the Ohio.[15]

An oblique limestone ridge crossing the Ohio River created the Great Falls, the worst single navigation hazard on the western waters. Four towns (Louisville and Shippingsport in Kentucky, and Jeffersonville and Clarksville in what is now Indiana) sprung up to handle the commerce of this transshipment point, but Louisville was the first and by far the most successful. The reasons for this were simple: directly above Louisville lay a good little harbor at the mouth of Bear Grass Creek, and only at Louisville could boats lay up before braving the Falls. The area had been settled in 1778 by twenty families accompanying Colonel George Rogers Clark during his Revolutionary War forays in the West. By 1803, Louisville claimed a population of four hundred, a score of hotels, saloons, inns, and stores, as well as warehouses, boatbuilding establishments, and a healthy number of boatmen, wagonmasters, and draymen. Before the Louisiana Purchase, Louisville served as the official port of entry and headquarters for a United States customs agent. While the town fathers wrestled with problems caused by residents "raising and now posessed of large *numbers* of Swine," other citizens talked of national politics, read the *Farmer's Library* and Louisville *Gazette,* and even dabbled in drama. According to the Louisville historian Ben Casseday, writing in the 1850s, the erection of a theater in Louisville in 1808 "established the golden era of Drama in the West" and "created a high standard of taste and judgement . . . still perceptible here."[16]

While the "golden era of Drama in the West" flourished in Louisville, western boatmen wrestled with the more pressing concern of how to get over the Falls in one piece. In high water there was no great problem. The Falls were actually rapids, and experienced boatmen could navigate through one of three "chutes" that descended twenty-five feet in a distance of two miles; most followed the "Indian [Indiana] chute." In low water, however, the task became much more hazard-

15. Volney, *A View,* 331; Cramer, *Ohio and Mississippi Navigator,* 35.

16. All quotations are from Ben Casseday, *The History of Louisville, from Its Earliest Settlement to the Year 1852* (Louisville, 1852), 114, 117. See also Wade, *Urban Frontier,* 13–18; Allan J. Share, *Cities in the Commonwealth: Two Centuries of Urban Life in Kentucky* (Lexington, Ky., 1982), 1–4; Cramer, *Ohio and Mississippi Navigator,* 36–37.

ous. The pounding of the waves against the rocks was audible half a mile upstream. Many boatmen chose to unload their cargoes and portage down, although by 1802 reliable, licensed pilots could be hired to steer boats through the rapids. Earlier, Francis Bailey, an Englishman traveling to New Orleans in 1797, considered himself fortunate to have taken passage with two farmer flatboatmen who "were going upon their second adventure" and thus "would be better able to conduct the boat through the dangerous navigation" ahead. He described their low-water passage through the Falls as awe-inspiring: "the torrent begins to roar, and loud-sounding rocks to foam with unabated vigour, then the boat twists its unyielding sides to the force of the compelling current, and the long-accustomed pilot with dismay exerts himself, and stirs on his associates to lend a willing hand to save him from impending destruction; till at last, escaped from all danger, the vessel (like an arrow from the bow) is propelled with great violence from this Charybdis, and in peace once more possesses the wonted gentle course." Having braved the Great Falls, the rivermen and their passengers could look back and enjoy the spectacular view. Josiah Espy did so in 1805 and even caught a glimpse of the "celebrated warrior" Colonel George Rogers Clark, who was by this time a "frail and rather helpless" old man residing in Clarksville, Indiana, at the base of the Falls. Clark's tiny village was one of the last settlements between the Falls and St. Louis.[17]

Joseph Hough, an Ohio merchant flatboatman, made many trips down the Lower Ohio during the early decades of the nineteenth century, and he remembered that "the cabins on the river below Louisville were few and far between" and the "banks of the Mississippi from the mouth of the Ohio to Natchez were still more sparsely settled." The landscape also changed. Now, "instead of those romantic scenes which a broken and hilly country often afforded us," wrote Francis Bailey, "we had an entirely flat and overflowed, though at the same time rich and fertile country, presented to our view." Settlements were scarce and tiny. Henderson, Kentucky, had just been surveyed in 1802, and served mainly as a port for Kentucky's Green River region. Sailing south past Diamond Island, the boatmen viewed the mouth of the Wabash River, one of the largest navigable rivers of the Northwest

17. Bailey, *Journal of a Tour,* 113, 121; Espy, *Memorandums of a Tour,* 13–14.

Territory, and soon to form the Illinois-Indiana state line. Just below the Wabash lay Shawneetown, a scruffy frontier village that Cramer did not even mention in his 1802 *Ohio and Mississippi Navigator*. There was probably not much to talk about in 1802, although in the first decades of the nineteenth century Shawneetown became the most important river town between Louisville and St. Louis.[18]

Many historians and journalists have written about the villainous river pirates of Cave-In Rock, a limestone cavern on the "Indian side of the Ohio" just below Shawneetown. Yet piracy seems not to have been much of a problem in 1803. Indeed, most boatmen treated the cave as a natural curiosity and tourist attraction. Its walls reportedly were covered with "inscriptions, names of persons, dates, etc., etc." South of Cave-In Rock, the Cumberland and Tennessee rivers joined the Ohio within the space of a few miles. Both were very large rivers, navigable for small boats as far up as Nashville and Muscle Shoals, respectively. Paducah, Kentucky, was not yet established, but at the mouth of the Cumberland a tiny village called Smithtown existed by at least 1807. Christian Schultz termed it "a kind of inland port, where runaways, idle young men, and unemployed boatmen, assemble to engage as hands on board any boats that may happen to call." Two such boats in 1804 were captained by a young former United States congressman and Tennessee judge named Andrew Jackson. Jackson recorded that it took his thirteen hands sixteen days and "20 gallons whiskey" to travel from Nashville to the mouth of the Cumberland and back.[19]

Thus, in approximately two hundred miles, four major rivers—the Green, Wabash, Cumberland, and Tennessee—all joined their forces with the Ohio. La belle rivière was not so beautiful anymore, but it

18. R. Pierce Beaver (ed.), "Joseph Hough, an Early Miami Merchant," *Ohio Archeological and Historical Quarterly*, XLV (January, 1936), 43; Bailey, *Journal of a Tour*, 124; Cramer, *Ohio and Mississippi Navigator*, 38; Rohrbough, *Trans-Appalachian Frontier*, 357–58.

19. Otto A. Rothert, *The Outlaws of Cave-In Rock: Historical Accounts of the Famous Highwaymen and River Pirates Who Operated in Pioneer Days upon the Ohio and Mississippi Rivers and Over the Old Natchez Trace* (Cleveland, 1924); Cramer, *Ohio and Mississippi Navigator*, 38–40; Schultz, *Travels on an Inland Voyage*, I, 202–203; "Account of Expenses," June, 1804, in J. S. Bassett (ed.), *Correspondence of Andrew Jackson* (7 vols.; Washington, D.C., 1926–35), I, 95.

was becoming grand. As the river rolled on with mounting strength, the boatmen passed Fort Massac, an Illinois post that one Cumberland River flatboatman noted was built by the French in 1757. Eleven miles below Massac, and nearly 1,100 miles below Pittsburgh, stood Wilkinsonville, a rather shabby little frontier station named after army brigadier general James Wilkinson, a man who dabbled in soldiering, flatboating, and treason. (Wilkinson boasted yet another namesake on the Lower Mississippi, but like their progenitor, both villages faded and disappeared with time.) Wilkinsonville lay only a few miles from the confluence of the Ohio and the Mississippi.[20]

By the time the boatmen and their passengers neared the mouth of the Ohio, they had passed through a range of environmental and climatic extremes. From the mountains and forests of the Upper Ohio, they had floated southwesterly into the Mississippi Valley, a region of flooded lowlands and great flat stretches of brushy wilderness. They also had mingled with an array of Scotch-Irish, English, and French pioneers, Yankees, Kentuckians, Indians, and black slaves and freemen. Indian tribes—Delaware, Miami, Peoria, Sauk, Piankashaw, and Shawnee—were a common sight along the Ohio in 1803, but the boatmen no longer lived in fear of Indian attack. The Ohio Valley tribes were disintegrating rapidly. Many of their remnants were moving west into the Illinois country and across the Mississippi.[21]

Even at this early date, the Ohio Valley was taking on a decidedly American tone, and before too many years passed would be completely Americanized. This was not so farther south. Arriving at the confluence of the Ohio and Mississippi near present-day Cairo, Illinois, in 1806, the braggadocious traveler and author Thomas Ashe purchased board and room at the tavern of "don Castro," a gentleman of Spanish blood who "furnishes travelers, merchants, and boatmen with every accommodation during their stay." Those travelers and rivermen who had never met a Spaniard would soon be meeting others, and many more blacks, Indians, Englishmen, Frenchmen, Acadians,

---

20. John R. Bedford, "A Tour in 1807 Down the Cumberland, Ohio, and Mississippi Rivers from Nashville to New Orleans," *Tennessee History Magazine,* V (April, 1919), 55; "Journals of Captain Meriwether Lewis," 46.

21. The best primary-source account of the Ohio Valley tribes, especially the Miamis, is Volney, *A View,* 352–427.

and Creoles as well. These were just some of the many changes that lay in store as the boatmen steered their flats and keels into the rushing current of the Mississippi River.[22]

The boatmen's first impressions of the Mississippi were neither idyllic "nor romantic," American diplomat Andrew Ellicott wrote in 1796. Thomas Ashe, traveling to New Orleans in 1806 with two hired boatmen, wrote that the dreadful accounts he had heard of the Mississippi combined with the "continued scene of terrific grandeur" to create frightening impressions of "veneration and awe." Indeed, how could one truly enjoy a river that, according to Volney, "rolls along a mass of yellow muddy water, a mile and a half wide, which annually lifts twenty or twenty-five feet above its banks . . . forms islands and destroys them, throws trees upon one side, and uproots them on the other . . . and at length overwhelms the spot which you thought most secure. The sublimity of this stream is like that of most other grand objects of nature, to be admired safely only at a distance."[23]

The Mississippi was intimidating. According to Cramer's *Navigator,* the river lay more than a mile wide in places, ran from thirty to fifty feet deep, was "remarkably crooked," and flowed at three to five miles an hour. This rapid current, combined with navigation hazards like snags, "planters, sawers, and wooden islands," put the boatmen immediately on guard. The velocity of the Mississippi and its constant erosive action led to continual changes of "the circuitous course of the river." This activity became especially severe during the five to six months of annual flooding. All of the boatmen and travelers described the Lower Mississippi Valley as a veritable floodplain. New Orleans merchant James Pitot spoke fearfully of "the fury of a river which during five or six months every year threatens to swallow up all the inhabitants along its banks." Only where the Louisianians had constructed their levee, from Pointe Coupée to New Orleans, did the population feel relatively safe from the great river. The muddy water

22. Thomas Ashe, *Travels in America, Performed in the Year 1806* (London, 1809), 260. Ashe's highly quotable account often has been used carelessly by historians.

23. Andrew Ellicott, *The Journal of Andrew Ellicott* (1803; rpr. Chicago, 1962), 119, Ashe; *Travels in America,* 254, 265; Volney, *A View,* 342. Ellicott was bound for Natchez in 1796 to arrange for carrying out the terms of Pinkney's Treaty, by which the Spanish granted Americans the right to navigate the entire length of the Mississippi.

of the Mississippi also "rendered a disagreeable drink to navigators," and Cramer recommended letting it sit overnight in jars, to cool and filter out the dirt. Then one supposedly could use the water as a refreshing drink, or even for its "medicinal qualities" as "a powerful cathartick and as a purifier of the blood."[24]

Geography, climate, flora, and fauna changed gradually as the boatmen descended the Mississippi to Louisiana. Rolling hills and bluffs skirted the river banks above the mouth of the Ohio, but the terrain soon flattened out. Chroniclers like Ellicott complained of the monotony of floating "for days together" through a flat, "uninhabitable, and almost impenetrable wilderness." Except for the Chickasaw Bluffs (modern-day Memphis, Tennessee), the next major change in scenery appeared near the mouth of the Arkansas River, where the edges of the Mississippi began to blend with swamps and bayous. This "dead swampy but very rich" marshland, Fortescue Cuming wrote, bordered the Mississippi "the length of the territory . . . from the Walnut Hills to Baton Rouge with the exception of some edges of ridges, or bluffs as they are called, at the Walnut Hills, the Grand and Petit Gulphs [and] Natchez and Baton Rouge." South of New Orleans, the Mississippi passed through a swamp of even greater proportion, "covered with reeds, having little or no timber, and no settlement whatever," and then flowed into the Gulf of Mexico.[25]

Travelers in the Mississippi Valley north of the Walnut Hills witnessed hard winters, freezing rains, ice, and snow. Navigation hazards on a river that "appeared like a vast mass of ice and snow in motion," halted the progress of the Andrew Ellicott party. As Volney noted, however, the temperatures warmed considerably as one neared Natchez and points south. John Stuart, a Kentucky flatboatman taking produce to New Orleans in the spring of 1806, complained of the "ardently hot . . . sultry weather" and the "most violent rain." The ultimate in "violent rain" came with the hurricanes about which some of the boatmen and travelers wrote. But no natural phenomenon so shocked

24. Zadok Cramer, *The Navigator* (1814; rpr. Ann Arbor, 1966), 149, 155, 164 (note that I use this later, more accurate, edition for the Lower Mississippi description); James Pitot, *Observations on the Colony of Louisiana from 1796 to 1802,* trans. Henry C. Pitot (Baton Rouge, 1979), 3.

25. Ellicott, *Journal,* 120; Cuming, *Tour to the Western Country,* in Thwaites (ed.), *Early Western Travels,* IV, 351; Ashe, *Travels in America,* 297.

Courtesy Newberry Library, Chicago. Reprinted from Christian Schultz, *Travels on an Inland Voyage . . . in the Years 1807 and 1808* (2 vols.; 1810).

the Lower Mississippi as the series of massive earthquakes that rocked that country in the winter of 1811–1812. Traveler John Bradbury was sailing near the Walnut Hills when the first severe quake felled trees and dislodged huge portions of the river bank near his boat and French-Canadian crew. In a journal entry he noted that "Immediately after we had cleared all danger the men dropped their oars, crossed themselves, then gave a shout which was followed by mutual congratulations on their safety." Earthquakes aside, the general impression of the climate as one traveled further south became most unfavorable. Travelers and rivermen complained constantly of the heat and humidity, and of the swamps, insects, fevers, and other illnesses that accompanied them. "The climate is horrid," one distraught European concluded.[26]

Just as geography and climate changed south of Ohio, so did the "trees, plants, and shrubs" of this different "theatre and country." Frenchman M. Perrin du Lac noted the immense forests that bordered the Mississippi north of the mouth of the Arkansas. There grew hickory, walnut, and poplar, all of which changed colors in the fall, providing a marvelous spectacle. Coniferous trees, particularly cedar, also grew in considerable abundance, but the deciduous held sway. Farther south the great cypress swamps began to appear—the trees covered with Spanish mosses "8 or 10 feet long," and separated by "almost impenetrable" canebrakes extending down into the bayou country.[27]

Wildlife flourished everywhere. In the Mississippi and tributary waters swam perch, trout, buffalo fish, soft turtle, pike, carp, and sturgeon. Captain Meriwether Lewis and his boatmen claimed to have caught a "128 lb. catfish." Wrote Cuming, "The woods abound with

26. Ellicott, *Journal*, 26–27; Volney, *A View*, 119–20; John G. Stuart, "A Journal: Remarks or Observations in a Voyage Down the Kentucky, Ohio, Mississippi Rivers etc.," *Register of the Kentucky Historical Society*, L (January, 1952), 20. An unedited typescript of the Stuart journal is in possession of the Kentucky State Historical Society, Frankfort. I quote from the published version except where noted. John Bradbury, *Bradbury's Travels in the Interior of America, 1809–1811*, in Thwaites (ed.), *Early Western Travels*, V, 204, 207–208; Ashe, *Travels in America*, 304.

27. Ashe, *Travels in America*, 274; M. Perrin du Lac, *Travels Through the Two Louisianas and Among the Savage Nations of the Missouri . . . 1801, 1802 and 1803* (London, 1807), 83; Ellicott, *Journal*, 285–88; Schultz, *Travels on an Inland Voyage*, II, 181–82; Stuart, "A Journal," 19.

bear and deer." He also noted eagles and "wild turkeys on the hills, and water foul [*sic*] of every description in the swamps." Francis Bailey reported seeing many deer but went hungry for want of hunting skills. Christian Schultz and his Canadian boatmen saw many wolves near the confluence and "were every night entertained with their horrible yells." Farther down they saw "wild horses . . . on the west side of the river" near Baton Rouge. Some boatmen even hunted alligators in the swamps, and all seemed fascinated by these "very strong, though dull and stupid" beasts. Thomas Ashe told an amusing if dubious tale of his battle with an alligator "at least twenty feet long" that "held on to the boat with one paw, while he was employed in rending off the [duck] coop with the other." None needed to exaggerate about the "myriads of mosquitoes and other insects" on the Lower Mississippi. According to flatboatman John Stuart, the mosquitoes were "almost twice as large as those in Kentucky." [28]

As for villages, towns, and "civilization" in this vast riverine wilderness, they were as scarce as mosquitoes were abundant. Only three centers of population deserved the name of "town": New Orleans, of course, and the considerably smaller St. Louis—each commanding its end of the Lower Mississippi Valley—and between them Natchez, respectable in size if not in reputation. These three, together with a score of tiny villages, trading posts, and military installations, made up the totality of the infant civilization that was growing on the banks of the Lower Mississippi.

Built on a limestone bluff near the confluence of the Missouri, Illinois, and Mississippi rivers, St. Louis seemed destined one day to become a great inland port and governmental center. The Frenchmen Pierre Laclede Liguest and Auguste Chouteau founded the city as a trading post in November, 1763, only to learn that the region had been ceded to Spain. St. Louis grew into a decidedly French community, despite Spanish governance and an oddly assorted resident

28. Gilbert Imlay, *A Topographical Description of the Western Territory of North America* (1792; rpr. New York, 1969), 178; "Journals of Captain Meriwether Lewis," 49; Cuming, *Tour of the Western Country,* in Thwaites (ed.), *Early Western Travels,* IV, 353; Bailey, *Journal of a Tour,* 232–33; Schultz, *Travels on an Inland Voyage,* II, 185, 144; Ellicott, *Journal,* 34; Samuel Donnell, "Journal of a Trip on the Mississippi in 1806" (MS in Samuel Donnell Collection, Indiana Historical Society, Indianapolis); Ashe, *Travels in America,* 274, 266; Stuart, "A Journal," 19.

population of Frenchmen, a few Spaniards, Indians, black slaves, British citizens, and American frontiersmen. At the time of the Louisiana Purchase, the town was hardly a metropolis: flatboat merchant Moses Austin had noted in 1797 that it boasted "a Number of wealthy Mercht [merchants]" and "contains about 200 Houses, most of which are of stone, and some of them large but not Elegant." At the waterfront, canoes, keels, and flatboats arrived from and departed to the Ohio, Missouri, Illinois, and Upper and Lower Mississippi rivers. The wealthy maintained a social calendar and some semblance of culture, but St. Louis still retained the rough aspects befitting its frontier status.[29]

Moving south along the Lower Mississippi, rivermen found the villages of Cahokia, Ste. Genevieve, Kaskaskia, and Cape Girardeau. Moses Austin described Ste. Genevieve as a small town located "about 2 Miles from the Missisipe on the high land from which You have a Commanding Vew of the Country and River." Captain Meriwether Lewis wrote that the village contained about 120 families, principally French. The economy of Ste. Genevieve revolved around boating, agriculture, land speculation, and lead mines. Directly across the river, six miles inland, stood Kaskaskia, a hundred years old and the scene of George Rogers Clark's famous Revolutionary War victory. Once a flourishing French village of four hundred inhabitants, Kaskaskia in 1803 more closely resembled a ghost town, with scarcely twelve French families in residence.[30]

29. Auguste Chouteau, "Narrative of the Settlement of St. Louis," in John Francis McDermott (ed.), *The Early Histories of St. Louis* (St. Louis, 1952), 45–59, is the best contemporary history. See also Wade, *Urban Frontier,* 3–7. For the Spanish view, see the description in "Trudeau to Governor, St. Louis, January 15, 1798," in Abraham P. Nasatir (ed.), *Before Lewis and Clark: Documents Illustrating the History of the Missouri, 1785–1804* (2 vols.; St. Louis, 1952), II, 535, and Don Esteban Miró, "A Description of Louisiana," in Lawrence Kinnaird (ed.), *Spain in the Mississippi Valley, 1765–1794: Translations of Materials from the Spanish Archives in the Bancroft Library* (4 vols.; Washington, D.C., 1946), III, 160 (part of American Historical Association's *Annual Report, 1945*). Miró, governor of Spanish Louisiana, wrote his "Description" in 1785. Austin quotations are from Moses Austin, "A Memorandum of Mr. Austin's Journey from the Lead Mines in the County of Wythe in the State of Virginia to the Lead Mines in the Province of Louisiana West," *American Historical Review,* V, (April, 1900), 535. Wade, *Urban Frontier,* 4, estimates the population in 1803 at approximately one thousand, one-third of whom were black slaves.

30. Austin, "Memorandum of Mr. Austin's Journey," 540; "Journals of Captain Meriwether Lewis," 70; du Lac, *Travels Through the Two Louisianas,* 82; Ashe, *Travels in America,* 261–62; Volney, *A View,* 341–42.

Farther south, Captain Lewis noted, rivermen used Grand Tower Rock as the site for a ritual similar to that of ocean sailors crossing "the tropics or Equanoxial line." Greenhorns were compelled to "furnish spirits to drink or be ducked" in the river. Downstream from the rock stood Cape Girardeau, on the west bank of the Mississippi. Founded by the Spanish in 1793, the town contained predominantly "anglo-American families" who, according to du Lac, made a living at farming wheat, barley, corn, and potatoes. Lewis reported the 1803 population of the little town and its surrounding district to be 1,111 persons, all governed by an amiable French commandant with thick dark hair "nearly as low as his knees."[31]

As the land flattened and the river meandered along, settlement grew sparse. Boosters and land speculators would have had it otherwise: they touted the nonexistent "Town of America," at the confluence of the Ohio and Mississippi (modern-day Cairo), as a potentially great "inland commercial city." The Mississippi drowned their dreams and schemes. The great floodplain precluded extensive settlement between the mouth of the Ohio and Natchez, with the exception of New Madrid, the Chickasaw Bluffs, and Walnut Hills. New Madrid, on the west bank of the Mississippi below the mouth of the Ohio, was another Spanish outpost inhabited almost entirely by Americans. Sponsored by Spain but founded by New Jersey land speculator Colonel George Morgan in 1790, the village fought a losing battle with the mighty river for twenty years. Around 1810, John Bradbury found only a "few straggling houses" sheltering an indolent population of a few Spaniards, "French Creoles from Illinois, United States Americans and Germans." Cuming noted two poorly stocked stores selling goods at enormously high prices. The great earthquakes of 1811 and 1812 ended what the floods had begun. New Madrid was not destined to be a great city.[32]

A better fate awaited the fourth Chickasaw Bluff, the future site of Memphis. Sailing south from New Madrid, past Little Prairie and the treacherous stretches of the Mississippi known to rivermen as Devil's

---

31. "Journals of Captain Meriwether Lewis," 65, 59; du Lac, *Travels Through the Two Louisianas*, 82.

32. Wade, *Urban Frontier*, 31–32; Max Savelle, "The Founding of New Madrid," *Mississippi Valley Historical Review*, XIX (June, 1932), 30–56; Bradbury, *Travels in the Interior of America*, in Thwaites (ed.), *Early Western Travels*, V, 201, 204–208; Cuming, *Tour to the Western Country*, in Thwaites (ed.), *Early Western Travels*, IV, 281.

Raceground and Devil's Elbow, boatmen encountered the fourth bluff. High atop it perched the lonely watchtower of the United States Army's Fort Pickering, overlooking the great Mississippi and broad expanses of forest sweeping in all directions. The settlement, originally the home of a Spanish garrison, was in 1803 comfortably situated in a land that was, according to Thomas Ashe, "as rich as possible." Ashe enjoyed a sumptuous dinner of "fish, venison, squirrels, and bear's meat, with a profusion of wine and dessert of Illinois nuts, a forest fruit," compliments of the fort's commanding officer. A few years later, Cuming was not as impressed with the commandant, a rather precocious young lieutenant named Zachary Taylor.[33]

Farther south, and about thirty miles up the Arkansas River, stood an old French village and Spanish fort known alternately as Ozark Village and the Arkansas Post. Here, approximately four hundred French-descended frontiersmen hunted, traded, and behaved in a manner quite similar to that of the Indians among whom they lived. South of the Arkansas Post, at the mouth of the Yazoo River, the American Fort McHenry stood atop the Walnut Hills. Formerly the Spanish Fort Nogales, this pleasant and well-cultivated settlement would be incorporated as Vicksburg in 1811. Many travelers and boatmen expressed relief at seeing this "bold but gradually rising ground" after the "dull uniformity of a flat swampy forest for six or seven hundred miles." But real relief was not yet at hand. The countryside surrounding Grand Gulf, Bayou Pierre, and Petit Gulf remained for the most part a swampy and inhospitable wilderness. Natchez was certainly a welcome enough sight, but the populous stretches of the Mississippi Valley in lower Louisiana still lay far to the south.[34]

Arrival in Natchez represented a great milestone in the boatmen's journey down the Mississippi. With the most treacherous portions of

33. "Journal of a Trip from Champaign County, Ohio Down the Mississippi River to New Orleans with a Cargo of Flour, November 25, 1805–July 26, 1806" (MS in Illinois State Historical Library, Springfield, cited courtesy of the Illinois State Historical Library), 25; Ashe, *Travels in America*, 268–70; Cuming, *Tour to the Western Country*, in Thwaites (ed.), *Early Western Travels*, V, 306.

34. Miró, "Description of Louisiana," in Kinnaird (ed.), *Spain in the Mississippi Valley*, III, 160; Stanley Faye, "The Arkansas Post of Louisiana: Spanish Dominion," *Louisiana Historical Quarterly*, XXVII (July, 1944), 629–716; Ellicott, *Journal*, 37; Cramer, *Navigator*, 312; Moses Austin, "Journal of a Voyage," in Eugene C. Barker (ed.), *The Austin Papers* (2 vols.; Washington, D.C., 1924), Vol. II, Pt. 1, p. 73 (part of American Historical Association's *Annual Report, 1919*).

the great river now behind them, they found Natchez an excellent place to resupply and rest up for the final run to New Orleans. Originally an encampment of the Natchez Indians, the bluff settlement had been wrangled over by the French, British, Spanish, and the young United States during the 1700s, before the Americans finally reigned supreme. This conflict left Natchez a rich history and international flavor that ranked it with St. Louis and New Orleans as one of the great towns of the Mississippi Valley. In 1803 the population of the entire Natchez district probably numbered six or seven thousand. The area boasted rich soil, well-developed farms and plantations, and something of a social life. Perrin du Lac observed that "the town, which is built on high ground at the distance of one mile from the river, contains fine houses and rich shops." Cuming added, "I was much struck with the similarity of Natchez to many of the smaller West India towns, particularly St. Johns Antiqua. . . . The houses all with balconies and piazzas . . . free mulattoes, and French and Spanish creoles—the great mixture of colour of the people in the streets . . . might have made one suppose . . . that by some magick power, I had been suddenly transported [to the Caribbean]." Unfortunately, a ragged "Company of Indians" soon made an appearance, shattering Cuming's Caribbean daydreams.[35]

Indeed, enough sordid behavior occurred in Natchez to more than offset its many charming aspects. "Natchez-Under-the-Hill," the area near the river beneath the bluff, became a famous rendezvous for boatmen and frontiersmen who stopped to celebrate the approach of lower Louisiana. Saloons, whorehouses, and gambling dens lined the main (and only) street of Natchez-Under-the-Hill. Bradbury observed that "there is not, perhaps, in the world a more dissipated place. . . . Almost all of the Kentucky men stop here on the way to Orleans, and as they now consider all the dangers and difficulties of their voyage as past, they feel the same inclination to dissipation as sailors, who have been long out of port, and generally remain there a day or two to indulge it."[36]

35. The best secondary account is D. Clayton James, *Antebellum Natchez* (Baton Rouge, 1968). Quotations are from du Lac, *Travels Through the Two Louisianas*, 83–84; and Cuming, *Tour to the Western Country*, in Thwaites (ed.), *Early Western Travels*, IV, 320–21.

36. Bradbury, *Travels in the Interior of America*, in Thwaites (ed.), *Early Western Travels*, V, 211.

The Mississippi River between Natchez and Pointe Coupée, although easier to navigate than the upstream reaches, still lay in a vast wilderness of forest and cypress swamps. On Loftus' Heights, at the thirty-first parallel, stood Fort Adams, the southernmost military installation on American soil during the years before the Louisiana Purchase. Here General James Wilkinson made his headquarters and conducted his numerous business, military, diplomatic, and political affairs. Thomas Ashe noted in 1806 that the general was "collecting troops to drive the Spaniards beyond the Louisiana line." Directly below the bluff stood the village of Wilkinsonburg, an unhealthy spot that seemed to please no one. At Fort Adams and Wilkinsonburg, the Mississippi narrowed to a mere three hundred yards. Riverman John Stuart floated by in the summer of 1806 and noted that "12 miles below the Heights we past the mouth of Red River on our right . . . & 3 miles below, [we passed] the Chaffelia [Atchafalaya River] on the same side." Stuart seemed quite pleased. His long, hard journey through the wilderness was nearly completed.[37]

Lower Louisiana began at Pointe Coupée and, according to Cramer, contained "three-quarters of the population and seven-eights of the riches of Louisiana." Here began the great levee, its construction started in French times and continued by the Spaniards in an attempt to prevent flooding of the rich agricultural lands of the lower Mississippi Valley. All the weary boatmen and travelers expressed delight at the spectacle that lay before them. Here was civilization! Plantations appeared frequently, as did small villages inhabited by friendly and hospitable French Louisianians. On the "German Coast," south of Pointe Coupée, planters grew cotton, rice, sugarcane, and groves of orange trees. Flatboatman Samuel Donnell described Baton Rouge in 1806 as an abandoned Spanish fort and small Acadian village, but from there to New Orleans the banks of the Mississippi had, according to Cramer, "the appearance of one continued village of handsome and

---

37. The American military installation was variously referred to as Loftus' Heights, Fort Wilkinson, Wilkinsonburg, and Fort Adams. Its correct name in 1803 was Fort Adams. See William Buckner McGroarty (ed.), "Diary of Captain Phillip Buckner," *William and Mary Quarterly,* n.s., VI (July, 1926), 173–207; Stuart, "A Journal," 20; Ashe, *Travels in America,* 293. For the Red River, see Miró, "A Description of Louisiana," in Kinnaird (ed.), *Spain in the Mississippi Valley,* III, 159–60. For the Atchafalaya River, see Pitot, *Observations,* 119.

neatly built houses." The travelers and rivermen reacted enthusiastically to these sights. Most were overjoyed. The Kentucky flatboatman John Stuart aptly summed up these feelings in his journal entry of June 2, 1806: "We had a fine pleasant night for floating last night. We past several houses where they were dancing in full glee. We have the most beautiful prospects about 60 or 70 miles above New Orleans. Low level Banks fine plantations & handsome houses surrounded with beautiful orange and fig trees."[38]

Founded by the French in 1718, New Orleans had grown to a population of approximately eight thousand inhabitants by the time of the Louisiana Purchase. The great fire of 1788 had destroyed many dwellings, but most travelers seemed impressed with the quality of the tile-roofed wood and brick housing of the early 1800s. Public buildings included the cathedral, town hall, prison, army barracks, hospital, convent, and market house. Commerce boomed. The economic activities not only of the Ohio and Mississippi flatboatmen and keelboatmen, but of many Caribbean, African, and European interests revolved around the city. Ships, flats, and keels reportedly extended "the entire length of the Levee . . . three abreast . . . composed of all nations." One riverman estimated seeing "150 ships & sailing Vessels of burthen & upwards of 300 flats." The market house teemed with shoppers in search of "beef, pork . . . veal; fish of several sorts in abundance and cheap; wild ducks and other game in season; tame turkies, fowls, ducks, and geese." Stuart noted that "Plenty of watermelons, cucumbers, plumbs, sweets, Irish potatoes & almost everything" could be purchased.[39]

Of course, there was much more to life in New Orleans in 1803 than business, and the boatmen were anxious to go ashore. Thomas Ashe wrote that as soon as the sun set, "animation begins to rise, the public walks are crowded; the billiard rooms resound, music strikes up, and life and activities resume their joyous career." In the tradition of the Spanish *paseo,* residents congregated along the levee for the eve-

38. Cramer, *Navigator,* 330, 221; du Lac, *Travels Through the Two Louisianas,* 86; Donnell, "On the Mississippi in 1806"; Stuart, "A Journal," 21.

39. For a lively secondary account of early New Orleans, see Herbert Asbury's *The French Quarter: An Informal History of the New Orleans Underworld* (New York, 1938). Quotations are from Ashe, *Travels in America,* 302–303, 311; Cramer, *Navigator,* 315–18; Stuart, "A Journal," 21.

ning stroll, and it was "no uncommon thing to see the sprightly dance on the deck, or the bottle circulate under the awning, while the whole town promenades the Levee." A Pittsburgh flatboat merchant saw "vast numbers of negro slaves, men, women, and children, assembled together on the levee drumming, fifing, and dancing, in large rings."[40]

Other scenes proved less enchanting. For example, du Lac complained of muddy roads, filth, and the "putrid" smell of the markets, and Louisianian James Pitot condemned the "Hundreds of licensed taverns" selling liquor to boatmen and blacks, and the "gambling houses . . . where the swindler and adventurer rob the inexperienced young man as well as the father of a family who is forgetful of his duties." Gambling was "very frequent," observed another visitor to New Orleans, "and our foolish Kentucky men spend and lose their money in this place most infamously." New Orleans was, after all, a town that catered to boatmen and merchant seamen, and it definitely retained an unsavory aspect. Yet New Orleans in 1803 was undoubtedly a fascinating and exciting place to be. Certainly there were other cities in the world that offered excitement, but New Orleans had emerged in a milieu that could never be duplicated, and it appropriately served as the capital city of the Mississippi Valley.[41]

Like its leading city, the Mississippi Valley in 1803 hosted a curious amalgam of French, Spanish, English, American, African, Caribbean, and Indian peoples. Every traveler wrote about the Indian population. According to Schultz, white encroachments had forced some Ohio Valley Indians such as the Shawnee to take up residence on the west bank of the Mississippi, near Cape Girardeau. The Shawnee, the Miami, and, below the confluence, the Creek, Chickasaw, Choctaw, Cherokee, and Natchez made up most of the Indian population of the lower Mississippi Valley. Francis Bailey waxed a bit romantic aboard his flatboat in 1797, describing a "well-made, handsome race of men . . . a number of them sitting on the banks and others standing at the top of the hill, enjoying the mildness of evening and the beauty of the setting sun." He added, however, that none of the Indians would approach the flatboats, "whose motions they watched with an attentive

40. Ashe, *Travels in America,* 311; Cuming, *Tour to the Western Country,* in Thwaites (ed.), *Early Western Travels,* IV, 363.

41. Du Lac, *Travels Through the Two Louisianas,* 90; Pitot, *Observations,* 29, Whitaker, *Mississippi Question,* 44.

eye." Boatman Joseph Hough concurred—he saw the Indians only at a distance. As time passed, many would come closer to investigate these rivermen and the goods they brought with them—and some of the southern Indians chose to fight the invasion foreshadowed by the arrival of the boatmen.[42]

Black slaves and freemen formed a sizable portion of the varied society of the Lower Mississippi in 1803. Most outsiders seem to have viewed this element of the population basically as a novelty; only a few travelers expressed any great outrage at the institution of slavery. One of these was Francis Bailey, who wrote indignantly in 1797 about how "that miserable class of men . . . the unfortunate blacks [of New Orleans] bear up under the haughty frowns of their masters."[43]

The French Louisianians—"Acadians" and "Creoles"—seemed a warm and hospitable people. Flatboatmen walking or riding home horseback during the late 1700s and early 1800s often enjoyed the food, shelter, and generous hospitality of French Louisianians. However, James Pitot noted that the "gay, noisy, hospitable" Acadians also could display undue "emotionalism" and love for "pleasure and dissipation." Evidently they liked to drink whiskey and wine and enjoy themselves.[44]

All seemed to agree, in 1803 at least, that the French influence still dominated the lower valley of the Mississippi. The Spanish had held political control since 1763, and a handful of their troops and officials were still dispersed over the realm. Yet the Spanish population's influence, although somewhat evident in architecture and culture, remained relatively small in comparison with that of the French, who dominated in "tastes, customs, habits, religion, and language." The English held strong in West Florida, but the Americans seemed to be as-

42. Schultz, *Travels on an Inland Voyage*, II, 220; Bailey, *Journal of a Tour*, 143; Beaver (ed.), "Joseph Hough, an Early Miami Merchant," 44.

43. Bailey, *Journal of a Tour*, 165.

44. "Autobiography of John Hutchins" (Typescript in Breckinridge Family Papers [M–1311], in Southern Historical Collection, Library of the University of North Carolina at Chapel Hill); Pitot, *Observations*, 31. The word *Acadian* is derived from Acadia—that region of the maritime provinces of Canada from which French settlers were evicted by the British in 1755. Many of the Acadians ultimately made their way to Louisiana, where the name long since has been corrupted to *Cajuns*. *Creole* is a much-debated term used to refer to native Louisianians of French (and sometimes Spanish) ancestry. See Asbury, *French Quarter*, 92.

cendant in 1803—they had, after all, just purchased the Louisiana Territory. American military and governmental officials began to make an appearance, and native Louisianans and travelers were heard to complain of the "influx of American speculators" and the "violence and competition" they brought with them. The western boatmen, often referred to simply as "Kentuckians," were in the vanguard of this American advance. By 1803, these "Kentuckians" already had gained a reputation for their alleged uncouth behavior, "drunkenness, fighting and violence."[45]

The society of the Lower Mississippi was thus incredibly diffuse. Where else but Natchez, Baton Rouge, or New Orleans could an Englishman enjoy a repast of gumbo in his French-style home, take an afternoon siesta, only to be awakened by two American boatmen engaged in a rough-and-tumble over an Indian squaw? Such a fantastic scenario was not at all improbable on the Lower Mississippi in 1803. In culture and society, as well as in geography, climate, flora, and fauna, this was a diverse and fascinating place.[46]

Geography and climate in fact provide another important key to understanding the world the boatmen knew. All of the rivermen seemed profoundly affected by the lower Mississippi Valley's wild aspect, the steamy humidity, and the stifling summer heat. Even as far north as St. Louis, the rich vegetation and warm summer rains contributed to a semitropical feeling. To be sure, the Mississippi Valley was no Barbados, but the palmettos and bayous (and alligators) that characterized much of this region made it a far cry from Salem, Massachusetts. The African, Spanish, French, and Caribbean cultural influences provided a fitting complement to the natural setting.

The descent south from New Orleans, along the Mississippi through the great Louisiana swamplands, was thus the final stage of a natural evolution for the boatmen, geographically and climatically as well as culturally. At the river's mouth lay the Gulf of Mexico and the world of the Caribbean. In 1803 very few of the western boatmen

45. Pitot, *Observations*, 31; Ashe, *Travels in America*, 310, 263; Governor Manuel de Salcedo to Governor W. C. C. Claiborne, February 28, 1802, in Dunbar Rowland (ed.), *Official Letter Books of W. C. C. Claiborne, 1801–1816* (6 vols.; Jackson, Miss., 1917), I, 60–62.

46. After writing this paragraph rather fancifully, I found a very similar scenario documented in Schultz, *Travels on an Inland Voyage*, II, 145–46.

made the trip south from New Orleans and into the Gulf. Many flat-boatmen walked home over the Natchez Trace or rode horseback. Keelboatmen began their arduous upstream journey home by river—a journey that would last several months. A surprising number of these early rivermen simply took up residence in Louisiana and the territo-ries, and never returned to the states from which they had sailed. The remainder shipped as seamen on merchant vessels or bought passage to the northeastern United States on those same vessels; these boatmen followed the Mississippi to its mouth.[47]

Settlement was sparse along the hundred miles of the Mississippi south of New Orleans. A small village at English Turn and another at Fort Plaquemine (an old French installation) protected New Orleans from a naval assault. But du Lac reported that agriculture flourished only "within twenty miles" of the city "on account of the whole being part of the year inundated by the river." Cramer's *Navigator* stated that this "low and swampy" region appeared "chiefly covered with reeds, having little or no timber, and no settlement whatever." Indeed, this "morass, almost impassable for man or beast," was inhospitable country.[48]

About twenty-four miles south of Fort Plaquemine, the Mississippi branched into three passes, all of which led to sea. Most boatmen took the southeast route, passing the old Spanish (and, earlier, French) fort and lighthouse at Balize. Here local pilots boarded to navigate the ships down the river's treacherous final miles. A Pittsburgh flatboat merchant described this final stage of his journey down the Mississippi in 1799, noting among other things "the beauty of nature as exhibited by the setting sun reflecting its rays upon the clouds in the western hemisphere, which were beautifully tinged with red." A few years later, another flatboatman recorded the end of his journey down the great Ohio and Mississippi rivers and through the world the boatmen knew: "Taking leave of the Mississippi sands, we launch forth to plough the Mexican Gulph."[49]

47. Whitaker, *Mississippi Question*, 141; "Journal of Henry Troth, 1799" (Photocopy in Louisiana Historical Center, New Orleans; original MS in possession of Tyrrell W. Brooke, Vienna, Virginia), 9.

48. Du Lac, *Travels Through the Two Louisianas*, 101; Cramer, *Navigator*, 336–37.

49. Cuming, *Tour to the Western Country*, in Thwaites (ed.), *Early Western Travels*, IV, 370–71; "Journal of a Trip from Champaign County, Ohio," 61.

THREE

Hard Way to Make a Living

After a hard day's push [the boatmen] would take their "fillee" or ration of whisky, and having swallowed a miserable supper of meat half burnt, and of bread half baked, stretch themselves without covering, on the deck, and slumber till the steersman's call invited them to the morning "fillee."

—Captain Frederick Marryat, *A Diary in America*

Poor business this, the Patroon cursing the hands, the hands cursing the boat," keelboatman William Adams wrote bitterly in his journal entry of July 14, 1807. The upstream journey of his barge *Lovely Nan* from New Orleans to the mouth of the Cumberland River had proved exhausting and frustrating. After grueling days of poling, rowing, cordelling, and literally pushing their boat upstream, Adams and his fellow boatmen sometimes found they were "not out of sight of our last place of encampment." Fights broke out among the crew, and several men deserted. Only after four long months did the *Lovely Nan* finally reach the mouth of the Cumberland.[1]

Adams' experiences were not unusual. Throughout the Ohio and Mississippi valleys, flatboatmen, keelboatmen, and raftsmen daily faced great difficulties. Primitive living conditions, sickness, navigation hazards, summer storms and winter ice, attacks by Indians and robbers, and a thousand-mile walk home through a dangerous wilderness were all very much a part of the lives of the early western boatmen. Boating, in the late eighteenth and early nineteenth centuries, was a hard way to make a living.

1. William Adams, "Journal of the Barge Lovely Nan, Lewis West, Master, July 9, 1807–November 20, 1807" (MS in Ohio Historical Society, Columbus). Quotations are from entries of July 14 and September 11.

The evolution of Ohio and Mississippi river commerce, from the early Indian traders to the keelboat and flatboat boom of the early nineteenth century, is a complex and cumbersome subject much investigated by historians.[2] The Indians—the first Ohio and Mississippi boatmen—were joined by French *voyageurs* and English traders in the late seventeenth and early eighteenth centuries. The European traders sailed in canoes and dealt mainly in animal skins, which they bartered from the Indians and transported to the French and English Ohio Valley forts and to St. Louis and New Orleans. The French and British battled fiercely over this lucrative inland commerce, eventually squaring off in the French and Indian War. Even Britain's victory in 1763 did not resolve the question of commercial supremacy in the Ohio and Mississippi valleys. Indeed, the end of the French and Indian War brought two more competing powers into this complex scene: Spain and the soon-to-be-independent American colonies.[3]

From 1762 to 1803, the Spanish controlled the Mississippi from its mouth to St. Louis. Throughout this time they dealt shrewdly with British and, later, American boatmen, often through resident French middlemen. The Spanish yearned for economic independence in the Old Southwest, but economic necessity drove them to a reluctant, foot-dragging cooperation with the Anglos. Slowly a trade in pelts, lead, and staples such as flour, salt, and whiskey began to grow. The American Revolution presented the Spanish with an opportunity to harm their old enemies, the British. With Spanish consent and aid, an illicit trade in gunpowder and military stores moved up the Mississippi, and soldier-boatmen such as "Captain" James Willing enjoyed a

2. The best secondary accounts of this early commerce are John G. Clark, *New Orleans, 1718–1812: An Economic History* (Baton Rouge, 1970), and Nancy M. Surrey, *The Commerce of Louisiana During the French Regime, 1699–1763* (New York, 1916). For the late eighteenth and early nineteenth centuries, I have relied heavily on Arthur P. Whitaker's classics, *The Spanish-American Frontier, 1783–1795* (1927; rpr. Lincoln, Neb., 1969) and *The Mississippi Question, 1795–1803: A Study of Trade, Politics, and Diplomacy* (1934; rpr. Gloucester, Mass., 1962).

3. Surrey, *Commerce of Louisiana*, 55–76, 288–365; William O. Scroggs, "Early Trade and Travel in the Lower Mississippi Valley," *Proceedings of the Mississippi Valley Historical Association*, II (1908–1909), 235–56; George Johnston, Esqr., Governor of West Florida, to John Pownall, Esqr., May 4, 1765, in Dunbar C. Rowland (ed.), *The Mississippi Provincial Archives: English Dominion, 1763–1766* (Nashville, Tenn., 1911), 279; Fairfax Harrison, "The Virginians on the Ohio and Mississippi in 1742," *Louisiana Historical Quarterly*, V (July, 1922), 316–22.

brief moment of fame. By having helped to defeat the British, however, the Spanish had insured their own demise, for now they had to deal with the Americans.[4]

In 1783 the American surge west of the Appalachians began in earnest. Granted the "right" to navigate the entire length of the Mississippi by Great Britain in the Treaty of Paris of 1783, American frontiersmen believed naïvely that Spain would allow them to do business in New Orleans. The Spanish, however, had not signed the Paris accord, and they viewed the growing American economic presence as a portent of military and political penetration into the Old Southwest. In 1784, Count Floridablanca ordered the Mississippi below New Madrid closed to American navigation. Furious westerners were then treated to an even greater surprise. Negotiating with Don Diego de Gardoqui in 1785, New York diplomat John Jay offered to suspend American navigation of the Mississippi for twenty-five years. This less-famous "Jay's Treaty" was never implemented, and it never would have succeeded on the frontier. The Spaniards' problem was that they needed American goods, especially flour. Also, by 1787 the American army officer and flatboat entrepreneur James Wilkinson already had begun to develop a technique through which American boating commerce in Spanish Louisiana would survive and prosper.[5]

James Wilkinson was not the only flatboatman to penetrate the Spanish barrier, but he was one of the first and most enterprising. He understood the Spaniards' fears and aimed to salve them. If the Spaniards wanted new subjects and loyalty oaths—and after 1788 they did—then that is exactly what they would get. With "a view to promote my own fortunes and to benefit my fellow citizens," Wilkinson in 1787 made his first descent to New Orleans. He later sent personally

---

4. "Spanish Detailed Statistical Report of St. Louis and Ste. Genevieve" (1772–74), in Louis Houck (ed.), *The Spanish Regime in Missouri* (2 vols.; New York, 1971), I, 55, 87, 93; Ben Casseday, *The History of Louisville from Its Earliest Settlement to the Year 1852,* (Louisville, 1852), 62; James Hall, *Notes on the Western States* (Philadelphia, 1838), 219; John Caughey, "Willing's Expedition Down the Mississippi, 1778," *Louisiana Historical Quarterly,* XV (January, 1932), 5–36; John Caughey, *Bernardo de Galvez in Louisiana, 1776–1783* (Berkeley, 1934).

5. The complicated events of the period from 1783 through 1787 are treated thoroughly in Whitaker, *Spanish-American Frontier,* 1–88. I have summarized them and discussed the Jay-Gardoqui affair in "The Mississippi River Debate, 1785–1787," *Tennessee Historical Quarterly,* XXXVI (Winter, 1977), 447–67.

or sponsored scores of southbound flatboats laden with flour and tobacco. Wilkinson instructed his pilots "to put on your best Bib &
Tucker," treat all Spanish commandants with great courtesy and a
bribe, announce "a determination to settle in Louisiana," and take "the
Oath of Allegiance." Say "nothing that is not flattering & favorable to
Louisiana," he warned, "and pay me any . . . Compliments you may
think I deserve." To what extent Wilkinson was a "Spanish subject"
and "secret agent" is debatable, but the general was most certainly an
ambitious businessman.[6]

Under careful Spanish supervision, Ohio and Mississippi river
commerce was revolutionized in the 1780s and 1790s. Hundreds of
boatmen floated south, took the oath of allegiance, and sold their
cargoes in Natchez and New Orleans. When a terrible fire burned
New Orleans to the ground in 1788, the Spanish government was
forced into an even greater expansion of its trade connection with
the Ohio Valley. Governor Manuel de Lemos Gayoso continued the
American trade from 1789 to 1799, and Philadelphia and Pittsburgh
merchants sent agents and boatmen to handle their growing business
affairs in New Orleans. All of the boatmen took the loyalty oath, but
Gayoso's dreams of making Spanish subjects of these American adventurers never materialized. The burgeoning trade served only to increase American diplomats' bargaining power. The Treaty of San
Lorenzo of 1795—Pinkney's Treaty—gave the United States the Natchez District, legalized American navigation of the Mississippi, and
granted a place of deposit for American goods in Spanish New Orleans. Although final American diplomatic victory seemed imminent,
the struggle was not yet finished.[7]

6. Clark, *New Orleans, 1718–1812*, p. 213; James Wilkinson, *Memoirs of My Own
Times* (4 vols; Philadelphia, 1816), II, 110–14 and Appendix 6; Arthur P. Whitaker,
"James Wilkinson's First Descent to New Orleans in 1787," *Hispanic American Historical
Review*, VIII (February, 1928), 82–97; James Wilkinson to Hugh McIlvain, March 17,
1791, as transcribed in George D. Todd, "How the Pioneers of the West Marketed Their
Products and the Difficulties They Had to Contend With" (Typescript of a talk before
the Filson Club, May 4, 1903, in George D. Todd Papers, Filson Club Library, Louisville, Ky.). The Spanish oath of allegiance is reproduced in James A. Robertson (trans.
and ed.), *Louisiana Under the Rule of Spain, France, and the United States* (2 vols.; Cleveland, 1911), I, 162–64. For Wilkinson's role in the "Spanish Conspiracy," see Whitaker,
Mississippi Question, 58–59, 103–104, 120, 157–58.

7. Whitaker, *Mississippi Question*, 79; Clark, *New Orleans, 1718–1812*, pp. 213–14;
"Passport Granted the Galley Lavanganza, 1794" (Microfilm copy in Ste. Genevieve,

During the administration of the baron de Carondolet as Spanish governor, American boatmen continued to flock to New Orleans. More flour arrived in that port between 1799 and 1802 than in any comparable period until after the War of 1812. Despite this flow, the boatmen complained of Spanish harassment. True, the Spaniards maintained a Mississippi River squadron and sometimes boarded American boats to inspect cargoes, and, at New Orleans, violators of the rules of deposit were sometimes fined. Usually, however, a bribe could grease the machinery of government and commerce, and from 1799 to 1802 American boatmen actually fared quite well. One can hardly blame the Spanish for not welcoming these "Kentuckians" (as they called them) with open arms. New Orleans and the Louisiana Territory were valuable possessions, and the prospect of losing them did not sit well with the Spanish colonial governors. In this light, the Spaniards' closure of the port of New Orleans to American deposit on October 16, 1802, can be seen as a final, desperate act of defiance. The following year Louisiana was handed over to the French, who, even as the tricolor was being raised over New Orleans, already had sold the territory to the United States.[8]

"What a reverse in the situation of a trader, since the banks of the

Missouri, Archives, Joint Collection, State Historical Society of Missouri, Columbia), folder 375; John Halley Journal, May 2–June 2, 1789, April 27–June 8, 1791 (Photostat of original, in Manuscript Department, Filson Club Library, Louisville, Ky.); "Log of His Majesty's Galiot *La Flèche,*" January 5–March 25, 1793, in Lawrence Kinnaird (ed.), *Spain in the Mississippi Valley, 1765–1794: Translations of Materials from the Spanish Archives in the Bancroft Library* (4 vols.; Washington, D.C., 1946) Vol. IV, Pt. 3, pp. 122, 126 (part of American Historical Association's *Annual Report, 1945*); Carlos de Grand Pré's reports to Don Esteban Miró of flatboat arrivals in Natchez, February–July, 1790, in Kinnaird (ed.), *Spain in the Mississippi Valley,* Vol. III, Pt. 2, pp. 299–300, 313–14, 323–31, 336–37, 343–56, 368; Minter Wood, "Life in New Orleans in the Spanish Period," *Louisiana Historical Quarterly,* XXII (July, 1939), 666; C. Richard Arena, "Philadelphia–Spanish New Orleans Trade in the 1790s," *Louisiana History,* II (1961), 438; Pittsburgh *Gazette,* April 18, 1789; Whitaker, *Spanish-American Frontier,* 201–22.

8. Whitaker, *Mississippi Question,* 91–92, 96, 130, 176–200, 234–36; Clark, *New Orleans, 1718–1812,* pp. 212–15; Sir Jack D. L. Holmes, *Gayoso: The Life of a Spanish Governor in the Mississippi Valley, 1789–1799* (Baton Rouge, 1965), 244–46; Abraham P. Nasatir, *Spanish War Vessels on the Mississippi, 1792–1796* (New Haven, 1968). For an example of how a flatboatman dealt with the Spanish, see "William Johnson's Journal," *Louisiana Historical Quarterly,* V (January, 1922), 34–50, or "A Young Man's Journal of 1800–1813," *Proceedings of the New Jersey Historical Society,* n.s., VII (January, 1922), 49–59. See also E. Wilson Lyon, "The Closing of the Port of New Orleans," *American Historical Review,* XXXVII (January, 1932), 280–86.

Mississippi have become the soil of the United States," wrote Zadok Cramer in his famous how-to book for boatmen, *The Navigator*. "What a conquest gained! A conquest equal to a second revolution! A vast and unlimited territory acquired without a drop of blood! Happy Columbians!" Cramer's enthusiasm was shared by a nation hungry for trade. After 1803 a counterclockwise, circular trade at last was freed from diplomatic restraints. Goods could be shipped down the Ohio and Mississippi and then via the Gulf of Mexico to American coastal cities or on to Europe. Although some sugar, molasses, coffee, and rice moved upstream by keelboat after 1803, this trade amounted to less than 10 percent of the total river commerce. Natchez was, for practical purposes, the Mississippi's northernmost commercial depot for upstream-bound goods. Thus, the late eighteenth and early nineteenth centuries did not really constitute a "keelboat age on western waters." The less glamorous and unheralded flatboat was the foremost river vessel of the era, and the number of flatboat arrivals in New Orleans grew phenomenally, finally peaking fifty years later in 1846 and 1847. The early days of boating were in fact a "flatboat age" on western waters, and nine-tenths of America's early boatmen were flatboatmen.[9]

What kinds of cargoes did the flatboats carry? One could say accurately that they carried everything but the kitchen sink. Early cargoes were simple: furs, salt, lead, lime, flour, pork, and whiskey were the most common loads from 1700 through the Revolution. But the great post–1783 migration west of the Appalachians fostered a demand for a variety of products. By the late 1790s, there existed several permanent army garrisons to be supplied, and a class of sutler-boatmen arose to fill the need. Pioneers bought household goods and hardware from "store boats" flying calico flags. Boatmen continued to haul flour, salted pork, and tobacco, but by the turn of the century loads might as easily include hemp, cotton, potatoes, brandy, ale, logs, lumber, fur-

9. Zadok Cramer, *The Navigator* (1814; rpr. Ann Arbor, 1966), 225; George Rogers Taylor, *The Transportation Revolution, 1815–1860* (New York, 1961), 158; Malcolm J. Rohrbough, *The Trans-Appalachian Frontier: People, Societies, and Institutions, 1775–1850* (New York, 1978), 99–106; Whitaker, *Mississippi Question*, 139. For keelboat cargoes and commerce, see Daniel Drake, *Natural and Statistical View; or, Picture of Cincinnati and the Miami Country* (Cincinnati, 1815), 149; Marshall Smelser, *The Democratic Republic, 1801–1815* (New York, 1968), 38; and Whitaker, *Mississippi Question*, 146–47.

niture, manufactured goods, or livestock—although white horses and cows were believed to bring bad luck, rivermen would haul animals of any other hue.[10]

Thus, by the mid-1820s, the traveler Charles Sealsfield could describe the flatboat landing at Natchez by noting that "one of these flatboats is from the Upper Ohio, laden with pineboards, planks, rye, whiskey, flour; close to it another from the falls of the Ohio, with corn in the ear and bulk, apples, peaches; a third, with hemp, tobacco and cotton. In the fourth you may find horses, regularly stabled together; in the next, cattle from the mouth of the Missouri; a sixth will have hogs, poultry, turkeys. . . . They have come thousands of miles and still have to proceed a thousand more before they arrive at their place of destination." Sealsfield also observed a cargo of "slaves transported from Virginia to Kentucky, to the human flesh mart at New Orleans," and there are many other documented accounts of slave cargoes. As for more willing passengers, westerners had been buying passage on southbound flats and keels for decades, and a packet service existed on Ohio River keelboats twenty years before steamboat days. Some of these packet boats conducted the first regular mail service in the Ohio Valley.[11]

In the year 1807, a reported total of 1,223 flatboats arrived in New Orleans. Inland commerce was crippled by Jefferson's embargo and by the War of 1812, but the river trade bounced back in 1815. Compe-

10. Randolph C. Downes, "Trade in Frontier Ohio," *Mississippi Valley Historical Review,* XVI (March, 1930), 480; Wilkinson, *Memoirs of My Own Times,* II, 269–70; Edgar B. Wesley (ed.), "The Diary of James Kennerly, 1823–1826," *Missouri Historical Society Collections,* VI (1928), 41–97; Fountain and Roderick Perry Papers (MSS in Special Collections and Archives, University of Kentucky Library, Lexington); Works Progress Administration, "Flatboats on the Mississippi in 1807: A Compilation of Craft Names, Marine Hospital Tax, and Cargoes Carried on Flat and Keelboats Down the Mississippi River During One Month, May 1 to May 29, in the Year 1807" (Typescript in Louisiana Room, Louisiana State University, Baton Rouge); Christian Schultz, *Travels on an Inland Voyage . . . in the Years 1807 and 1808* (2 vols.; 1810; rpr. Ridgewood, N.J., 1968), II, 100.

11. Charles Sealsfield, *The Americans as They Are* (London, 1828), 108–109; Eliza Chotard Gould, "Autobiography" (Typescript in Alabama Department of Archives and History, Montgomery), 5, 7; William Higgins to William Lucas, July 3, 1825, in Lucas Collection, Missouri Historical Society, St. Louis; *Centinel of the Northwest Territory* (Cincinnati), November 16, 1793; Pittsburgh *Gazette,* October 19, 1793; Postmaster General to Judge Putnam, May 24, 1794, in Clarence Carter (ed.), *The Territorial Papers of the United States* (28 vols.; Washington, D.C., 1934–75), II, 482–84.

tition from steamboats after 1811 drove keelboatmen up the tributaries, but flatboatmen continued to grow in number and prosper. Theirs was a risky but lucrative business, and by 1823—a year that can be used to divide roughly the periods of preindustrial and industrial (steam) boating in America—the flatboat trade had become a very substantial and profitable enterprise. Ohioan Felix Renick wrote his friend William McNeill in 1823, saying that "our ears are now continually greeted with the musical sound of the boatman's horn" and estimating that "something like three hundred [flatboats will] float out of the Scioto this year." He told his friend that "you can form no conjecture nor could you possibly believe was you to hear the quantity of produce that descends the River to the Orleans Market." Indeed, the flatboats carried goods that "no other person, except a yankey, would think of takeing to market."[12]

"No form of water craft so whimsical, no shape so outlandish, can well be imagined," wrote the Reverend Timothy Flint, "but what, on descending from Pittsburgh to New Orleans, it may some where be seen lying to the shore, or floating on the river." Boats and boatbuilding have been researched thoroughly by historians who confirm Flint's observations.[13] Besides the flats and keels there were crude "bullboats," dugout canoes and pirogues, "batteaux," and a few huge lumber and log rafts. Some boatmen experimented with horse- or cattle-driven watercraft, and Colonel Henry Atkinson even used sol-

12. Stephen F. Austin to Moses Austin, July 12, 1812, in Eugene C. Barker (ed.), *The Austin Papers* (2 vols.; Washington, D.C., 1924), Vol. II, Pt. 1, p. 216 (part of American Historical Association's *Annual Report, 1919*); Works Progress Administration, "Flatboats on the Mississippi in 1807"; Felix Renick to William McNeill, March 15, 1823, in McNeill Papers, West Virginia and Regional History Collections, West Virginia University Library, Morgantown. The best quantitative study of the profitability of keels and flats before the advent of the steamboat is summarized in Erik F. Haites and James Mak, "Ohio and Mississippi River Transportation, 1810–1860," *Explorations in Economic History*, VIII (Winter, 1970), 168–70, and presented in complete form in Erik F. Haites, James Mak, and Gary M. Walton, *Western River Transportation* (Baltimore, 1975).

13. Timothy Flint, *A Condensed Geography and History of the Western States, or the Mississippi Valley* (2 vols.; 1828; rpr. Gainesville, Fla., 1970), I, 229. The best secondary works on the subject are Leland D. Baldwin, *The Keelboat Age on Western Waters*, (Pittsburgh, 1941); Archer B. Hulbert, *The Paths of Inland Commerce* (New Haven, 1921) and *Waterways of Westward Expansion: The Ohio River and its Tributaries* (Cleveland, 1903); and John Amos Johnson, "Pre-Steamboat Navigation on the Lower Mississippi River" (Ph.D. dissertation, Louisiana State University, 1963).

diers to power sidewheel riverboats. In Marietta, Ohio, transplanted New Englanders built several seagoing sailing ships, only to learn at the Falls of the Ohio that a river is not an ocean. Add to this odd assortment the many store boats (referred to by locals as "chicken thieves" because of the alleged thieving propensity of their owners), the floating "tinner's" and blacksmith's establishments, and a variety of rivergoing taverns, "dram shops," and even whorehouses, and there appears a fascinating view of early boating on America's western rivers.[14]

Unusual rivercraft notwithstanding, keelboats and flatboats held sway on the western rivers during the eighteenth and early nineteenth centuries. Although not nearly so numerous or important as the flats, the more glamorous keelboats and their crews captured the imagination of the young Republic. The keel and its larger cousin, the barge, resembled small sailing ships. Keelboats were described by one Ohio pioneer as "long and narrow, sharp at bow and stern, and of light draft." Named for their four-inch-square keel shock absorbers, these boats averaged sixty feet in length, eight feet in width, and could carry a burden of from twenty to forty tons of freight up or down the main channel or a shallow tributary stream. A typical keel or barge was outfitted with sails, masts, and rigging, carried a leather boat pump, had cleated running boards from which the crew poled the craft, and featured a cabin "enclosed and roofed with boards or shingles." Although forced out of business by steamers on the Lower Ohio and Lower Mississippi in the 1820s and 1830s, the keels retreated to the Upper Ohio, Upper Mississippi, and tributary streams, where they continued to work well into the century.[15]

14. Flint, *Condensed Geography*, I, 230–31, 236–37; Baldwin, *Keelboat Age*, 39–42, 159–74; Vincennes (Ind.) *Western Sun*, July 31, 1819; Roger L. Nichols, "Army Contributions to River Transportation, 1818–1825," *Military Affairs*, XXXIII (April, 1969), 242–49; John G. Stuart, "A Journal: Remarks or Observations in a Voyage Down the Kentucky, Ohio, Mississippi Rivers etc.," *Register of the Kentucky Historical Society*, L (January, 1952), 15. An unedited typescript of the Stuart journal is in possession of the Kentucky State Historical Society in Frankfort. I quote from the published version except where noted.

15. S. Wilkerson, "Early Recollections of the West," *American Pioneer*, II (June, 1843), 271; Flint, *Condensed Geography*, I, 229; Haites and Mak, "Ohio and Mississippi River Transportation," 168–70. For detailed descriptions of keelboats, see also Odiborne Scott and Co. Papers, 1842 (MSS in Illinois Historical Society, Springfield) and Robert Dale Owen, "Travel Journal, 1825–26," ed. Josephine M. Elliott, *Indiana*

The flatboat was known by many aliases—"Kentucky boat" for its point of origin, "New Orleans" or "Natchez boat" for its destination, "broadhorn" for its huge steering oars, and "ark" for its supposed biblical predecessor—but by any name there was no mistaking these "large square boxes . . . abandoned to the current," floating clumsily down the Ohio and Mississippi. Flatboats won no beauty contests, but they got the job done. Averaging sixty feet in length and fifteen in width, and carrying forty to fifty tons of cargo, the flats "were usually sided up about six feet" above the water line. On the roof of the cabin "the bow hands could ply their Oars." Meals were prepared in an open sandbox fireplace on the deck below. Builders designed flatboats for downstream travel exclusively, and upon reaching their destination boatmen broke them up and sold them for scrap lumber. Many of the sidewalks and outbuildings of New Orleans were fashioned from dismantled flatboats, and there were even a few "flatboat churches" constructed with lumber from the flatboats of the Mississippi River. Popular among farmers and emigrant families as well as professional rivermen, flatboats were plying the western waters literally by the hundreds at the turn of the century.[16]

Professional boatbuilders appeared on the Upper Ohio as early as the 1750s and, by 1800, were working in boatbuilding centers such as Pittsburgh, Wheeling, Cincinnati, Louisville, and St. Louis. Although flatboats and keelboats became larger and more comfortable during the nineteenth century, the techniques for building them remained much the same. Keels and barges were always built by professional boatbuilders, but a flatboat could be assembled by any farmer or frontiersman who had some tools and a little help and advice. Flatboatman Miles Stacy of Marietta, Ohio, built all his own boats, felling and drafting "8,000 feet of lumber to build a boat 75 feet long." He framed the craft with "straight yellow poplar . . . gunnels," cross-ties, and "stringers,"

Historical Society Publications, Vol. XXIII, Pt. 4, p. 237. For barges, see *Missouri Gazette* (St. Louis), December 2, 1815. The best secondary account is Baldwin, *Keelboat Age,* 43–47.

16. Josephine E. Phillips, "Flatboating on the Great Thoroughfare," *Cincinnati Historical Society Bulletin,* V (June, 1947), 12; Samuel Chew Madden Notebook (Typescript in Indiana Historical Society, Indianapolis), 2; "Notebook," n.d. (MS in James Earl Bradley Papers, Louisiana and Lower Mississippi Valley Collections, Louisiana State University Libraries, Baton Rouge); New Orleans *Police Code* (1808), Tulane University, New Orleans, 94; Baldwin, *Keelboat Age,* 47–49.

all hammered together with "some two thousand" wooden pins made of "seasoned white oak." Planks "were fastened to this framework and all the seams calked tight with oakum." The boat was built upside-down at the water's edge, and Stacy and his crew launched it and then piled rocks on one side until the weight tipped the boat rightside-up. At such launchings, old hands made a show of standing on the boat's bottom, "one on the bow and the other on the stern," walking up the bottom as the boat tilted, then swinging over and walking "down the other side." Those who were not quick enough, Stacy remembered, got "a ducking and the rest of us got a laugh."[17]

Early rivermen always named their boats, sometimes in honor of a political leader or member of the owner's family (*John Adams, Madison, Craig, James Ross, Paul Jones, Young Mary Jane*), but just as often for the boat's home port or point of destination (*Missourian, Vicksburg, Bayou Pierre, Belle Rivière*), an animal (*Eagle, Sea Serpent, Dolphin, Snail, Hornet*), an ideal (*Freedom, Democrat, Adventure, Good Luck, Philanthropist, Perseverence* [sic], *Fear Not, Invincible*), the boat's cargo (*Swiness, Potato, Tavern Ship, Sandy Sow*), or a personal fancy or whim (*Bachelor's Joy, Drunkard, Three Friends, Plough Boys*). Fitted out with "check posts," a capstan, 150-yard-long lines ("hawsers"), and a leather boat pump, flatboats during the presteam period sold for about $1.25 per foot; keels cost about $2.25 per foot. Thus, a newly built, average-sized flatboat cost about $75, and a keelboat $135. Optionally, the prospective riverman could buy a used boat (making sure the timber was not rotten), build one himself, or, like George Hamilton of Ste.

---

17. Zadok Cramer, *The Ohio and Mississippi Navigator* (Pittsburgh, 1802), 7; *Pennsylvania Journal* (Philadelphia), February 13, 1788. I have quoted Miles Stacy's mid-nineteenth-century account of boatbuilding because, with the exception of increased boat size, his boats and building techniques were quite similar to those of earlier builders. See "Flatboating Down Old Man River, 1849–1869: Reminiscences of Captain Miles A. Stacy as Related to His Daughter Adelaide Frost Stacy, February, 1913. Rearranged and Typed by Her, April, 1945" (Typescript in Ohio Historical Society, Campus Martius, the Museum of the Northwest Territory, Marietta, Ohio), 4–6. Compare this with *George Hamilton v. Theophilus Williams*, 1806 (Microfilm copy in Ste. Genevieve, Missouri, Archives, Joint Collection, State Historical Society of Missouri, Columbia), folders 537, 548; or with Sangamon/Logan County Documents, 1830 (MS in Illinois Historical Society, Springfield), folder 1. The most accessible firsthand account is Donald F. Carmony (ed.), "Flatboat Building on Little Raccoon Creek, Parke County, Indiana," *Indiana Magazine of History*, LX (December, 1964), 305–22.

Genevieve, barter "a brown horse three years old" for a new flatboat.[18]

Having purchased a boat, the owner proceeded to hire a crew and begin his journey. There was considerable variation in crew composition and caste. If the owner of the boat and cargo accompanied the load south, he was called *captain* or *supercargo*. If he knew how to steer, he also served as pilot and was referred to in the trade as a *merchant navigator*. If he could not steer the difficult stretches of the river, he hired a pilot, either for the entire trip or temporarily. If the owner stayed home, then the pilot became captain, even if he had no financial interest in the load. In the early West such agent boatmen were called *patroons,* a word apparently adopted from the French *patron,* conceivably with some Dutch influence; Americans generally substituted the term *master* for patroon. Other than their own salaries, neither patroons nor masters usually retained any financial interest in the load. This rather confused situation was further complicated by inevitable exceptions and variations to the rules and by a watch system that gained popularity toward the end of this era of flatboating and keelboating. As long as the boat was sailing smoothly and there were no emergencies, nineteenth-century boatmen stood watches—each man on duty six hours and off duty six hours. This meant that a second pilot, or *steersman,* guided the boat while the captain, patroon, or master slept. This second pilot was usually the lead deckhand—today he would be called the first mate. Early flatboat owners hired two or three common hands. As boat size increased, so did the number of crew members. Five or six hands, however, were sufficient to navigate even the largest flatboat. An upstream-bound keelboat, by way of comparison, carried a crew of at least ten. Barges, the short-lived cousins of the keels, engaged approximately twenty-five hands.[19]

Even with such large crews, keelboatmen and bargemen found their daily work exhausting. Much has been written about the daily

18. Works Progress Administration, "Flatboats on the Mississippi in 1807"; Baldwin, *Keelboat Age,* 53–54; Receipt, October 2, 1826 (MS in Fountain and Roderick Perry Papers); *Hamilton* v. *Williams,* folder 537.

19. Flatboat and keelboat crew composition and caste have never been discussed or analyzed adequately. The above generalizations are derived from numerous boatmen's and travelers' reminiscences, including Adams, "Journal of the Barge Lovely Nan"; Madden Notebook, 2; and Flint, *Condensed Geography,* I, 232.

regimen of the keelboatmen, yet it is still difficult for any person in today's world to grasp the magnitude of the ordeals these men endured on the upstream leg of their journeys. From sunrise to sunset, the keelboatmen inched their way up the western rivers, spending three to six months on a single voyage. Traveling during flood stage to avoid shoals, they faced the strongest currents of the Ohio and Mississippi rivers. On a good day, one riverman remembered, "a breese arose," and the crew "hoisted sail." Occasionally, too, eddies worked in the upstream man's favor. But most of the time the boatmen rowed, cordelled, poled, "warped," and "bushwacked" their boats up the river, averaging, if they were fortunate, fifteen to twenty miles a day.[20]

When the current allowed, the upstream men rowed, seated in the bow of their keel or barge and using wooden oars. Rowing songs created both a rhythm to which boatmen could synchronize their work and a medium for transmitting commands from the captain, and at the same time served to take a bit of the drudgery out of the rivermen's toil. Around 1810, traveler John Bradbury observed a crew of "Canadian" boatmen on the Lower Mississippi, "measuring the strokes of their oars by songs, which were generally responsive betwixt the oarsmen at the bow and those at the stern; sometimes the steersman sung and was chorused by the men" (see Appendix). This "call and response" pattern also can be traced to black slave rivermen, who rowed to tunes such as the spiritual "Michael Rowed the Boat Ashore." An observer of Ohio River keelboatmen noted the words of a popular river worksong of the early nineteenth century: "Some rows up, but we rows down / All the way to Shawnee town / Pull away— pull away!"[21]

Cordelling required the crew to carry ashore a long thick rope known as a cordelle or hawser. Using this, the men literally pulled the

20. Adams, "Journal of the Barge Lovely Nan," November 8, 1807, *passim*.

21. "Ulloa's Instructions to Rui, 1767," in Houck (ed.), *The Spanish Regime in Missouri*, I, 1–2; John Bradbury, *Bradbury's Travels in the Interior of America, 1809–1811* in Thwaites (ed.), *Early Western Travels, 1748–1846* (32 vols.; Cleveland, 1904–1907), V, 39–40; Lawrence Levine, *Black Culture and Black Consciousness: Afro-American Thought from Slavery to Freedom* (New York, 1977), 202–17; John Blassingame, *The Slave Community: Plantation Life in the Antebellum South* (New York, 1972), 53; Constance Rourke, *American Humor: A Study of the National Character* (New York, 1959), 79, 87–88; James Hall, *Letters from the West* (1828; rpr. Gainesville, Fla., 1967), 93–94.

boat ahead from the bank. *Warping* was the reverse process, used when the bank was too brushy or rugged for foot travel. The men rowed ahead of the boat in a skiff and attached a line to a big tree. Returning to the boat, they would "lay hold of the warp," pulling the keel or barge up to the tree by using a wooden reel or capstan. If the shore was especially wooded, boatmen simply grabbed onto the limbs of trees and bushes and inched their way upstream. This method of "pulling it along by the brush" they termed *brushwacking* or *bushwacking*.[22]

The upstream man's signature piece, however, was the poling of his craft. At the patroon's commands "Stand to your poles!" and "Set poles!" each crew member planted the iron-shod end of his staff in the river and braced the opposite end with his shoulder. "Down on her!" the patroon would yell, and with a grunt the boatmen began "creeping along on their hands and toes" down the cleated running board, from the bow to the stern. "Lift poles!" barked the patroon, and the keel-boatmen quickly returned to the bow to begin again. In a rapids, "chute," or any particularly strong current, only one man rotated at a time while the others, with great difficulty, held the boat steady in the current. As an old Ohioan remembered, "A boatman who could not boast that he had never swung nor backed in a shoot was regarded with contempt and never trusted with the head pole, the place of honor among the keel-boatmen." The shallow, sandy bottoms of the Ohio were the best suited for poling, but the technique proved exhausting even under ideal conditions—and when one places it alongside the other methods of upstream navigation, the picture that emerges of the daily regimen of the upstream men is not a pretty one. "Made the best of our way by rowing, cordelling, & warping," wrote the weary bargeman William Adams at the end of a sweltering August day in 1807. "A hard day's work this to find only 8 miles cut off the Distance we have to run." If Adams found his work particularly romantic, he did not say so. The trademark of these early frontier rivermen was not a feathered cap and a girl in every port, but rather a sweaty and blood-

22. Adams, "Journal of the Barge Lovely Nan," August 10, 1807; Moses Meeker, "Early History of the Lead Region of Wisconsin," *Wisconsin Historical Collections,* VI (1872), 277–78; Thomas Forsyth, "Journal of a Voyage from St. Louis to the Falls of St. Anthony, June 1–September 17, 1819" (MS in State Historical Society of Wisconsin, Madison), 7.

stained shirt and "callouses on their shoulders where the poles rested that would make a hodcarrier blush." [23]

Downstream navigation was less time-consuming, but certainly as dangerous. Although no self-respecting keelboatman would have given the lowly flatboatman any credit, the downstream men's work was very demanding. Many of their problems can be traced to the navigation seasons. Flatboatmen traveled when the river was high, and on the Ohio and the Mississippi that meant during the winter (approximately November through January) and during the spring flooding (approximately March through May). Most boats descended in the spring, but among the many flatboatmen who also farmed, the winter season was popular: it facilitated the marketing of pork and the produce of the autumn harvest during the very months when these farmer flatboatmen could not work at home. If everything went well, a flatboat could descend from the Upper Ohio to New Orleans in three or four weeks. Unfortunately, things did not always go well during the treacherous winter months or at spring flood stage on the Ohio and Mississippi rivers. [24]

Inclement weather brought constant hardship and sickness to the western boatmen. In winter, floating ice crashed against boats, sending some to the bottom. A "noise resembling peals of thunder in consequence of the ice breaking up" and the cry of "Ice ahead! Ice floating in the Mississippi!" sometimes foreshadowed a horrible plunge into the freezing river and a struggle for survival. Spring brought thunderstorms, and boatmen found themselves working and sleeping for days in soaking-wet clothes. In heavy fog, boatmen could only tie up to the bank or proceed blindly downstream. One old flatboatman "would strike the deck at occasional intervals, the Pilot meantime listening for each echo, and by the sense of hearing keep the boat in the center of

23. This sketch is drawn from Wilkerson, "Early Recollections," 271; Jane Ross, "Flatters and Keelers on the Western Rivers," *Early American Life,* VIII (1977), 23; Adams, "Journal of the Barge Lovely Nan," August 10, 11, 1807; Forsyth, "Voyage from St. Louis," *passim;* Otto M. Knoblock, "Early Navigation on the Saint Joseph River," *Indiana Historical Society Publications,* VIII (1925), 191; John J. Audubon, *Delineations of American Scenery and Character* (New York, 1926), 24–27.

24. Works Progress Administration, "Flatboats on the Mississippi in 1807"; Cramer, *Ohio and Mississippi Navigator,* 7; James Hall, *Notes on the Western States* (Philadelphia, 1838), 29–30; Gilbert Imlay, *A Topographical Description of the Western Territory of North America* (1792; rpr. New York, 1969), 81.

the river." To avoid other boats, boatmen carried "tin horns with them, from which they sent forth a wild music through the fog" to announce their presence, and these "boatmen's horns" became a trademark and romantic symbol of the early boating profession (see Appendix). Horns, however, were useless against a final hazard, strong headwinds, which forced many boats to tie up to the bank.[25]

The dangers and discomforts caused by ordinary rain, fog, and wind were paltry when compared with those attached to monumental acts of nature—blizzards, hurricanes, even earthquakes; indeed, some of the most vivid accounts of the New Madrid Earthquakes of 1811 and 1812 were recorded by flatboatmen like Ohioan James McBride, who wrote dramatically about "the desolating effects of the Earthquakes. . . . The shores of the river in this region presented a most melancholy spectacle, the banks cracked and fractured, trees broken off and fractured and in many places acres of ground sunk down so that the tops of trees just appeared above the surface of the water. All nature appeared in ruins, and seemed to mourn in solitude over her melancholy fate."[26]

Beginning a voyage, novice boatmen bought a recent edition of Cramer's *Navigator* for counsel, but any flatboat crew descending without an experienced pilot on board was asking for trouble. Veteran boatmen like Fountain Perry of Kentucky kept extensive notes and logs from previous journeys. Rivermen often lashed their flats together and traveled in fleets for greater speed and safety. "Running with the current" was a general rule of thumb, and many other techniques were common knowledge among flatboatmen. Moses Austin, a merchant navigator in the Louisiana Territory before his eyes turned toward Texas, touched upon several of these techniques in a letter to his son Stephen, who in May of 1812 was heading south to New Orleans with a flatboat loaded with his father's merchandise:

25. Owen, "Travel Journal, 1825–1826," 253; Fountain Perry, "River Logs" (MSS in Fountain and Roderick Perry Papers), December 13, 1829; "Excerpts from the Stone Diary" (Typescript in Ohio Historical Society, Campus Martius, the Museum of the Northwest Territory, Marietta, Ohio), 3 (the original of the diary is in possession of the Ross County Historical Society, Chillicothe, Ohio); William Cooper Howells, *Recollections of Life in Ohio from 1813 to 1840* (1895; rpr. Gainesville, Fla., 1963), 84; Forsyth, "Voyage from St. Louis," 10.

26. James McBride to Miss Mary McRoberts, April 1, 1812, reprinted under the title "A Voyage Down the Mississippi," *Quarterly Publications of the Historical and Philosophical Society of Ohio*, V (1910), 28–31.

In the first place I intended to state to you some general rules to be observed in descending the Mississippi in opposition to every other advice do you observe the following rules—first never run late at Night but always make a landing under a Willow Point in time, its always better to loose a few hours than to be exposed at Night. Never land under a high bank and large timber. When you Intend to land begin in time to pull your boat in shore and always before the boat striks turn her stern down-Stream. Never trust your boat to float unless you have a man on the look out—let this rule be always strictly observed, to much care cannot be taken in Descending this river, when you make your Boat fast at Night see yourself that the Cable is properly made fast—Never suffer any water to be in your boat a[t] Nigh[t] always put to land in Winds I advise you always to Keep out from the bends of the rivers, and guard against Points of Islands, haveing observed this much I must committ you to the Care of that being that govern us all.[27]

Downstream navigation entailed alternate periods of great labor and great leisure. If the boat ran in the current and without problems, no one but the pilot need do anything. But when it came time to work the flat "out of bends in the river, out of eddies" and to make "crossings and landings," the pilot called "To oars!" and all hands went to work. A flatboat came equipped with four oars or "sweeps"—long poles with boards attached. There was one huge stern oar, forty-five to fifty-five feet long and always manned by the pilot; two thirty-foot sweeps—one each on the starboard and port sides; and a small emergency oar, or "gouger," on the bow. To work these heavy sweeps required considerable strength. The boatman "would take the pole against one shoulder, and quartering across the breast would push, not pull, with a walk up about fifteen feet, carrying it back to get another hold in the water." Sometimes two men worked a sweep, and "it was extremely hard work, and very trying on clothes and shoe leather." If the boat headed for a snag or some other disaster, the captain yelled to "pull her out! pull her out!" Then "some pretty desperate pulling en-

27. Fountain Perry, "River Logs," *passim;* Cramer, *Ohio and Mississippi Navigator,* 8–9, *passim;* Moses Austin to Stephen Austin, April 28, 1812, in Barker (ed.), *Austin Papers,* Vol. II, Pt. 1, p. 203. As the nineteenth century advanced, Cramer continued to issue new editions of his *Navigator,* and a number of other how-to books for boatmen appeared. The most popular and accurate were Samuel Cummings' *The Western Navigator* (Philadelphia, 1822), and his *Western Pilot* (Cincinnati, 1825), both of which were issued in several editions.

sued." If the craft became trapped in a swirling eddy, all hands attempted to "crawfish out" using poles and sweeps, but sometimes their efforts failed: one old Memphian remembered that in the 1820s, "flatboats that intended giving Memphis the go-by not unfrequently found themselves forcibly drawn into the eddy, and made to rotate for hours, to the great delight of the boys on the bluff, who loved to hear the boatmen swear."[28]

The "landing of such an unwieldy craft called for no mean ability or lack of skill," an Ohio River boatman recalled. Spying a safe spot to land, the steersman called "Round to!" and two hands rowed the flat's skiff quickly to shore, pulling "some two hundred feet of line" behind them. Meanwhile, the rest of the crew began to slow the flat, steering the stern around until it was facing downstream and "drifting towards the shore at which the landing was to be made." When the skiff reached shore, the deckhands quickly tied their line to a stout tree. The men on the boat then gave the other end of the line "a round turn on the [bow] snubbing post." With a sudden jerk, the line became very taut and the boat swung to shore. The boatmen controlled the friction on the line by "paying it out," but often it "smoked" and threatened to snap. If it did snap, or if the hands' timing was off in any other particular, they had to start all over again. The only alternative to this tricky procedure was simply to steer the flat into a muddy bank or a stand of willows or cane, but that could prove disastrous. No wonder Cramer advised his readers to "contrive to land as seldom as possible."[29]

Flatboats were forever running into things. Grounding was a constant problem, even in high water. "[W]hat perplexity and embarrassment!" wrote Tennessee merchant navigator John Bedford in 1807. "[A]re we to stick and ground every 2 or 3 days? Some fatality seems directed to us particularly which, after torturing and perplexing us al-

28. Postmaster General to Major Isaac Craig, August 23, 1794, in Carter (ed.), *Territorial Papers of the United States,* II, 489; Hutchinson (Kans.) *Daily News,* October 11, 1890; Robert Carlton, *The New Purchase; or, Seven and a Half Years in the Far West* (2 vols.; New York, 1843), I, 44–45; "Memorandum of a Trip to New Orleans," (MS in Hawes Family Papers, Special Collections and Archives, University of Kentucky Library, Lexington), entry for December 16, 1842; James Dick Davis, *The History of the City of Memphis . . . [and] the "Old Times Papers"* (Memphis, 1873), 196.

29. Cramer, *Ohio and Mississippi Navigator,* 9. All preceding quotations in this paragraph are from "Excerpts from the Stone Diary," 1–2.

most out of life, will sink and drown us!" If unable to shove their flat off ground with poles, the boatmen had to unload cargo into a skiff or "lighter" until the larger boat floated free. Failing at this, they could either "scrape out channels . . . of sufficient width and depth" for navigation, wait for a "rise," or jump in the river and start pushing. Many took the latter course, regardless of season. Pushing his flatboat off ground in December of 1818, Joseph Lovell wrote that he had "never suffered so much from being in the Water. Whisky, however, preserved me from any ill effects." Whiskey notwithstanding, the idea of working waist deep in the Ohio River in December staggers the modern imagination.[30]

Running rapids, "chutes," Letart's Falls, the Falls of the Ohio, and other rough stretches of the Upper Mississippi, Tennessee, and Ohio rivers also could prove disastrous. The best policy was to pass through these places only in very high water. Another prudent step was to hire a "falls pilot" for a dollar or two to take the boat down the chute. Those who did otherwise risked the fate of Isaac Telfair, a Kentucky flatboatman whose "boat hit a rock and split, then filled with water" in 1792. Having braved the rapids, chutes, and falls of the Ohio, Upper Mississippi, and various tributaries, flatboatmen faced the swift and treacherous bends of the meandering Lower Mississippi. A stretch like Devil's Elbow, near the Chickasaw Bluffs, demanded navigation on the east bank or midstream, lest the current at flood stage sweep the flat "into the woods" and out onto the floodplain. On the other hand, running with the current into the constantly eroding banks of the lower river could be fatal: Andrew Ellicott referred in 1796 to a boatman named "M'farling and part of his crew being lost by the falling of a bank."[31]

30. John R. Bedford, "A Tour in 1807 Down the Cumberland, Ohio, and Mississippi Rivers from Nashville to New Orleans," *Tennessee History Magazine,* V (April, 1919), 63; "A Brief Account of Mr. Hough's Life Written by Himself in 1852," *Bulletin of the Cincinnati Historical Society,* XXIV (October, 1966), 308; Joseph Lovell to Nancy Lovell, December 24, 1818, in Joseph Lovell Collection, Indiana Historical Society, Indianapolis.

31. James Trimble to John Trimble, December 28, 1822, in Trimble Family Papers, Ohio Historical Society, Columbus; Francis Bailey, *Journal of a Tour in Unsettled Parts of North America in 1796 and 1797,* ed. Sir Jack D. L. Holmes, (London, 1969), 57–58; Edith Wyatt Moore, *Natchez Under-the-Hill* (Natchez, 1958), 37; Samuel Postlethwaite, "Journal of a Voyage from Louisville to Natchez in 1800," *Bulletin of the Missouri Historical Society,* VIII (April, 1951), 317; Andrew Ellicott, *The Journal of Andrew Ellicott* (1803; rpr. Chicago, 1962), 122.

Rapids, bends, and "cave-in banks" were constant dangers, but the real scourge of the western boatmen was uprooted trees. During flood stage there were many trees adrift, but far more dangerous were those that somehow became secured and remained stationary in the river. These were the "snags"—differentiated as "planters" and "sawyers"— to which so many boatmen's accounts refer, and these "Mississippi produce buyers" could put a quick end to a flatboat trading venture. On the Lower Mississippi at places like the Devil's Raceground and the so-called Council of Snags, they were "so thick as to appear like a little wood of dead trees." Coming unexpectedly upon a snag, a boatman had little choice but to avoid a head-on collision by steering into the hazard obliquely. With luck, his flat would bounce off without being "stove in" and sunk—but many had no such luck. Merchant navigator Moses Austin reported that eighteen "Kentucky Boats . . . had been lost above Walnutt Hills in March and Early in April" of 1801, and flatboatman John Stuart passed "the wrecks of a great many Boats" on the Lower Mississippi five years later.[32]

If a flatboat "stove in" and drew more water than pumping, bailing, and makeshift repairs could keep out, the boatmen found themselves in serious trouble. If they could not nurse the craft to shore, they abandoned ship in their skiffs or started swimming, but the Ohio and Lower Mississippi at flood stage were cruel and many men drowned in their cold, swift currents. In 1808 Christian Schultz witnessed a horrible accident in which two men "were drowned immediately" and one survivor was in such a state of shock that Schultz's boatmen could barely break "his hold from the tree" in the river to which he clung for his life. Eighteen years later, near Devil's Elbow, a Tennessee flatboatman named David Crockett ran upon "a large raft of drift timber" and found himself "in a worse box than ever." Trapped in the cabin of his sinking boat, Crockett yelled to his crew to jerk him through a tiny hatch. He lived, but only after spending a miserable night on a Mississippi island, naked and "skin'd like a rabbit." That was "the last of my boats, and my boating," he wrote a few years later, "for it went so

32. Thomas S. Teas, "A Trading Trip to Natchez and New Orleans, 1822: Diary of Thomas S. Teas," eds. Julia Ideson and Sanford W. Higginbotham, *Journal of Southern History*, VII (August, 1941), 322, 383; Cramer, *Ohio and Mississippi Navigator*, 12–13; Bailey, *Journal of a Tour*, 132; Schultz, *Travels on an Inland Voyage*, II, 168–70; Moses Austin, "Journal of a Voyage," in Barker (ed.), *Austin Papers*, Vol. II, Pt. 1, p. 74; Stuart, "A Journal," 18.

badly with me, along at the first, that I hadn't much mind to try it any more." Crockett then decided he might have better luck in another vocation, so he returned home to run in the congressional election.[33]

Having endured strenuous labor, summer and winter weather, rapids, cave-in banks, eddies, sandbars, and snags, the downstream men arriving in Natchez or New Orleans encountered yet another difficulty: figuring out a way to return north. Many solved this problem by simply staying in the South; the Spanish governmental records prior to 1803 frequently complain of these "vagabonds," who formed a considerable portion of the early population of lower Louisiana. Northern boatmen who chose to go back home did so by one of three routes. Some merchant navigators and a few others with enough money booked passage "by sea to Philadelphia or Baltimore, whence they go by land to Pittsburgh and the environs." A few hardy souls shipped upstream as hands on keelboats and barges. The vast majority of returning rivermen, however, had neither the money for ship passage nor the stomach for the life of an upstream man. These boatmen faced a thousand-mile trek home, much of it on the Natchez Trace.[34]

The Natchez Trace is perhaps the most fabled trail of the trans-Appalachian West. Following a series of old Choctaw and Chickasaw Indian trails, the Trace served until approximately 1815 as the major means of land communication between Natchez, Nashville, and the Ohio Valley. A two-hundred-mile wagon road from New Orleans to Natchez served as a prelude to the Trace and provided relatively easy

33. "Journey Down the Ohio and Mississippi" (MS in Case Collection, Newberry Library, quoted courtesy of the Newberry Library, Chicago), 13–14; Schultz, *Travels on an Inland Voyage*, II, 28–29; David Crockett, *A Narrative of the Life and Adventures of David Crockett of the State of Tennessee* (1834; rpr. Knoxville, Tenn., 1973), 195–200.

34. Governor Manuel de Salcedo to Governor W. C. C. Claiborne, New Orleans, February 28, 1802, in Dunbar Rowland (ed.), *Official Letter Books of W. C. C. Claiborne, 1801–1816* (6 vols.; Jackson, Miss., 1917), I, 60–62; Sir Jack D. L. Holmes, "Law and Order in Spanish Natchez, 1781–1798," *Journal of Mississippi History*, XXV (July, 1963), 192–93, and "Livestock in Spanish Natchez," *ibid.*, XXIII (January, 1961), 23; F. A. Michaux, *Travels to the West of the Allegheny Mountains by François André Michaux*, in Reuben Gold Thwaites (ed.), *Early Western Travels, 1748–1846* (32 vols.; Cleveland, 1904–1907), III, 159; "Journal of Henry Troth, 1799" (Photocopy in Louisiana Historical Center, Louisiana State Museum, New Orleans; original MS in possession of Tyrell W. Brooke, Vienna, Virginia), New Orleans; 9–10; Hisey and Batson to McDonogh and Brown, October 19, 1803, in John McDonogh Papers, Tulane University, New Orleans.

going for the traveler, with many settlements and way stations along its course. The Natchez Trace, however, was altogether different. For six hundred miles, from Natchez to Nashville, there appeared not a single town. Three Indian villages, James Colbert's Tennessee River ferry, and a few squatters' cabins were, in 1800, the only evidence of civilization amid the forests, swamps, and canebrakes along the Trace. Although the trail served as a mail route and was of limited commercial and military importance, its main function, from the Revolution until the advent of the steamboat, was as a route north for returning flatboatmen.[35]

Thousands of flatboatmen walked or rode horseback over the Trace during the late eighteenth and early nineteenth centuries. Spanish officials in Natchez reported approximately 240 boatmen returning to their homes through the wilderness in 1790. In July of 1800, the Reverend Joseph Bullen estimated that "not less than one thousand" men annually followed the Trace. By 1810, ornithologist Alexander Wilson provided data indicating that this number had quadrupled. Beginning their trek in New Orleans, many rivermen traveled in companies of twenty men or more for protection. One pioneer remembered that those who had the money "purchased mules or Indian ponies . . . but few could afford to ride." Because the first half of the Natchez Trace passed through a "flat, unhealthy country, with bad water," fevers, malaria, and other sicknesses broke out, and "many died on the way, or were left to the care of Indian or hunter who had settled on the road." Kentucky boatman John Stuart complained of "a violent dysentery" and "a bloody flux," and Marietta riverman Charles DeVol "was reduced to a mere skeleton, with hollow eyes," but managed to return home alive. Even in good health, returning boatmen like Joseph Hough had to walk hundreds of miles through swamps and forests, "encamp out without tents regardless of rain or other unfavorable weather,"

35. Much has been written about the Natchez Trace, but a solidly documented, book-length treatment has yet to appear. I have relied on the old but sturdy accounts in Dawson A. Phelps, "Travel on the Natchez Trace: A Study of Its Economic Aspects," *Journal of Mississippi History*, XV (July, 1953), 155–64; Lena Mitchell Jamison, "The Natchez Trace: A Federal Highway of the Old Southwest," *ibid.*, I (January, 1939), 82–99; and Virginia Matthias, "Natchez Under-the-Hill as It Developed Under the Influence of the Mississippi River and the Natchez Trace," *ibid.*, VII (October, 1945), 201–21. Jonathan Daniels' *The Devil's Backbone: The Story of the Natchez Trace* (New York, 1962), the most recent study, is unsatisfactory.

swim across streams and rivers, all the while enduring "Muskeetos & Gnats," poisonous snakes, and dangers from bears, panthers, and other wild animals. No wonder Alexander Wilson was struck by the wild aspect of the flatboatmen he passed on the Trace in 1810: "I . . . met several parties of boatmen returning from Natchez and New Orleans. . . . These were dirty as Hottentots, their dress a shirt and trousers of canvas, black greasy and sometimes in tatters; their skin burnt wherever exposed to the sun; each with a budget wrapped up in an old blanket; their beards eighteen days old added to the singularity of their appearance, which was altogether savage." [36]

Boatmen on the Natchez Trace were threatened not only by sickness, the wilderness, the weather, and other natural phenomena. There were human dangers as well—highwaymen. Unfortunately, so much nonsense has been written about the river pirates of Cave-In Rock and the "land pirates" of the Natchez Trace that it is extremely difficult to determine the nature and extent of wilderness crime at the turn of the century. [37] Yet even in the absence of a well-founded secondary work on banditry on the Trace, the historian still can piece together a formulation concerning the highway robberies of this era. The extent of such robberies has been exaggerated in folklore and history. There were, however, acts of crime perpetrated on the Natchez Trace during the late eighteenth and early nineteenth centuries. Spanish court records as early as 1786 complain of "highway robbers who by force of

36. Phelps, "Travel on the Natchez Trace," 159, 161; Dawson A. Phelps (ed.), "Excerpts from the Journal of Rev. Joseph Bullen, 1799 and 1800," *Journal of Mississippi History,* XVII (October, 1955), 272; Samuel P. Hildreth, "History of an Early Voyage on the Ohio and Mississippi Rivers with Historical Sketches of the Different Points Along Them, etc.," *American Pioneer,* I (April, 1842), 141, 143; S. Wilkerson, "The Commerce of the West," *American Pioneer,* II (March, 1843), 163−64; John G. Stuart, "A Journal: Remarks or Observations in a Voyage Down the Kentucky, Ohio, Mississippi Rivers, etc." (Typescript), 22−25; "Account of Mr. Hough's Life Written by Himself," 309; William Buckner McGroarty (ed.), "Diary of Captain Phillip Buckner," *William and Mary Quarterly,* n.s., VI (July, 1926), 191; Emerson Gould, *Fifty Years on the Mississippi: or, Gould's History of River Navigation* (St. Louis, 1889), 137−38.

37. The most famous and widely read book on land piracy is also the least accurate: Robert M. Coates, *The Outlaw Years: The History of the Land Pirates of the Natchez Trace* (New York, 1930). Otto A. Rothert's *The Outlaws of Cave-In Rock: Historical Accounts of the Famous Highwaymen and River Pirates Who Operated in Pioneer Days upon the Ohio and Mississippi Rivers and over the Old Natchez Trace* (Cleveland, 1924) is better researched, but Rothert tends to interpret folktales literally. Nearly everyone else who has written anything about piracy on the Trace or at Cave-In Rock has followed Coates and Rothert.

arms strip travelers and enter the houses of citizens and plunder their most valuable effects," and horse thieves reportedly plagued returning boatmen and local residents alike. In 1801 the *Kentucky Gazette* noted that a party of boatmen returning home on the Natchez Trace had been robbed of their money by four "blacked" highwaymen. Most of the documented accounts, however, tell of the activities of the infamous Samuel Mason and his gang of land pirates.[38]

Samuel Mason's story is a tangle of folklore and fact. Unfortunately, the tale of this Revolutionary War hero turned highwayman and river pirate has been interwoven with the folklore of Wiley ("Little") Harpe, a legendary Kentucky murderer with whom Mason probably had no association. What we do know is that in April, 1802, Mississippi territorial governor W. C. C. Claiborne wrote Colonel Daniel Burnett of Walnut Hills complaining of "a set of Pirates and Robbers who alternately infest the Mississippi River and the Road leading from this District to Tennessee." This "Banditti," the governor explained erroneously, was led by "a certain Samuel Mason & a Man by the name of Harp." Claiborne called upon Burnett to "procure 15 or 20 men as volunteers" and "use all means in your power to arrest them."[39]

Claiborne later offered a reward of nine hundred dollars, but beyond this point the story is blurred by a myriad of folktales concerning Little Harpe and the capture of "Mason's Head." As Otto Rothert argued in *The Outlaws of Cave-In Rock,* Claiborne had no good reason to believe that Little Harpe, a fugitive Kentucky murderer, had become one of Mason's band, but the governor knew that if he linked the names of these two notorious outlaws together, the public would become more fearful of Mason and therefore assist in his capture. The problem is that Claiborne's white lie seems to have been swallowed by everyone ever since. Moreover, a legend that the head of "Little" Harpe's brother, Micajah ("Big") Harpe, had been severed from his body by a posse and hanged from a tree or stuck to a pole in Kentucky

38. May Wilson McBee (ed.), *The Natchez Court Records, 1767–1805: Abstracts of Early Records* (2 vols.; Greenwood, Miss., 1953), II, 247; Holmes, "Law and Order in Spanish Natchez," 192–93, and "Livestock in Spanish Natchez," 23; Whitaker, *Mississippi Question,* 141; *Kentucky Gazette* (Lexington), September 14, 1801.

39. W. C. C. Claiborne to Col. Daniel Burnett, April 27, 1802, in Rowland (ed.), *Official Letter Books of W. C. C. Claiborne,* I, 91–92.

in 1799 also became part and parcel of Mason's "history"—these are the sorts of stories that fascinate folklorists and aggravate historians. In one version of "Mason's Head," two men named Sutton and May supposedly capture Mason, cut off his head, and bring it to Washington, Mississippi, to claim the reward. But Sutton is proved to be Wiley Harpe and both men are hanged. In another folktale, "regulators" cut off Mason's head and hang it from a tree. Still another story ends with Mason's and Harpe's heads both on pointed stakes on the Natchez Trace, serving as a warning to all highwaymen. There are several other similarly gory and unsubstantiated versions of this tale.[40]

The truth, as far as one can discern, seems to be that Claiborne's men drove Mason and his gang across the Mississippi into Spanish territory, where Mason was captured, tried, and brought to New Orleans in 1803 by Roberto Mackay, the Spanish captain of New Madrid. In April, 1803, Mackay left New Orleans with Mason, bound for Natchez to turn the captive over to American authorities. En route Mason killed Mackay, escaped, and was never seen again. Governor Claiborne then offered the aforementioned reward for Mason, but the culmination of the whole affair seems not to have been the staking of Mason's head but rather the 1804 execution in Natchez of "two of Mason's Party"—men named Sutton and May. Thereafter, the Natchez Trace became a relatively safe route for travelers. There is no official governmental account of the staking of Mason's head. Although Mason's subsequent life is unknown, his career as a grand villain in American folklore had just begun. By the mid–nineteenth century, he and the Harpes were being credited with criminal operations and nefarious activities throughout the Ohio and Mississippi valleys. The most famous of their folkloric lives, however, was as river pirates at Cave-In Rock.[41]

40. Rothert, *Outlaws of Cave-In Rock,* 199. Harpe's decapitation is described *ibid.,* 126–28, but the definitive folkloric account is James Hall's *The Harpe's Head: A Legend of Kentucky* (Philadelphia, 1833). For a review of the Mason story, see Matthias, "Natchez Under-the-Hill," 210–11, and J. F. H. Claiborne, *Mississippi as Province, Territory, and State, with Biographical Notices of Prominent Citizens* (1880; rpr. Baton Rouge, 1964), 225–28.

41. "A Letter from Governor Manuel de Salcedo to the Cabildo Requesting a Sum of Money to be Advanced to Captain Roberto Mackay to Meet the Expenses Incurred in Capturing Some River Pirates," in Ronald Rafael Morazán, "Letters, Petitions, and Decrees of the Cabildo of New Orleans, 1800–1803: Edited and Translated" (2 vols.; Ph.D. dissertation, Louisiana State University, 1972), II, 191–200. Complete details of Mason's New Madrid trial are in Rothert, *Outlaws of Cave-In Rock,* 207–40. Rothert

If Samuel Mason or Big and Little Harpe actually did plunder flat-boats at Cave-In Rock on the Lower Ohio in the 1790s and early 1800s, it was a happy circumstance indeed for storytellers and drama-tists for years to come. Tales of Mason and his gang luring unsuspect-ing rivermen ashore with promises of liquor and women, and then robbing and killing them, made for attention-getting fiction. So, too, did stories of a secret treasure room in an upper portion of Cave-In Rock, loaded with booty. One can search in vain for such a room in the cave today, just as one can search in vain for firsthand accounts by the boatmen of the 1790s concerning any river pirates at Cave-In Rock. It was not until well after actual river piracy ceased to be a threat on the Ohio and Mississippi rivers that the marvelous details of the Cave-In Rock tenure of Mason's band, Big and Little Harpe, Camilla, Colonel Plug (alias Phlügger) and his wife Pluggy, and the infamous rogue Nine Eyes began to emerge in folktales, and eventually in news-paper humor and the Mike Fink stories. It is no coincidence that Otto Rothert, the only serious scholar of the history of Cave-In Rock, was also a fine folklorist, dramatist, and writer of fiction. Yet much of folklore is based on a kernel of truth, and documented instances of river piracy certainly did occur on the Ohio and Mississippi during this period.[42]

Early boatmen considered the infrequent confiscations of flatboat cargoes by the Spaniards during the 1780s and 1790s to be piracy. Then, too, there are recorded instances of petty thievery and looting aboard boats tied up in port at Natchez and New Orleans. More to the point, however, are examples of robbery that more closely resemble the scenes painted in *The Outlaws of Cave-In Rock*. Real river pirates operated in the Spanish territory during the 1780s, in the swamps and bayous south of New Orleans, on the Mississippi north of the mouth of the Ohio at Grand Tower Rock, and at Stack Island on the Lower Mississippi near the mouth of the Arkansas.[43]

refers to Mackay as "McCoy." See also W. C. C. Claiborne to James Madison, March 15, 1804, in Rowland (ed.), *Official Letter Books of W. C. C. Claiborne*, II, 40–41.

42. Casseday, *History of Louisville*, 67–71; James Hall, *The Harpe's Head and Legends of the West* (Cincinnati, 1869); Emerson Bennett, *Mike Fink: A Legend of the Ohio* (1852; rpr. Upper Saddle River, N.J., 1970). See Rothert's play scenario "Mike Fink: A Legend of Kentucky" and his epic poem *The Outlaw* (MSS in Otto A. Rothert Papers, Manu-script Department, Filson Club Library, Louisville, Ky.).

43. Works Progress Administration, "Dispatches of the Spanish Governors" (Type-script translation in Louisiana Historical Center, Louisiana State Museum, New Or-

Flatboatman Joseph Hough made annual trips from Ohio to New Orleans during the early 1800s, and he remembered that "bands of robbers who had infested the lower part of the Ohio and Mississippi Rivers had not been entirely dispersed, and were yet much dreaded by the merchant navigators of those rivers." John Turner and James Colbert, who harassed Spanish keelboat crews and stole valuable cargoes in the early 1780s, were succeeded by more desperate and dangerous characters. The Vincennes *Western Sun* warned Indianans that several "bands of pirates . . . infested the lower part of the Mississippi" and the adjacent swamps, where they retired and hid with their plunder. And far to the north, the Grand Tower Rock near Cape Girardeau provided a perfect location for river desperadoes. But the stretch of country most often mentioned in firsthand accounts of river piracy is the old Spanish dominion, later called the Arkansas Territory, near the mouths of the White and Arkansas rivers. The activities of thieves inhabiting this swampy wilderness no doubt have been exaggerated, yet Mason operated here, and there are official records of piracy in the area as early as 1802. Travelers and rivermen mention robbers and counterfeiters at "the Crow's Nest" and Stack Island—both near the Walnut Hills— in 1809 and 1811. By 1817, however, traveler J. G. Flugel could describe Stack Island, the "former seat of counterfeiters, murderers, and thieves," as being now "only a bar with a few willows." [44]

Interestingly, the Arkansas Territory near Stack Island was reputed

leans) XI, 37; Holmes, *Gayoso*, 244–46; Nasatir, *Spanish War Vessels on the Mississippi*, 55; City of New Orleans, Decisions of the Mayor in Criminal Court Cases, New Orleans, 1823–1827 (MSS in Louisiana Division, New Orleans Public Library), 24–26; Moore, *Natchez Under-the-Hill*, 27–28.

44. James McBride, *Sketches of the Lives of Some of the Early Settlers of Butler County, Ohio* (2 vols.; Cincinnati, 1869), I, 319; Caughey, *Galvez in Louisiana*, 229–30; Vincennes (Ind.) *Western Sun*, October 2, 1819; Works Progress Administration, "Louisiana Pirates: Historical Data Taken from Case Papers in the Archives of the United States District Court" (Typescript in Louisiana Historical Center, Louisiana State Museum; New Orleans), nos. 1–449, *passim;* Emerson Gould, *Fifty Years on the Mississippi*, 57–59; Jess E. Thilenius and Felix E. Snider, *Grand Tower Rock (la Roche de la Croix)* (Cape Girardeau, Mo., 1968), 22–24; W. C. C. Claiborne to [Spanish] Governor of Louisiana, February 10, 1802, and Claiborne to Richard Sparks [American commander at Fort Pickering], in Rowland (ed.), *Official Letter Books of W. C. C. Claiborne*, I, 44–45, 46; Thomas Nuttall, *Journal of Travels into the Arkansas Territory . . . 1819*, in Thwaites (ed.), *Early Western Travels*, XIII, 295–96; J. G. Flugel, "Pages from a Journal of a Voyage Down the Mississippi in 1817," ed. Felix Flugel, *Louisiana Historical Quarterly*, VII (July, 1924), 418, 428.

to have served years later as an early headquarters for the famous pirate John A. Murrell of Tennessee. According to legend, Murrell cut his teeth in the criminal world by robbing flatboatmen on the Lower Mississippi and the Natchez Trace. The real John Murrell, of course, did no such thing. During his brief stint as a petty criminal in the 1830s, boatmen no longer walked the Trace, and there is no documented account of Murrell's involvement in Mississippi River flatboat robberies. Yet Stack Island and Natchez Trace piracy were so often employed for dramatic effect by storytellers and journalists in Murrell's time that it was quite natural to add these acts to his already-exaggerated criminal résumé. This same point can be made for all discussions of early land and river piracy. There *were* pirates on the Ohio and Mississippi rivers and on the Natchez Trace, and firsthand accounts of piracy written before the mid-1820s are probably true. But accounts written after that should be taken with a grain or two of salt. Just as storytellers, newspapermen, and novelists exaggerated the exploits of Mike Fink and the western boatmen, so too did they exaggerate the crimes of the boatmen's nemeses, the pirates. One notable aspect of all of this is that it was during the Steamboat Age, when river life was becoming relatively tame, that writers began to embellish and romanticize the rougher and wilder river life of earlier decades.[45]

It is easier to document Indian attacks on boatmen during the 1780s, 1790s, and early 1800s than to verify the depredations of land and river pirates. Many of these Indian attacks occurred on the Ohio River, for during this period there was open warfare between the Ohio Valley tribes and encroaching American settlers and soldiers. Flatboats and keels provided inviting targets for Indian warriors, and there are many stories of boatmen going ashore in search of game or to assist stranded rivermen, only to find an Indian war party waiting in ambush. As the Indians grew angrier and bolder, they utilized more direct tactics, running down flatboats in their canoes or pouncing upon boats or fleets of boats temporarily tied to the bank. Terrified rivermen took many precautions to avoid surprise Indian attacks. They stood watch twenty-

45. The best analysis of the Murrell myth is James Lal Penick, Jr., *The Great Western Land Pirate: John A. Murrell in Legend and History* (Columbia, Mo., 1981). Murrell's involvement in flatboat robberies is refuted *ibid.*, pp. 61–65. See also Larry D. Ball, "Murrell in Arkansas: An Outlaw Gang in History and Tradition," *Mid-South Folklore,* VI (Winter, 1978), 67.

four hours a day, "lashing . . . the boats together" so as to "be able to resist a pretty powerful Body" of warriors. Even so, the attackers persisted.[46]

The late eighteenth century was a dangerous time for boatmen on the Ohio and Mississippi rivers. There are several recorded instances of Indian war parties that "came out in their canoes," attacking and killing rivermen. In 1782 the merchant navigator and inventor John Fitch and his flatboat crew "ran aground . . . and gave ourselves up prisoners to savages" of the Delaware tribe. The Indians killed one of Fitch's men and turned the rest over to the British. Later boatmen did not fare so well. In 1791 Indians attacked two flatboats near the mouth of the Scioto and killed four crew members. In 1794 a government mail boat "received a whole volley from . . . Indians who lay in ambush, and had made . . . signs to entice them to shore." As Indian warfare escalated in the Ohio Valley, so did attacks on flatboatmen. In the mid-1790s it was reported that "the Indians were very troublesome on the river, having fired upon several boats," killing and wounding a number of boatmen. Fortunately, the attacks soon ended. Anthony Wayne's victory over the Wyandot at Fallen Timbers in 1794 and the resulting Treaty of Greenville greatly reduced the Indian problem for Ohio River boatmen.[47]

That was on the Ohio. On the Mississippi and tributary streams, Indians continued to attack and kill boatmen throughout the late eighteenth and early nineteenth centuries. Spanish records describe several attacks on flats and keels in the 1780s and 1790s. Moses Austin referred in 1801 to "a Battle between a number of Illinois Barges and a Party of Indians" on the Lower Mississippi. In Ste. Genevieve, near St. Louis, officials noted in 1804 that Indians had "lately attacked a Boat on the

46. R. David Edmunds, *Tecumseh and the Quest for Indian Leadership* (Boston, 1984), 12, 24, 26, 31; Emerson Gould, *Fifty Years on the Mississippi*, 31–33; W. Wallace Carson, "Transportation and Traffic on the Ohio and Mississippi Before the Steamboat," *Mississippi Valley Historical Review*, VII (June, 1920), 26–38; W. Espy Albig, "Early Development of Transportation on the Monongahela River," *Western Pennsylvania Historical Magazine*, II (April, 1911), 117; "Spencer Records' Narrative" (MS in Draper Collection, State Historical Society of Wisconsin, Madison), 23 CC, 73–74; Frank D. Prager (ed.), *The Autobiography of John Fitch*, in *Memoirs of the American Philosophical Society*, CXIII (1976), 62.

47. "Spencer Records' Narrative," 73–74; Edmunds, *Tecumseh*, 12, 24, 26, 31; *Autobiography of John Fitch*, 66–85; Emerson Gould, *Fifty Years on the Mississippi*, 32; Lewis Condict, "Journal of a Trip to Kentucky in 1795," *New Jersey Historical Society Proceedings*, n.s., IV (1919), 114.

Mississippi, and killed two white peaceable men attached to it." Boat-men on the Tennessee River near Muscle Shoals were attacked in 1806 by Indians who "fired several guns . . . killed one of the oarsmen and wounded two others," whooping wildly all the while. Of course, none of these accounts indicates whether acts of aggression by boat-men and others had preceded the attacks. Surely the Indians' actions were not always unprovoked. Whatever the case, Andrew Jackson's defeat of the Creeks at Horseshoe Bend in 1814 practically ended the southern Indian menace. On the Upper Mississippi and Missouri rivers, however, boatmen continued to fear Indian attack well into the nineteenth century.[48]

As with highway and river piracy, the historian studying Indian at-tacks on boatmen must ask just how frequently they occurred and how many boatmen were directly affected. A precise answer is impos-sible to ascertain, but from a considerable body of documented ac-counts it appears that such attacks occurred frequently during the 1780s and 1790s, being less common both before and after those two decades. Even when the threat was minimal, however, boatmen wor-ried about hostile Indians, and this anxiety existed well into the first quarter of the nineteenth century. Like the risks of highway and river piracy, the dangers of Indian attack have been exaggerated and used for dramatic effect by storytellers and literary historians. As they be-came further separated from the era of the early boatmen, chroniclers increasingly magnified their emphasis on robbery, murder, and Indian onslaughts until it seemed as though every southbound flatboat ran a bloody gauntlet of thieves, pirates, and painted savages. This is ob-viously a distorted picture. At the same time, it is apparent that boat-ing during these early, presteamboat days was not only a hard way to make a living, but sometimes a very dangerous one.[49]

48. Piernas to Miró, March 23, 1783, in Kinnaird (ed.), *Spain in the Mississippi Val-ley*, Vol. III, Pt. 2, p. 74; "Log of His Majesty's Galiot *La Flèche*," January 5–March 25, 1793, *ibid.*, Vol. IV, Pt. 3, p. 127; Moses Austin, "Journal of a Voyage," in Barker (ed.), *Austin Papers*, Vol. II, Pt. 1, p. 72; Ste. Genevieve, Missouri, Archives (Microfilm copy in Joint Collection, State Historical Society of Missouri, Columbia), folder 376; Eliza Chotard Gould, "Autobiography," 7; J. B. Brant to General Jesup, July 10, 1827, in In-dian Papers, Missouri Historical Society, St. Louis.

49. For examples of exaggeration, see James Hall, *Notes on the Western States* (Phila-delphia, 1838), 48–49, 220–21; Thomas D. Clark, *The Rampaging Frontier: Manners and Humors of Pioneer Days in the South and Middle West* (Indianapolis, 1939), 81; and Bald-win, *Keelboat Age*, 116–33, 142–49.

FOUR

Kentucky Boatmen

The Kentuckians are known as excellent boatmen on all the rivers of the United States. . . . One need not fear that this vigorous breed of men will lose their bold and attractive manly spirit. Thus I am induced to sing their praises here.
—Paul Wilhelm, duke of Wurttemberg, *Travels in North America*

I have seen nothing in human form so profligate as [boatmen]. Accomplished in depravity, their habits seem to comprehend every vice. They make few pretensions to moral character; and their swearing is excessive and perfectly disgusting.
—James Flint, *Letters from America*

The reminiscence of Ohioan Claudius Cadot, a deckhand who worked for the celebrated Mike Fink, serves as an excellent example of the pitfalls awaiting the historian in pursuit of the "typical" riverman. Cadot's story is important for several reasons. For one, it is among the very few existing firsthand accounts of Mike Fink. Also, it provides an excellent view of a common hand—Cadot himself. But the most intriguing aspect of the account, to me, is its depiction of the rivermen Fink and Cadot as two almost totally different types of human being.[1]

The Mike Fink that Claudius Cadot describes bears a resemblance to the Alligator Horse of literature, but without romance and glamor. Cadot remembers Fink as a "wild and reckless" man who spent much of his time and money in drinking and carousing. Cadot does credit Fink with having some good character traits, but notes that Mike could "scarcely be called a good man." Perhaps the best that can be said of Mike Fink is that he had enough sense to hire and retain the likes of Claudius Cadot. A veteran of the War of 1812, Cadot "went on the river to follow keelboating for the purpose of raising money to buy a piece of land." He proved capable and trustworthy and often` was chosen to guard the boat when Fink and the rest of the crew went "up into town" to "get on a spree." Mike Fink repeatedly raised Ca-

---

1. James Keyes, *Pioneers of Scioto County* (1880; rpr. Louisville, Ky., 1960), 3–4.

dot's wages, and Cadot worked for him for four years. But Claudius Cadot did not relish the life of a riverman. He quit the river as soon as he had "saved enough money to purchase a quarter section of land and settle down to the life of a farmer."[2]

Thus the real Mike Fink is depicted as a drunken brawler, while his hired hand Claudius Cadot appears to have been a sober man whose sole aim was to do his job and save his money. The point, of course, is that two men as different as Fink and Cadot could be found working together on the same keelboat during the early days of boating. If one is searching for a "typical" boatman, then, would that boatman more closely resemble Mike Fink or Claudius Cadot? I think the average boatman more closely resembled Mike Fink, but I am talking about the *real* Mike Fink, not the romantic Alligator Horse of literature and folklore. The real Mike Fink was probably not a very pleasant fellow, and many of his fellow rivermen probably were not, either.

Perhaps as many as three thousand boatmen were working the western waters at any given time during the presteamboat era, from approximately 1763 to 1823. This estimate is supported by existing figures for flatboat arrivals in New Orleans and by contemporary estimates of the number of flatboatmen returning home over the Natchez Trace.[3] The evidence suggests that the vast majority of these rivermen were young and single. For instance, nearly one-third of them remained in the Louisiana country and never returned north; surely few of these were family men. Some merchant navigators and pilots were middle-aged, married men, but their hired hands were, according to one Ohio pioneer, "young men who had been brought up in the fron-

2. *Ibid.*

3. Richard E. Oglesby, "The Western Boatman: Half Horse, Half Myth," in John Francis McDermott (ed.), *Travelers on the Western Waters* (Urbana, 1970), 265; Works Progress Administration, "Flatboats on the Mississippi in 1807: A Compilation of Craft Names, Marine Hospital Tax, and Cargoes Carried on Flat and Keelboats Down the Mississippi River During One Month, May 1 to May 29, in the Year 1807" (Typescript in Louisiana Room, Louisiana State University, Baton Rouge). Erik F. Haites and James Mak compute the average flatboat crew at five men for the 1810–1819 period in "Ohio and Mississippi River Transportation, 1810–1860," *Explorations in Economic History,* VIII (Winter, 1970), 162, table 2. See also Arthur P. Whitaker, *The Mississippi Question, 1795–1803: A Study of Trade, Politics, and Diplomacy* (1934; rpr. Gloucester, Mass., 1962), 151; Dawson A. Phelps, "Travel on the Natchez Trace: A Study of Its Economic Aspects," *Journal of Mississippi History,* XV (July, 1953), 159, 161; and Dawson A. Phelps (ed.), "Excerpts from the Journal of Rev. Joseph Bullen, 1799 and 1800," *Journal of Mississippi History,* XVII (October, 1955), 272.

tier settlements, many of whom had acquired a restless and a lawless spirit." Census checks of the post-1823 generation of boatmen confirm the age difference between captains and pilots and their young hands. In this later period, however, marriage was more common among all rivermen than in the late eighteenth and early nineteenth centuries. In those early years, the young Kentucky flatboatman John Stuart undoubtedly spoke for many others like him when, departing for New Orleans in 1805, he noted in his journal, "I neither wept nor was wept for."[4]

No women worked professionally aboard flats or keels during the presteamboat era. Some women no doubt shared steering duty and other tasks aboard the emigrant family flatboats that dotted the Ohio during the great migration west, but women did not begin to ship as employees until the mid-nineteenth century. At that time a few flatboat operators and lumber raftsmen began to hire women cooks, and this practice increased (especially aboard the rafts) after the Civil War. In its early days, however, riverboating was an all-male profession. Ethnically, on the other hand, the rivermen were a polyglot collection, especially during the eighteenth century before the advent of the British-American "Kentucky" boatmen. There were, during these early days, Indian, black, French, Spanish, German, and various other European-descended boatmen plying the western waters.

The Indians were the least numerous of these ethnic groups. Excellent canoemen, they were "accustomed to the paddle only," one disgruntled employer reported, and "made a sad [s]plashing and floundering" with the huge sweeps of a flatboat. Although some Indians worked as rivermen, and French-Indian mixed bloods excelled in the

4. Whitaker, *Mississippi Question,* 141–42; Governor Manuel de Salcedo to Governor W. C. C. Claiborne, February 28, 1802, in Dunbar Rowland (ed.), *Official Letter Books of W. C. C. Claiborne, 1801–1816* (6 vols.; Jackson, Miss., 1917), I, 60–62; Minter Wood, "Life in New Orleans in the Spanish Period," *Louisiana Historical Quarterly,* XXII (July, 1939), 695; [?] Lawrence to Catherine Lawrence, May 25, 1805, in Catherine Lawrence Collection, Indiana Historical Society, Indianapolis; S. Wilkerson, "Early Recollections of the West," *American Pioneer,* II (June, 1843), 273; John Halley Journal, May 2–June 2, 1789, April 27–June 8, 1791 (Photostat of original, in Manuscript Department, Filson Club Library, Louisville, Ky.); John G. Stuart, "A Journal: Remarks or Observations in a Voyage Down the Kentucky, Ohio, Mississippi Rivers, etc." (Typescript in Kentucky State Historical Society, Frankfort), 1. An edited version of this journal appears under the same title in *Register of the Kentucky Historical Society,* L (January, 1952), 5–25. I quote from the published version except where noted.

profession, most professional flatboat and keelboat operators found full-blooded Indians to be unsatisfactory hands. Apparently, most of them simply did not adapt well to the rigors and confinements of boating.[5]

Black men, slave and free, were both more numerous and more successful as boathands. French records show black slave boatmen working on the Lower Mississippi as early as the 1740s and 1750s. In 1803 the American consul in New Orleans, Daniel Clark, wrote James Madison, "It has lately become a practice with many traders and planters bringing their produce to market to navigate their boats with their Slaves, when hirelings could not be had." There are several firsthand accounts mentioning slave and free black rivermen during this period, but it is difficult to determine exactly what proportion of the entire class of boatmen were black. A study of existing wharf registers for Natchez in 1790 and New Orleans in 1807 indicates that black rivermen constituted only about 2 percent of the total labor force. Interestingly, the number of black men working on the river increased dramatically during the steamboat era, as white men found safer and more lucrative occupations.[6]

5. John Melish, *Travels Through the United States of America* (2 vols.; Philadelphia, 1812), II, 88; Thomas Nuttall, *Journal of Travels into the Arkansas Territory . . . 1819,* in Reuben Gold Thwaites (ed.), *Early Western Travels, 1748–1846* (32 vols.; Cleveland, 1904–1907), XIII, 121; John Peter Kluge, "Diary from Goshen on the Muskingum to White River, March 24 to May 25, 1801," ed. Lawrence Henry Gipson, *Indiana Historical Collections,* XXIII (1938), 94; Frederick Marryat, *A Diary in America,* ed. Jules Zenger (1839; rpr. Bloomington, 1969), 215.

6. Nancy M. Surrey, *The Commerce of Louisiana During the French Regime, 1699–1763* (New York, 1916) 74–75; Daniel Clark to Secretary Madison, 1802, in "Dispatches from the U.S. Consulate in New Orleans," *American Historical Review,* XXXII (July, 1927), 821; Christian Schultz, *Travels on an Inland Voyage . . . in the Years 1807 and 1808* (2 vols.; 1810; rpr. Ridgewood, N.J., 1968), II, 28–29, 137–38; William Buckner Mc-Groarty (ed.), "Diary of Captain Philip Buckner," *William and Mary Quarterly,* n.s., VI (July, 1926), 179; Emerson Gould, *Fifty Years on the Mississippi; or, Gould's History of River Navigation* (St. Louis, 1889), 180; Works Progress Administration, "Dispatches of the Spanish Governors of Louisiana" (Typescript translation in Louisiana Historical Center, Louisiana State Museum, New Orleans), V, 355; William Adams, "Journal of the Barge Lovely Nan, Lewis West, Master, July 9, 1807–November 20, 1807" (MS in Ohio Historical Society, Columbus), entry for July 16, 1807; "Natchez Flatboat Arrivals, 1790," in Lawrence Kinnaird (ed.), *Spain in the Mississippi Valley, 1765–1794: Translations of Materials from the Spanish Archives in the Bancroft Library* (4 vols.; Washington, D.C., 1946), Vol. III, Pt. 2, pp. 299–337, *passim* (part of American Historical Association's *Annual Report, 1945*); Louis C. Hunter, *Steamboats on the Western Rivers: An Economic and Technological History* (Cambridge, Mass., 1949), 448–51.

A diverse collection of European adventurers manned the flats and keels on the Ohio and Mississippi during the presteamboat days. Spaniards began to appear after 1763, although mainly in the crews of His Majesty's galleys and gunboats. A smattering of immigrant Scotch, Irish, Scotch-Irish, English, German, and Swiss rivermen also worked the western waters. French-Canadian boatmen, however, greatly outnumbered all the others—Indians, blacks, Europeans, and even the British-Americans before 1783. A study of boat manifests, court and tax records, government documents, and travelers' accounts makes clear their importance in the trade: lists of early keelboat crews contain scores of names like Thibaut, Renet, Potin, Meraid, Pere, Bayette, Paut, and Breard. These boatmen were referred to variously as Frenchmen, Creoles, Canadians, and French-Canadians. The latter term perhaps best describes the majority of them, considering the fact that the Upper Mississippi and Ohio Valley were, before 1763, part of France's North American empire. Many of these men were second- or third-generation inhabitants of this country.[7]

Born to the rigors of the trans-Appalachian frontier, the hardy French-Canadians naturally took up hunting, trapping, and boating. "Capable of sustaining the greatest fatigue," one traveler noted, they were "seldom known to be impatient of labor, or to be affected by the heat; and on these accounts they are to be preferred to others." Indeed, the success of these Frenchmen in adapting to the harsh frontier environment led many travelers and observers to compare them with "the Indians themselves." They dressed in Indian fashion, stripped to

7. Abraham P. Nasatir, *Spanish War Vessels on the Mississippi, 1792–1796* (New Haven, 1968); F. Cuming, *Sketches of a Tour to the Western Country Through the States of Ohio and Kentucky,* in Thwaites (ed.), *Early Western Travels,* IV, 310; O'Fallon to Bruin, May 13, 1790, in Kinnaird (ed.), *Spain in the Mississippi Valley,* Vol. III, Pt. 2, pp. 338–40; J. G. Flugel, "Pages from a Journal of a Voyage Down the Mississippi in 1817," ed. Felix Flugel, *Louisiana Historical Quarterly,* VII (July, 1924), 416; Samuel Postlethwaite, "Journal of a Voyage from Louisville to Natchez in 1800," *Bulletin of the Missouri Historical Society,* VIII (April, 1951), 312; Ste. Genevieve, Missouri, Archives (Microfilm in Joint Collection, State Historical Society of Missouri), folder 197; Trudeau to Carondolet, May 27, 1794, in Abraham P. Nasatir (ed.), *Before Lewis and Clark: Documents Illustrating the History of Missouri, 1785–1804* (2 vols.; St. Louis, 1952), I, 214; Stanley Faye, "The Arkansas Post of Louisiana: Spanish Dominion," *Louisiana Historical Quarterly,* XXVIII (July, 1944), 662–63; "Natchez Flatboat Arrivals, 1790," in Kinnaird (ed.), *Spain in the Mississippi Valley,* Vol. III, Pt. 2, pp. 299–337, *passim;* Amos Stoddard, *Sketches of Louisiana* (Philadelphia, 1812), 304.

the waist for work, sometimes "having only . . . a piece of dirty looking cloth drawn between their legs and fastened with a belt around the
middle." No wonder an Ohio flatboatman in 1806 mistook a party of
French-Canadians for Indians and asked them the name of their tribe.
One of the Frenchmen, "not so well pleased jumped up and answered
vehemently 'we no Indians, we French, French.'" A rather stuffy traveler who made the same mistake in 1796 received a more creative response: "I examined [the supposedly Indian keelboatmen] with my
spy glass & found them all quite naked except an handkerchief tied
round their heads & a breachclout round their middles; as we approached their boat they perceived my Glass & immediately two of
them lifted up their breechclout & stuck out their bare Posteriors."[8]

French-Canadian rivermen continued to work the western waters
well into the early nineteenth century, but the great migration to the
trans-Appalachian West during the postrevolutionary decades was accompanied by a dramatic increase in the number of British-descended
American boatmen. New Orleans wharf records for the years 1805 to
1823 show an overwhelming number of English, Scotch, and Scotch-
Irish surnames. These were the famed "Kentucky boatmen" or, more
simply, "Kentuckians." Since Kentucky was originally the most heavily settled of the frontier regions bordering the Ohio River, many
rivermen of the 1790s and early 1800s actually were Kentuckians. But
many were not, and in fact Ohio, Indiana, and other "north of the
Ohio" boatmen came to dominate the profession in the first half of the
nineteenth century. A boatman's actual home state was of no concern
whatsoever to the citizens of Natchez and New Orleans, or to the
scores of journalists and storytellers who later recorded the adventures
of these rivermen. To them, the early boatmen were Kentuckians, and
Kentuckians they remained. Creole mothers in early New Orleans

8. Stoddard, *Sketches of Louisiana,* 304; C. F. Volney, *A View of the Climate and the
Soil of the United States of America,* trans. C. B. Brown (1804; rpr. New York, 1968), 336;
John Watson, Jr., "The Journey of a Pennsylvania Quaker in Frontier Ohio," eds.
Dwight L. Smith and S. Winifred Smith, *Bulletin of the Cincinnati Historical Society,*
XXVI (January, 1968), 36; "Journal of a Trip from Champaign County, Ohio, Down
the Mississippi River to New Orleans with a Cargo of Flour, Nov. 25, 1805—July 26,
1806" (MS in Illinois State Historical Library, quoted courtesy of the Illinois State His-
torical Library, Springfield), 19; John Francis McDermott (ed.), *The Western Journals of
Dr. George Hunter, 1796–1805,* in *Transactions of the American Philosophical Society,* n.s.,
Vol. LIII, Pt. 4 (1963), p. 21.

were said to have scolded their children, "*Toi, tu n'es qu'un mauvais Kaintock*"—"You, you're nothing but a filthy little Kentuckian!"[9]

Besides ethnic differences, many other factors divided and subdivided the early boatmen. One obvious difference was between the men who owned and/or navigated the boats and those who shipped as common hands. Of course, there were differences among the owners, too—for instance, some were farmers, others urban businessmen. For most purposes, however, the boatmen of the presteamboat era can be grouped into four broad categories: merchant navigators, farmer flatboatmen, agent boatmen, and common hands.[10]

The story of the merchant navigators is interesting and important if only because it greatly qualifies the myth of the Alligator Horse boatman as a lone frontiersman divorced from the constraints and norms of "civilized" society. The merchant navigator was very much a part of that society. He belonged to that most "progressive"—and least romantic—class of settlers, the frontier merchants. The merchant navigators arose during the seventeenth and eighteenth centuries, when the first shrewd frontiersmen figured out that there was a profit to be turned in taking a boatload of goods west on the Ohio and south on the Mississippi. Some of the men involved in this trade never worked on the river a day in their lives. Men like John McDonogh, Shepherd Brown, John Reed, Standish Forde, and Israel Ludlow stayed as far away from flats and keels as they possibly could while still making a profit. These men were purely speculators, and they traveled the river only to make an occasional business connection or seal an important bargain. In contrast to them, the real merchant navigators were as much boatmen as businessmen. Unwilling to entrust their cargoes and fortunes to a professional agent boatman, they elected to become pro-

9. Works Progress Administration, "Returns of Seamen for Marine Hospital Tax, Port of New Orleans, 1805 to 1833" (Typescript in Louisiana Historical Center, Louisiana State Museum, New Orleans), *passim;* Works Progress Administration, "Flatboats on the Mississippi in 1807"; Herbert Asbury, *The French Quarter: An Informal History of the New Orleans Underworld* (New York, 1938), 94. For an excellent discussion of the use of the term *Kentuckian* in history, folklore, and literature, see Arthur K. Moore, *The Frontier Mind* (New York, 1963), 114–15.

10. My categories of boatmen for the years 1763–1823 correspond roughly to those proposed by Harry N. Scheiber for a later period in his outstanding essay "The Ohio-Mississippi Flatboat Trade: Some Reconsiderations," in David M. Ellis (ed.), *The Frontier in American Development: Essays in Honor of Paul Wallace Gates* (Ithaca, 1970), 277–98.

fessional rivermen themselves. The history of river navigation during the late eighteenth and early nineteenth centuries is interwoven with the stories of these men.[11]

The term *merchant navigator* itself is drawn from the autobiographical sketch of one such man, Joseph Hough. Apprenticed in his teens to a Pennsylvania clockmaker, Hough left western Pennsylvania in 1806 at the age of twenty-one; he and his brother headed for Cincinnati in a flatboat loaded with "a small stock of merchandize, purchased in Philadelphia, with which we designed to commence business." He did just that, soon moving to Hamilton, Ohio, on the Great Miami River. There he kept his general store supplied with eastern merchandise imported on "flat boats or keel boats" that he commanded himself three months of the year, enduring "toil and privations, and . . . exposures of every kind." Hough's ambitions eventually turned southward, and in 1808 he formed a partnership with nineteen-year-old James McBride, flatboating "Wheat & Flour . . . to New Orleans on speculation." Hough and McBride ended their partnership in 1815, having "realized a handsome profit on our investments"—but Hough did not retire from flatboating. Although he married and raised a family, he remained a merchant navigator for the rest of his life. Indeed, when he wrote his autobiographical sketch in 1852, Hough was "making preparations for descending the river the twenty-ninth time since I first commenced business." He died on that trip, stricken by typhoid fever in Vicksburg, Mississippi, at the age of sixty-eight.[12]

Like Hough, Henry Miller Shreve began a successful business career as a merchant navigator on the Ohio and Mississippi rivers. Born in New Jersey in 1789, Shreve made his way to western Pennsylvania,

11. Lewis E. Atherton, *The Frontier Merchant in Mid-America* (Columbia, Mo., 1971). For nonboatmen speculators, see James Wier Letterbooks, 1805–16, 1816–24 (MSS in Draper Collection, State Historical Society of Wisconsin, Madison), 21CC, 22CC; John McDonogh Papers (MSS in Tulane University, New Orleans); Shepherd Brown & Co. Papers (MSS in Louisiana Division, New Orleans Public Library); Lewis E. Atherton, "John McDonogh and the Mississippi River Trade," *Louisiana Historical Quarterly*, XXVI (January, 1942), 37–43; Arthur P. Whitaker, "Reed and Forde: Merchant Adventurers of Philadelphia," *Pennsylvania Magazine of History and Biography*, LXI (July, 1937), 237–62; Randolph C. Downes, "Trade in Frontier Ohio," *Mississippi Valley Historical Review*, XVI (March, 1930), 489–90. For French St. Louis speculators and merchants, see Frederick L. Billon, *Annals of St. Louis* (St. Louis, 1886), 411–92, *passim*.

12. "A Brief Account of Mr. Hough's Life Written by Himself in 1852," *Bulletin of the Cincinnati Historical Society*, XXIV (October, 1966), 302–12.

where, at the age of eighteen, he built a thirty-five-ton barge and began a trade in furs between Pittsburgh and St. Louis. In 1810, Shreve ran the first keelboat load of lead from Galena, on the Upper Mississippi, to St. Louis, netting eleven thousand dollars. Soon thereafter he married, started a family, and became one of the first steamboat captains on the western rivers. At the end of his illustrious career, this one-time keelboat merchant navigator had pioneered snag removal and river improvements on the western waters and could claim responsibility for making the Red River navigable. Shreveport, Louisiana, is named in his honor.[13]

Not all merchant navigators became as famous as Henry Shreve, but many prominent and respected midwesterners started their careers by running flatboats to New Orleans. Many of the French St. Louis merchants of the 1770–1800 era engaged actively in this trade. In 1801, William Johnson, a New Jerseyite and son of a Revolutionary War officer, agreed with his brother Sammy "to purchase a load of flour, whisky, etc. and go to New Orleans with it, and from thence take Spanish produce and get it freighted to New York." Thomas Teas, a devout Quaker and abolitionist, left his native Philadelphia in 1820, moved to Ohio, gathered a cargo, and floated it down the Ohio and Mississippi, returning to Philadelphia in 1822. Thomas James and John McCoy of Chillicothe, Ohio, were involved in the river trade in the 1790s, as were Kentuckians William Stanley and Daniel Gano. Nathaniel Massie, one of the greatest land speculators in central Ohio, became prosperous with capital he acquired as a merchant navigator in the New Orleans trade. So did the Kentucky land speculator, flatboatman, and entrepreneur Captain Phillip Buckner. Other notable merchant navigators include the DeVol family of Marietta, Isaac B. Dunn, Kentuckian Fountain Perry, army sutlers James Kennerly and John May, North Carolina trader Thomas Amis, Moses and Stephen F. Austin, Tennessean Andrew Jackson, and the ubiquitous General James Wilkinson.[14]

13. William J. Peterson, *Steamboating on the Upper Mississippi* (Iowa City, 1968), 68–69; Edith McCall, *Conquering the Rivers: Henry Miller Shreve and the Navigation of America's Inland Waterways* (Baton Rouge, 1983), 16–51.

14. "Spanish Detailed Statistical Report of St. Louis and Ste. Genevieve" (1772–74) in Louis Houck (ed.), *The Spanish Regime in Missouri* (2 vols.; New York, 1971), I, 55, 87, 93; William Johnson, "A Young Man's Journal of 1800," *Proceedings of the New Jersey Historical Society*, n.s., VIII (January, 1922), 51; Thomas S. Teas, "A Trading Trip to

The farmer flatboatmen constituted a group similar in some ways to the merchant navigators, but large enough and different enough to be considered in its own right. Throughout the Ohio Valley in the late eighteenth and early nineteenth centuries, frontier farmers found themselves with agricultural surpluses, forests full of boatbuilding materials, and navigable creeks and rivers within a stone's throw. During the idle winter months and the early spring, these farmers built flatboats, loaded them with their own produce and that of their neighbors, and headed for New Orleans on their own speculative ventures. Many met disaster in the form of snags or glutted markets, but some returned home with cash in their pockets and a notion to try it again the next year.[15]

The English tourist Francis Bailey took passage with two such flatboatmen near Louisville in 1797. They were "farmers in the upper country, and had joined their produce together and were going upon their second adventure." John Halley of Kentucky made two such trips, in 1789 and 1791, accompanied by neighboring farmers and relatives. This contingent was typical: the crews of these produce flatboats were often composed of a farmer and a son or two, or a brother or brother-in-law, and some neighboring farm boys. In 1814, Thomas Bolling Robertson traveled on a keelboat captained by the son of "an independent farmer of Kentucky" whose whiskey the boy was hauling to New Orleans. James and John Trimble ran loads of barreled pork from the Upper Ohio to the south, making "a coasting voyage of it." Throughout the history of the trade, these rivermen took great eco-

Natchez and New Orleans, 1822," eds. Julia Ideson and Sanford W. Higginbotham, *Journal of Southern History,* VII (August, 1941), 378–99; Claire V. Mann Records (Microfilm in Joint Collection, State Historical Society of Missouri, Columbia), folder 134, pp. 41–42; Downes, "Trade in Frontier Ohio," 471–72, 476–77; McGroarty (ed.), "Diary of Captain Phillip Buckner," 173–207; Louis Pelzer, "Economic Factors in the Acquisition of Louisiana," *Mississippi Valley Historical Association Proceedings,* VI (1912–13), 114–17; Fountain and Roderick Perry Papers (MSS in University of Kentucky Library, Lexington); Edgar B. Wesley (ed.), "The Diary of James Kennerly, 1823–1826," *Missouri Historical Society Collections,* VI (1928), 41–97; Eugene C. Barker (ed.), *The Austin Papers* (2 vols.; Washington, D.C., 1924), Vol. II, Pt. 1, pp. 69–75, 202–209 (part of American Historical Association's *Annual Report, 1919*), J. S. Basset (ed.), *Correspondence of Andrew Jackson* (7 vols.; Washington, D.C., 1926–35), I, 94–95; James Wilkinson, *Memoirs of My Own Time* (4 vols.; Philadelphia, 1816), II, 110–14, Appendix 6.

15. Whitaker, *Mississippi Question,* 142–143; Atherton, *Frontier Merchant,* 19–20.

nomic risks. The letters of farmer flatboatmen such as the Trimbles constantly refer to competitors, potential markets, gluts, and "prices current." The farmer flatboatmen were speculators in every sense of the word—they were men who sought the main chance. Compared with the merchant navigators, however, most of the farmer flatboatmen were a bit rough around the edges. They were, after all, frontier farmers, not town dwellers. As Francis Bailey observed of his two boatmen, "They appeared to be very good sort of men, though not the most refined I have seen frequent these waters."[16]

A third type of riverman was the agent boatman. Such men were professional pilots. This group developed only very slowly in the days before steam, mainly because river conditions and the lengthy and hazardous return trip by keelboat or over the Natchez Trace precluded a pilot's making more than one or two trips a year. Not until the proliferation of steamboats did a large class of seasoned, professional flatboat and keelboat pilots burgeon. Yet a small number of professional pilots existed even during the 1763–1823 period. Some of these men owned their own boats; others navigated the boats of the merchants and farmers who hired them. They generally did not retain any speculative financial interest in the loads they carried. The first agent boatmen were exclusively French patroons from St. Louis and the Ohio Valley. As the nineteenth century approached, the Frenchmen gradually were replaced by British–American agent boatmen, captains, and masters.[17]

Mike Fink is the most famous of these American agent boatmen, but he had many less-spectacular contemporaries. His kinsman John Fink worked as a Wheeling ferryboatman and a keelboat cook before building and piloting his own flatboats on the Upper Ohio, eventually buying a steamboat in 1833. Captain Isaiah Sellers was a keelboat mas-

16. Francis Bailey, *Journal of a Tour in Unsettled Parts of North America in 1796 and 1797*, ed. Jack D. L. Holmes (London, 1969), 113; Halley Journal; Thomas Bolling Robertson, "Journal of a Tour Down the Ohio and Mississippi" (Typescript in Thomas Bolling Robertson Papers, Louisiana and Lower Mississippi Valley Collections, Louisiana State Libraries, Baton Rouge); R. Buchanan to John Trimble, January 5, 1826, James Trimble to John Trimble, April 25, 1823, Joseph McDowell to John Trimble, March 24, 1826, all in Trimble Family Papers, Ohio Historical Society, Columbus.

17. For French patroons, see "Bill of Lading, New Orleans to Ste. Genevieve, March 18, 1772," in Kinnaird (ed.), *Spain in the Mississippi Valley,* Vol. II, Pt. 1, p. 199 and "Log of His Majesty's Galiot *La Flèche,*" January 26, February 7, 1793, *ibid.,* Vol. IV, Pt. 3, pp. 116, 118.

ter "respected both ashore and on the river" who also went on to become a steamboatman, making "four hundred and sixty round trips to
New Orleans" during his long career on the western rivers. John James
Audubon described a "Mr. Aumack," the captain of a keel on which
Audubon took passage to New Orleans, as a "*plain* [and] easily *understood*" man, who "Seldom Deviates.—he is a good Strong, Young
Man, Generously Inclined rather Timorous on the River, Yet Brave
and accustomed to hardships." Audubon described another boat captain, named Loveless, as "a good Natured, rough fellow brought up to
Work without pride, rather anxious to make money—playfull & fond
of Jokes & Women—." On the Ohio River in 1811, Pennsylvanian
John Watson, Jr., met a keelboat master whose career had taken him
"up the Missourie from thence dow[n] the Columbia river and across
[to] the Pa[cific] . . . as Supercargo in the Fur Trade." It is difficult to
form any concise generalizations from these scattered reports, but a
few facts are obvious. The agent boatmen were hardy and adventurous men—frontiersmen to be sure. Yet they joined "civilized" society to the extent of becoming businessmen and entering into con-
tractual agreements with more urbane members of the merchant class.
Moreover, these frontier agent boatmen were, with some exceptions,
stable and trustworthy employees. They honored their contracts.[18]

How does all of this affect our image of the Alligator Horse? Does
the existence of entrepreneurial merchant navigators, farmer flatboatmen, and agent boatmen diminish somewhat the mystique of the individualistic, rugged, frontier riverman? Can one argue that the early
boatmen were by and large capitalists on the make, looking for a quick
profit and early retirement from their frontier pursuits? Not really, I
think. Such an argument *could* be made based on available firsthand
accounts of boatmen, but therein lies the problem. Most boatmen
were inarticulate—either unable or disinclined to leave any account of
themselves. Those few accounts that do exist are nearly all by the literate merchant navigators and entrepreneurs. These men, important as

18. Henry Howe, "A Talk with a Veteran Boatman," in *Historical Collections of Ohio*
(2 vols.; Columbus, 1888), I, 321–22; Samuel Clemens [Mark Twain], *Life on the Missis-
sippi* (1874; rpr. New York, 1960), 231–35; John James Audubon, *Journal of John James
Audubon Made During His Trips to New Orleans in 1820–1821,* ed. Howard Corning
(Boston, 1929), 16; Watson, "Journey of a Pennsylvania Quaker," 37; James Reynolds to
Shepherd Brown & Co., February 1, 1804, in Shepherd Brown & Co. Papers.

they were, made up at the very most only 20 percent of the working rivermen. Five men manned the average southbound flat. If one of them was a merchant navigator, farmer flatboatman, or agent boatman, who were the other four? Who were the common boatmen?[19]

Some preliminary answers are fairly easy to find. For example, as already shown, the crews of farm flatboats often consisted of relatives or neighbors of the farmer flatboatman. Most of these were teenagers looking for adventure and a few dollars to get their start in life. Commercial boats, on the other hand, generally hired young men who already had left their families—or who perhaps never had known a family life. Early accounts indicate that discharged soldiers often took up boating, as did frontier vagabonds and other homeless men. In river towns like Pittsburgh, Cincinnati, and St. Louis, a recognizable class of boat hands emerged in the late eighteenth and early nineteenth centuries. Many travelers commented on this group of "runaway boys, idle young men, and unemployed boatmen" loitering about until hiring on as hands on any boat that might need them. In the mid-1820s, Charles Sealsfield described the southern Indiana and Illinois villages as being "inhabited by some Kentuckians and loiterers, who spend part of their time in bringing down the Mississippi the produce of the country" and "the rest of their time sitting cross-legged over their whisky."[20]

Dyar Cobb, an Ohio farm boy, commenced what he "always called 'sowing my wild oats'" when he traveled to Cincinnati around 1825 and managed "to get the coveted prize of a job to go down the River" with an Irishman "who was loading two flat-boats with pork." Nineteen-year-old Indianan Alexander Dale "realized the necessity of making my own living," and so he "secured a place with a flat boat crew." Dale "made a trip to N[a]tchez of three months and another to St. Louis for 5 months," and then worked on "a trading boat" for four years before settling down as a distiller and farmer. Born in Montreal in 1804, Edward D. Beouchard moved to the upper Mississippi Valley in 1819 and went to work as a keelboatman "on the Mississippi for

19. Haites and Mak, "Ohio and Mississippi River Transportation," 162.

20. Charles Cist, "The Last of the Girty's," *Western Boatman*, I (June, 1848), 129; Gould, *Fifty Years on the Mississippi*, 32; Keyes, *Pioneers of Scioto County*, 1–5; Schultz, *Travels on an Inland Voyage*, I, 202–203; Charles Sealsfield, *The Americans as They Are* (London, 1828), 77–78.

Jean Brunet" and Colonel Richard Johnson. He later took up lead mining and fought in Black Hawk's War. The father of another veteran of this conflict made his first boat trip in the spring of 1806, when he built a flatboat for merchants "Bleakley & Montgomery" and hired on as a hand to New Orleans. This Kentuckian's name was Thomas Lincoln, and his son Abraham would make his own flatboat journey south about twenty-five years later.[21]

There are many other accounts of, though rarely by, the common boatmen of the presteamboat era. Traveling through the Ohio Valley in 1819, James Flint came upon a solitary, lame young man who "was on his return from New Orleans, having gone down the river in the capacity of a boatman," and was traveling "most of the way homeward on foot." Henry M. Brackenridge took passage aboard a keelboat manned by Bill Hulings and a "well-set broad-shouldered little fellow" named Ralph, "with watch in fob, and dressed in home-made cloth, cut out and made up by his good mother." Boatman Joseph Boyd solicited work aboard John Watson's keelboat in 1811 by seizing "the steering bar" and delivering "a volley of River Phraseology" before he "engaged to go with the Boat to the mouth of the Ohio" for forty dollars. Marietta riverman Joseph Dodridge had received a formal education and spoke Latin fluently, but he was certainly a rare exception among these men. More typical perhaps was Ned Kelly, "a wag of 21" employed as a boatman aboard Audubon's keel in 1820. Audubon described young Ned as a man "posessed of much Low Wit" who "Produces Mirth to the Whole even in his Braggardism." Kelly's crewmates were two Pennsylvanians who "Work Well" and "talk but little," and Joseph Seeg ("Lazy, fond of Grog") who "says nothing because it cannot help him" and "sleeps Sound." An Ohio boatman known as "Pappy," described by James Hall, appears to have possessed a more congenial and compelling personality. An "affected gravity, a drawling accent, and a kind benevolent manner . . . marked him as an eccentric being." Although he had endured "his share of those afflic-

---

21. Dyar Cobb, "Reminiscences of Dyar Cobb . . . 1819–1830" (Typescript in Dyar Cobb Collection, Indiana Division, Indiana State Library, Indianapolis), 19; Oliver Dale, "The History of the Dale Family" (MS in Dale Family Collection, Indiana Historical Society, Indianapolis); "Edward D. Beouchard's Vindication," in *Wisconsin Historical Collections*, VII (1908), 290–91; Louis A. Warren, *Lincoln's Youth: Indiana Years, Seven to Twenty-One, 1816–1830* (Indianapolis, 1959), 5.

tions which embitter life," he would "sit for hours scraping upon his violin, singing catches, or relating merry and marvellous tales." Hall's portrait of Pappy is, of course, romanticized. As a rootless, woman-less man engaged in a difficult line of work, Pappy endured "those af-flictions which embitter life" on a daily basis.[22]

Boatmen's pay, when compared with that of other unskilled American workmen of this era, appears to have been high. Wages in the trade varied greatly from 1763 to 1823, but available figures indicate an average wage of approximately $1.25 per day, plus room and board.[23] This was comparable with the wages of the highest-paid city workers, and well above that of rural working men. Such comparisons, how-ever, are deceptive: a trip to New Orleans lasted only a month, and at journey's end the boatman was left on his own. He had to spend his money to live between jobs—and the dollars could evaporate quickly for a young man without family or home, wandering about and buy-ing food piecemeal. Yet the romance prevailed even in the face of this reality. A riverman arriving in New Orleans, having spent absolutely nothing for a month, was paid perhaps thirty-five dollars, all in one lump sum. Imagine the feelings of a nineteen-year-old in Natchez or New Orleans in 1804 with that much money in his pocket. He was a

22. James Flint, *Letters from America,* in Thwaites (ed.), *Early Western Travels,* IX, 302; Henry M. Brackenridge, *Recollections of Persons and Places in the West* (Philadelphia, 1834), 208–209; Watson, "Journey of a Pennsylvania Quaker," 23; Samuel P. Hildreth, "History of an Early Voyage on the Ohio and Mississippi Rivers with Historical Sketches of the Different Points Along Them, etc.," *American Pioneer,* I (April, 1842), 134; Au-dubon, *Journal of John James Audubon . . . 1820–1821,* 17; James Hall, *Letters from the West* (1828; rpr. Gainesville, Fla., 1967), 180–83.

23. Haites and Mak, "Ohio and Mississippi River Transportation," 162. Haites and Mak estimate average total wages for a flatboat crew of five in the Louisville–New Or-leans trade, 1810–19, at $235 plus $5 per man for food. This averages out to about $47 per man, but the pilot was paid more than common hands, and there were differentia-tions among the crew as per experience, skills, etc. For more information concerning boatmen's wages during the presteamboat era, see Contract, April 7, 1803 (MS in Shep-herd Brown & Co. Papers, Louisiana Division, New Orleans Public Library); Ste. Genevieve, Missouri, Archives, folder 703; Receipt, January 7, 1827 (MS in Fountain and Roderick Perry Papers, Special Collections and Archives, University of Kentucky Library, Lexington); James Trimble to John Trimble, November 7, 1822, in Trimble Family Papers; William Richardson, *Journal from Boston to the Western Country and Down the Ohio and Mississippi Rivers to New Orleans, 1815–1816* (New York, 1940), 12; Schultz, *Travels on an Inland Voyage,* II, 108; Whitaker, *Mississippi Question,* 140; Leland D. Bald-win, *The Keelboat Age on Western Waters* (Pittsburgh, 1941), 88–89.

rich man, if only for a short time. Besides, the illusion of prosperity was not always entirely illusory. As an early chronicler wrote, the "fact that some of these boatmen would return with fifty Spanish dollars, which was a large sum at that day, was no small incentive to others, who perhaps never had a dollar of their own."[24]

As with the boatmen's pay, the matter of how they dressed is less straightforward than it at first might seem. If one were to believe the majority of descriptions of clothing of these early rivermen, one would have to conclude that they all wore red flannel shirts and red-feathered hats (the red feather denoted martial prowess). I find this notion of early frontier boatmen in matching red outfits a bit much to swallow, yet it permeates the literature.[25] Certainly some boatmen and raftsmen during the industrial era did wear red flannel shirts and black "boatman's caps," and in the post–Civil War period raftsmen adopted the red shirt virtually as a uniform. As less "literary" accounts make clear, however, most early boatmen dressed frontier-style, in leather trousers, smocks, and hunting shirts, or in handmade cloth trousers and shirts of homespun or linsey-woolsey. One contemporary described boatmen clothed in "buckskin breeches and blankets (capots), a grotesque combination of French and Indian styles which gave their attire a wild and peculiar appearance." Moccasins served these men for footwear, and hats of felt or animal skins protected them from the rain. In the sweltering Mississippi Valley summer, boatmen often were seen stripped to the waist or wearing only breechcloths, Indian fashion, and "their bodies exposed to the sun were turned to the swarthy hues of the Indian."[26]

It is interesting to speculate as to how these men might have talked and how their voices might have sounded. Accents change with time, but the early Ohio Valley boatmen probably spoke in a manner akin to

24. Marshall Smelser, *The Democratic Republic, 1801–1815* (New York, 1968), 37; S. Wilkerson, "The Commerce of the West," *American Pioneer,* II (March, 1843), 164.

25. For example, Morgan Neville, "The Last of the Boatmen," in Walter Blair and Franklin J. Meine (eds.), *Half Horse, Half Alligator: The Growth of the Mike Fink Legend* (Chicago, 1956), 48; "Mike Fink," in Charles Cist, *The Cincinnati Miscellany; or, Antiquities of the West* (Cincinnati, 1845), 31–32; Baldwin, *Keelboat Age,* 86–87. The red shirt myth probably started with Neville in 1829 and was perpetuated by everyone who borrowed from him until the knowledge trickled down to the boatmen themselves.

26. Peterson, *Steamboating on the Upper Mississippi,* 369; Noah M. Ludlow, *Dramatic Life as I Found It: A Record of Personal Experience* (St. Louis, 1880), 237; Gould, *Fifty Years on the Mississippi,* 53; Phelps, "Travel on the Natchez Trace," 161.

what we would call today an uneducated, "midland" accent. It is an accent that surprises those who do not realize that the Ohio Valley is in some ways very southern in culture and temperament. Because the western boatmen also spent time in the lower Mississippi Valley, they adopted more elements of Deep South speech than their neighbors who had never made the trek to New Orleans. The boatmen's accent, combined with the jargon of their trade and of the frontier lifestyle, with a few Indian, French, and Spanish words thrown in for good measure, was thus unique.[27]

A few writers have captured the essence of the boatmen's speech. The voices of Edward Eggleston's rural Indianans and of Mark Twain's lumber raftsmen in *Life on the Mississippi* are true to the early midland accent. So is the speech of the characters of Thomas Bangs Thorpe, Augustus Baldwin Longstreet, and John Henton Carter. Early travelers commented on this "River Phraseology"—the peculiar manner in which boatmen spoke. Rivermen gave treacherous stretches of the Lower Mississippi names like Devil's Raceground, Devil's Bake Oven, and Devil's Punch Bowl. A snag was a "Mississippi produce buyer," and an unreliable man would "never do to tie to." An out-of-work boatman was a "wharf rat," frozen lines were "cat's claws," peddling produce by boat was "ratting," a lightened flatboat was "sparsed," and a riverman's possessions were his "traps." Thomas Bolling Robertson described a group of Kentuckians "on the float" in 1814, lying "for hours to *pipe it,* and never pass[ing] a *lick* (a house where whiskey is sold) without stopping to take a *suck.*" He continued:

> the Cap & his men were all hail fellows well met, liberty & equality boys, Abe, Dave, Ike & Nate, or as they designated themselves, half horse half alligator, powers [?] hind leg, snapping *turtle,* steamboat & earthquak; they have a singular phraseology/we are *fornest* (opposite) the Island and the wind can't *faze* (affect) us—on falling in with other boatmen, the mutual salutation is the howl of the dog and the more expert and accomplished imitate to the very life the hooting of the owl—They have learnt this of the Indians among whom I have observed something of the same kind but less savage.[28]

27. Ravin I. McDavid, "The Dialects of American English," in Winthrop Nelson Francis (ed.), *The Structure of American English* (New York, 1958), 480–543.

28. McDavid, "A Note on Dialect in Literature," *ibid.,* 540–43; Cuming, *Tour to the Western Country,* in Thwaites (ed.), *Early Western Travels,* IV, 283, 289; Everett Dick,

By all accounts, these early boatmen were as filthy as the dogs whose howls they imitated. A few washed in the river or patronized the public baths in New Orleans at journey's end, but most rivermen seemed to have shunned regular contact with soap and were wetted only "with rain or by an accidental tumble into the river." It seems they wore one set of clothes until it rotted, whereupon they rustled up something else to wear. Sleeping accommodations were crude. Some boatmen brought a straw mattress on board, but many simply retired to bear and buffalo robes, "spread their blankets on deck," or "slept across flour barrels, without bed or covering."[29]

Food preparation and eating arrangements were equally crude. A few boatbuilders constructed a hearth and chimney in the cabin, but more common was a heavily planked sandbox for cooking on deck. There "the men lighted a fire and cooked the supper and dinner." Very few boats could afford the luxury of a full-time cook, so the men either took turns cooking or fended for themselves. Audubon's crew "seldom [ate] together, and very often the hungry Cooked." Those "preferring Bacon," Audubon observed, "would Cut a Slice from the Side that hung by the Chimney and Chew that raw with a hard biscuit." This diet of pork and hard biscuits was common. M. Perrin du Lac's French-Canadian crew cooked a concoction of "bacon and maize, which they called gue [burgoo]" and "seem[ed] to prefer above everything." Sometimes there was coffee, and always whiskey. With a little ingenuity, the boatmen could vary their diet by hunting or by trading with the local Indians and settlers. Kentucky flatboatman John Halley dined on "fine ripe mulberries" and birds' eggs in 1791, and wild turkey, turtle, and venison also found their way onto boatmen's dinner tables. John Stuart was pleased to have "got a kettle of milk" in 1806,

---

The Dixie Frontier (New York, 1948), 21; Robertson, "Journal of a Tour Down the Ohio and Mississippi." For some of these river terms, see Glossary.

29. "Journey Down the Ohio and Mississippi" (MS in Case Collection, Newberry Library, quoted courtesy of the Newberry Library, Chicago), 19; Flugel, "Voyage Down the Mississippi in 1817," 429; Schultz, *Travels on an Inland Voyage,* II, 198; John R. Bedford, "A Tour in 1807 Down the Cumberland, Ohio, and Mississippi Rivers from Nashville to New Orleans," *Tennessee History Magazine,* V (July, 1919), 116, and V, (April, 1919), 59; Robertson, "Journal of a Tour Down the Ohio and Mississippi"; John Palmer, *Journal of Travels . . . 1817* (London, 1818), 63; Estwick Evans, *A Pedestrious Tour of . . . Western States . . . 1818,* in Thwaites (ed.), *Early Western Travels,* VIII, 260.

but added that it was "the first I have eaten [sic] for two months." The boatmen's daily regimen during these early days was dull at best. At worst, it was inadequate and unhealthy.[30]

Poor diet, inclement weather, and strenuous work allied against the rivermen, creating or aggravating much sickness and disease among them. The diseases that afflicted boatmen were "the natural result of a life spent on the river, sometimes intemperately, always without care," lectured the Louisville *Public Advertiser*. The men worked strenuously during icy winter and blistering summer, drank very bad water, and slept out in the dews. Rain, snowstorms, or excessive heat sometimes forced them into the boat's crude cabin hold, but there the roof might leak or become "heated like an oven." Moreover, the stench of the unwashed, whiskey-drinking, tobacco-smoking crew proved "nauseous and suffocative" and drove some topside again, regardless of the weather, "glad to rise and rest and breath[e] fresh air." A little knowledge of proper diet and health care might have helped, but in their ignorance the boatmen were more or less at the mercy of their environment.[31]

Lice, mites, fleas, and other "diminutive creatures" flourished aboard flatboats, and the resulting "cursed Scotch-Irish itch" (also known as "Scotch Fiddle") was widespread among boatmen. Insects, however, were a minor irritation compared to "the Mississippi complaint, a sort of disentary" caused by bad water "wich weacans one very much" and was accompanied by vomiting and diarrhea. Unsanitary conditions and the inadequate cooking of food led to the spread of

30. Robertson, "Journal of a Tour Down the Ohio and Mississippi"; M. Perrin du Lac, *Travels Through the Two Louisianas and Among the Savage Nations of the Missouri . . . 1801, 1802, and 1803* (London, 1807), 44; Audubon, *Journal of John James Audubon . . . 1820–1821,* pp. 95–96; Adams, "Journal of the Barge Lovely Nan," entries for September 11 and 14, 1807; Halley Journal, entries for May 14, 1789, May 22, 1791; F. A. Michaux, *Travels to the West of the Allegheny Mountains by François André Michaux,* in Thwaites (ed.), *Early Western Travels,* III, 180; "Journey Down The Ohio and Mississippi," 24; Stuart, "A Journal," 6, 14.

31. *Public Advertiser* (Louisville, Ky.), November 10, 1821; Thomas Forsyth, "Journal of a Voyage from St. Louis to the Falls of St. Anthony, June 1–Sept. 17, 1819" (MS in State Historical Society of Wisconsin, Madison), 31; Logan Esarey (ed.), "The Pioneers of Morgan County: Memoirs of Noah J. Major," *Indiana Historical Society Publications,* V (1915), 397; Fountain Perry, "River Logs" (MSS in Fountain and Roderick Perry Papers, Special Collections and Archives, University of Kentucky Library, Lexington), entry for March 25, 1827; "Journal of a Trip from Champaign County, Ohio," 14.

various debilitating internal parasites—for example, tapeworm, which caused a sick flatboatman in 1817 to "vomit . . . up a worm 18 inches in length." Even more serious were smallpox, malaria, and yellow fever, diseases to which many rivermen fell prey throughout the late eighteenth and early nineteenth centuries. In 1798, W. McLuney found that "a great many of our Monongahela lads were at New Orleans lying sick," and William Adams' fellow bargemen fell ill continually in 1807. Thomas Forsyth reported considerable suffering among his keelboat crew on the Upper Mississippi in 1819. Samuel Postlethwaite recorded in his journal in 1800 that two of his flatboat hands, "Dersheit and McGowan, are skeletons but on the recovery." He further noted that "not a man on board save myself is able to pull half an oar."[32]

Most ailing rivermen had neither the opportunity nor the means to solicit aid from a physician. They sought medical advice from amateurs and tried to nurse one another with home remedies. Postlethwaite administered "Dr. Hahn's antibilious pills, and Port wine and Bark" to his ailing hands, and although traveler Estwick Evans' "knowledge of the Materia Medica was, no doubt, limited," he nevertheless found that "boatmen frequently becoming sick, applied to me for medical aid, and hence I acquired the title of Doctor." Evans used psychology, assuring the rivermen "that in a few days, they would be perfectly well" and he claimed that in this way he "did not lose a single patient." If so, then he was lucky indeed, for a New York medical publication reported in 1803 that many Ohio and Mississippi river flatboatmen at New Orleans had "died in the most forlorn conditions" imaginable.[33]

Governmental attempts to provide medical care for sick rivermen

32. "Journal of a Trip from Champaign County, Ohio," 14; Dwight L. Smith (ed.), *The Western Journals of John May, Ohio Company Agent and Business Adventurer* (Cincinnati, 1961), 146; Jacob Weaver to Johannis Weaver, July 24, 1823, in Jacob Weaver Collection, Indiana Historical Society, Indianapolis; "Journey Down the Ohio and Mississippi," 25; James Phillips to Shepherd Brown & Co., March 7, 1803, in Shepherd Brown & Co. Papers; W. McLuney to Smith and Findlay, September 4, 1798, in *Quarterly Publications of the Historical and Archeological Society of Ohio*, IV (January–March, 1909), 96–97; Adams, "Journal of the Barge Lovely Nan," *passim;* Forsyth, "Voyage from St. Louis," 8, 30; Postlethwaite, "Voyage from Louisville to Natchez in 1800," 324.

33. Postlethwaite, "Voyage from Louisville to Natchez in 1800," 315; Estwick Evans, *Pedestrious Tour . . . 1818,* in Thwaites (ed.), *Early Western Travels,* VIII, 259. The medical publication was the *Medical Repository,* quoted in *Appleton's Annual Cyclopaedia, 1879* (New York, 1880), 784.

during the presteamboat era did not make much headway. A 1798 federal law that taxed seagoing merchant vessels twenty cents per sailor per month toward a hospitalization program established an important precedent, and Governor W. C. C. Claiborne spoke the sentiments of many westerners when he asked in 1802 that this program be extended to include inland boatman as well. Congress then passed an act requiring the masters of all flatboats, keelboats, and rafts in New Orleans to pay a hospital tax similar to that paid by seagoing merchant vessels, but a combination of circumstances rendered these efforts ineffective. Thousands of boats went untaxed, and the system grew overly complicated and bureaucratic. Meanwhile, the old Catholic Charity Hospital in New Orleans treated many sick boatmen, as did state and local hospitals in Natchez, Louisville, and Cincinnati. But these efforts met with only limited success, and the need far outweighed the available facilities and manpower. Adequate medical and hospital facilities for sick boatmen did not really evolve until well into the nineteenth century. Almost always, early, preindustrial boatmen who became sick had to fend for themselves.[34]

Some of the most poignant accounts of these early boatmen tell of their deaths on the river. Sick boatmen without friends or aid were reportedly left "in [abandoned] boats, or get into wretched cabins, in which they die miserably." New Orleans merchant Shepherd Brown received a letter in 1802 from the father of Samuel B. White, a flatboatman who sailed to New Orleans in 1801, became sick, and "survived only two days before he died." White's father asked Brown to inquire where his son had been buried and what had become of his possessions. If a man died en route, he usually was buried at the first convenient spot along the bank. William Adams wrote in 1807 that "Lam Bird died this evening 8 o'clock P.M. very sudden," and his crewmates "had propper care taken of the Corps." Similarly, "Young Allen died about 8 o'clock on Tuesday morn," merchant navigator Jared Warner recorded several years later, "after an illness of 15 hours

34. W. C. C. Claiborne to James Madison, April 24, 1802, in Dunbar Rowland (ed.), *Official Letter Books of W. C. C. Claiborne, 1801–1816* (6 vols.; Jackson, Miss., 1917), I, 89–90. The history of this early movement for marine hospitals for inland boatmen is discussed in Hunter, *Steamboats on Western Rivers*, 461–64, and *Appleton's Annual Cyclopaedia, 1879*, pp. 778–98. See also Albert Gallatin to H. B. Trist, April 14, 1804, *Appleton's Annual Cyclopaedia, 1879*, pp. 783–84, and Works Progress Administration, "Returns of Seamen, Marine Hospital Tax, 1805–1833."

on Boat Red Rover 10 miles below Bayou Sara." Estwick Evans noted in 1818 that "upon the western rivers a great many boatmen die, and their graves are numerous, hence those who are taken sick are, generally, much alarmed." No doubt. A "rudely sculptured monument" along the banks of the Ohio or Mississippi must have seemed a dreadful fate to these early rivermen.[35]

Perhaps a need to block out the fear of sickness and death drove the boatmen to seek amusement as intently as they did. Their regimen of alternating work and rest certainly left time for such pursuits. When they worked, they worked hard, but sometimes there was "nothing to do but cook, eat, sleep," and seek respite from "this life of inactivity." Hunting and fishing provided recreation and food as well. "The boatmen of the western waters are great marksmen," one traveler wrote, "and pride themselves in sharp shooting." Duck, turkey, deer, and bear were favorite targets. One crew of bargemen even "killed with clubs about 120 pigeons," and another group carried "a stuffed panther on board which was killed by them." Catfish and buffalo fish could be taken easily: John Stuart "caught a fine white cat fish about 30 lbs weight" in 1806. Four-legged game also could be had in the river. Indeed, a favorite "sport" of boatmen throughout the eighteenth and nineteenth centuries was running down, shooting, or beating to death those deer and bear who unluckily happened to swim across the river in the path of a descending flat or keelboat.[36]

Besides fishing and the shooting or clubbing of animals, the rivermen amused themselves in a number of ways. Some engaged in sports such as racing, hiking, and swimming. Stuart's crewmates on the Lower Mississippi "Foot raced it on the Beach," swam in the river, and "ascended the Cliff on the hill opposite to our Boat" to enjoy "a tremendous view." Others competed in shooting matches à la Mike Fink or staged cockfights and even horse races. For the most part,

35. *Appleton's Annual Cyclopaedia, 1879,* p. 781; Henry White to Shepherd Brown, August 29, 1802, in Shepherd Brown & Co. Papers; "Journal of the Barge Lovely Nan," entry for July 11, 1807; Jared Warner, "Flatboat Book Number 5" (MS in Jared Warner Papers, University of Wisconsin–Platteville); Evans, *A Pedestrious Tour . . . 1818,* p. 309.

36. Dwight Smith (ed.), *The Western Journals of John May,* 116; Stuart, "A Journal," 7, 17; Evans, *Pedestrious Tour . . . 1818,* in Thwaites (ed.), *Early Western Travels,* VIII, 308; Adams, "Journal of the Barge Lovely Nan," October 5, 1807; Flugel, "Voyage Down the Mississippi in 1817," 421; Schultz, *Travels on an Inland Voyage,* I, 204–205.

however, the boatmen spent their spare time simply talking among themselves and spinning tales. Like Joseph Lovell's flatboat crew in 1818, they passed long evenings "setting around the fire telling over events of other days."[37]

Spying another boat or a fleet tied to the bank, a crew might land alongside them, hoping to meet with some of their acquaintances—which, in the small community of early professional rivermen, was entirely possible. The men would talk and entertain one another. Better still, if there were emigrant flatboats or a village nearby, there might be girls, and "a dance was got up." Kentucky flatboatman William Kelso and his men "collected some French ladies & made a Merry Collection to Dance" in 1782, but that was a stroke of luck: in the early Mississippi Valley wilderness, women were usually few and far between. In the absence of women, boatmen danced with one another, sang river songs, or simply sprawled back against a barrel, quite drunk, as "others struck up a tune on their fiddles." The flatboatmen carrying Lewis Condict to Kentucky in 1795 celebrated the Fourth of July by firing a volley with their rifles, and managed "with the help of a little whiskey & a turkey which we killed on shore, to pass the day with as much hilarity & glee as our Countrymen on land." Exactly twenty-four years later, on the Upper Mississippi, adventurer Henry Rowe Schoolcraft noted that the keelboatmen aboard his vessel, "to testify their observance of [the Fourth of July] . . . made their appearance this morning in *clean shirts,* and were indulged with an extra dram by the captain." But Schoolcraft was not impressed: "I could not help thinking it less a tribute of honour to the day, than a comfort to themselves."[38]

Schoolcraft's cynicism was typical of those who criticized the leisure pursuits of the western boatmen. While hunting, fishing, hiking, swapping tales, singing, and listening to music were common pas-

37. McGroarty (ed.), "Diary of Captain Phillip Buckner," 184; "Journey Down the Ohio and Mississippi," 19; Stuart, "A Journal," 10, 18, 20; Audubon, *Journal of John James Audubon . . . 1820–1821,* pp. 36, 50; Joseph Lovell to Nancy Lovell, December 24, 1818, in Joseph Lovell Collection, Indiana Historical Society, Indianapolis.

38. Schultz, *Travels on an Inland Voyage,* II, 118–19; Wilkerson, "Early Recollections," 272; William Kelso, "A Diary, May 10, 1782–June 22, 1782, of William Kelso . . . from Fort Pitt to New Orleans with a Cargo of Flour" (MS in Ohio Historical Society, Columbus), 6; Lewis Condict, "Journal of a Trip to Kentucky in 1795," *New Jersey Historical Society Proceedings,* n.s., IV (1919), 117; Henry Rowe Schoolcraft, *A View of the Lead Mines of Missouri* (1819; rpr. New York, 1972) 224–25.

times, the early boatmen were better known for their more unsavory recreational activities. Swearing, smoking, gambling, drinking, fighting, and promiscuity are part and parcel of the Alligator Horse legend. The question is, to what extent can these characteristics be ascribed to the actual boatmen? To quite a large extent, I believe. The available evidence clearly suggests that many early rivermen were indeed as wild and reckless as the rivermen of folklore and literature. Why? The reasons are not difficult to understand. During the late eighteenth and early nineteenth centuries, the Mississippi Valley was a wild and lawless region—it was what one historian has called "a spillway of sin." There were few adequate law enforcement agencies, and no disposition on the part of many of the residents to create such agencies. The vast majority of boatmen certainly did not desire law and order. They were vagabonds engaged in a dangerous occupation. Their pleasures in life were few and often illegal—or would have been declared illegal in a law-abiding society. In short, most boatmen stood outside the law. They were a rough, hard-drinking class of frontiersmen who not only attracted professional criminals to their company but committed crimes themselves.[39]

Swearing and smoking were the least of the boatmen's sins, yet they proved most annoying to passengers and other more saintly observers. James Flint characterized the boatmen's swearing as "excessive and perfectly disgusting." Estwick Evans, more philanthropic than Flint, offered a young riverman "a dollar upon the condition of his not swearing for the remainder of the day," but the lad refrained for only an hour before returning "to his long established practice." Aboard an Ohio flatboat in 1806, "a lusty fellow" named Glasscock was reprimanded by a passenger "for his notorious profanity . . . but he persisted in his folly with unmannered obstinancy." There are a number of such accounts. Unfortunately, none of them quote succinctly this "notorious profanity," and so the blasphemy of these boatmen is forever lost or left to the modern reader's imagination to reconstruct. The boatmen's love of tobacco may be more easily imagined by anyone who frequents crowded cafes and bars. According to Dr. Daniel Drake of Cincinnati, tobacco was smoked and chewed by frontiersmen of

39. Phillip D. Jordan, *Frontier Law and Order: Ten Essays* (Lincoln, Neb., 1970), 23–27, 35; Dennis Charles Rousey, "The New Orleans Police, 1805–1889: A Social History" (Ph.D. dissertation, Cornell University, 1978), 24.

"all ages, from ten years old upwards," and the boatmen were particularly fond of the weed. Many observers found the resulting smoke, "tobacco breath," coughing, and "tobacco spittle" intolerable and escaped the "nauseous and suffocative" abodes of rivermen at every opportunity.[40]

Rivermen loved to gamble. Card games such as poker, three-card monte, *vingt-et-un* ("21" or blackjack), and faro, as well as roulette, billiards, cockfights, and horse racing were, by the early nineteenth century, extremely popular among the residents of the Mississippi River towns. St. Louis, Natchez, and New Orleans (and later Memphis and Vicksburg) were famous for their gambling dens, and the western boatmen were steady patrons. The adventurous rivermen were among the best known and most zealous of the Mississippi Valley's early gamblers. Once ashore, many would wager on almost anything. Christian Schultz noted that some boatmen received their pay at journey's end, only to gamble and lose "in one hour . . . the hard earned wages of a two month voyage." Henry Bradshaw Fearon, describing New Orleans' gambling houses, noted that "when the Kentuckians arrive at this place, they are in their glory, finding neither limit, nor punishment of their excesses."[41]

The boatmen gambled afloat and ashore. The keelboatmen bringing John Audubon south in 1820 ran a boat race "that was well nigh terminating in a dispute," and Audubon noted in his journal one evening that "All our Hands Play[ed] Cards untill bed Tim about 9." There are other accounts of these games, and some do not describe such a relaxed and tranquil scene. Playing cards for jewelry and for otter and raccoon skins in 1817, two boatmen ("John and Strauss") aboard J. G. Flugel's flatboat got into an altercation, one calling the other "a cheat, liar, etc." More "sharp words passed" between them, and a fight broke out. Flugel complained that this gambling and fighting con-

40. Oglesby, "Half Horse, Half Myth," in McDermott (ed.), *Travelers on Western Waters,* 264; Evans, *Pedestrious Tour . . . 1818,* in Thwaites (ed.), *Early Western Travels,* VIII, 260–61; "Journal of a Trip from Champaign County, Ohio," 14; Daniel Drake, *Notices Concerning Cincinnati* (Cincinnati, 1810), 31; Paton Yoder, *Taverns and Travelers: Inns of the Early Midwest* (Bloomington, 1969), 126; Flugel, "Voyage Down the Mississippi in 1817," 428.

41. Much of this paragraph is based on John M. Findlay, *People of Chance: Gambling in American Society from Jamestown to Las Vegas* (New York, 1986), 44–55. See also Jordan, *Frontier Law and Order,* 43–61; Schultz, *Travels on an Inland Voyage,* I, 203; Henry

tinued throughout the voyage. Ashore, Spanish officials achieved limited success in isolating the gambling dens of Natchez and New Orleans to the river districts, but during these early days of boating,
gamblers did pretty much as they pleased. The extirpation of the professional gamblers and the taming of the boatmen who patronized
them did not occur until the 1830s and 1840s, when the Mississippi
Valley became a more law-abiding and civilized region.[42]

In *The Alcoholic Republic,* W. J. Rorabaugh documented the fact
that between 1790 and 1830, Americans drank more alcoholic bev-
erages per capita than ever before or since. Moreover, while early national Americans composed "a nation of drunkards," the Ohio and
Mississippi rivermen proved to be some of the drunkest of the lot.
Rorabaugh argues that the lonely and unstructured lives of these rootless, womanless rivermen led to anxiety, which they attempted to
drown in alcohol. Contemporaries of the boatmen agreed that these
men were problem drinkers; today many of them would be labeled
alcoholics. Like one 1805 Kentucky flatboatman, these early rivermen
were frequently "obliged to apply to the Bottle to 'Drive away care,
And banish despair.'"[43]

"[W]hiskey is drunk like water," wrote a traveler on the Upper
Ohio River in the 1820s. Corn whiskey was universal, and boatmen
also drank a good deal of beer, cider, and rum. When the opportunity
arose, they drank in taverns and inns in the river towns. Traveler John
Melish patronized an Ohio tavern where boatmen were making "a
terrible rumpus, drinking . . . and swearing unmeaning oaths." Recorded instances abound of "riotous and disorderly" rivermen in taverns. American envoy Andrew Ellicott complained in 1796 that "in all
small trifling villages" along the Ohio and Mississippi, the "inhabi-

---

Bradshaw Fearon, *A Narrative of a Journey of Five Thousand Miles Through the Eastern and Western States of America* (London, 1819), 274.

42. Audubon, *Journal of John James Audubon . . . 1820–1821,* pp. 50, 36; Flugel, "Voyage Down the Mississippi in 1817," 417, 426; "A Letter from the Attorney General to the Cabildo Requesting the Reduction of Public Dance Halls and the Prohibition of Gambling," February 7, 1800, in Ronald Rafael Morazán, "Letters, Petitions, and De- crees of the Cabildo of New Orleans, 1800–1803: Edited and Translated" (2 vols.; Ph.D. dissertation, Louisiana State University, 1972), I, 39–53; D. Clayton James, *An- tebellum Natchez* (Baton Rouge, 1968), 36.

43. W. J. Rorabaugh, *The Alcoholic Republic: An American Tradition* (New York, 1979), ix–xi, 140, 142–43; Stuart, "A Journal," 9.

George Caleb Bingham's *Boatmen on the Missouri* (1846)

Oil on Canvas, 25 × 30 in. Gift of Mr. and Mrs. John D. Rockefeller 3rd, 1979.7.15
© The Fine Arts Museums of San Francisco.

A Kentucky riverman, portrayed as an Alligator Horse, bites off the leg of
John Bull. This print celebrated the American victory over the British at the
Battle of New Orleans in 1815.

Courtesy American Antiquarian Society

Mike Fink, rifle in hand, is pictured here on the stern of his keel in this engraving from the *Crockett Almanac*.

From Walter Blair and Frederick J. Meine (eds.), *Half-Horse, Half-Alligator: The Growth of the Mike Fink Legend* (University of Chicago Press, 1956).

The death of Mike Fink in a shooting fray at the mouth of the Yellowstone River provided the dramatic conclusion to many of the published tales about him. This illustration accompanied an 1847 story by Joseph M. Field.

From Walter Blair and Frederick J. Meine (eds.), *Half-Horse, Half-Alligator: The Growth of the Mike Fink Legend* (University of Chicago Press, 1956).

Warping a Keelboat, by Pierre Chouteau. In this contemporary illustration, three modes of locomotion—poling, sailing, and warping—occur simultaneously.

Courtesy Missouri Historical Society (GPN Riverfront #7)

This meticulous engraving of a flatboat by Victor Collot depicts a partially covered flat. Many boatbuilders decked over the hold to protect the cargo.

Courtesy Ohio Historical Society

The bluffs in the background indicate that this log raft is afloat north of Cairo, Illinois. Note the six oarsmen, the cook's fire, and the tent shelter.

Reprinted from T. B. Thorpe, "Remembrances of the Mississippi," *Harper's New Monthly Magazine,* XII (December, 1855), 39.

George Caleb Bingham's *In a Quandary* (1851). Here the raftsmen are on a raft of sawed lumber, not logs. Note the peg and plank construction.

Virginia Steele Scott Collection, Huntington Library and Art Gallery

THE FIVE CENT

WIDE AWAKE
LIBRARY

Entered at the Post Office at New York, N. Y., as Second Class Matter.

No. 1017. | COMPLETE. | FRANK TOUSEY, Publisher, 34 & 36 North Moore St., N. Y. | PRICE 5 CENTS. | Vol. II.
New York, December 24, 1890. ISSUED EVERY WEDNESDAY.

Entered according to Act of Congress, in the year 1890, by FRANK TOUSEY, in the office of the Librarian of Congress, at Washington, D. C.

FLAT BOAT FRED; or, THE YOUNG SWAMP HUNTER OF LOUISIANA.

By H. K. SHACKLEFORD.

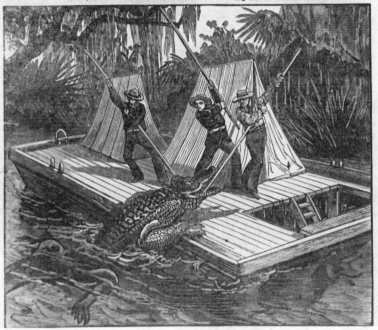

The fascination with rough-and-ready boatmen declined as the nineteenth century progressed, but never faded completely. Here Flatboat Fred and fellow boatmen grace the cover of a pulp novel of the 1890s.

Reprinted from *The Five-Cent Wide-Awake Library*, II (December 24, 1890). Courtesy Special Collections, Tulane University Libraries

Three Western Rivermen

T. C. Collins of Little Hocking, Ohio, worked his way up from common hand to merchant navigator on flatboats during the antebellum and postbellum decades.

Reprinted with permission from Herbert L. Roush, Sr. (ed.), *The Adventures of T. C. Collins—Boatman: Twenty-Four Years on the Western Waters, 1849–1873* (Baltimore, 1985).

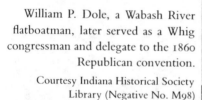

William P. Dole, a Wabash River flatboatman, later served as a Whig congressman and delegate to the 1860 Republican convention.

Courtesy Indiana Historical Society Library (Negative No. M98)

Joseph Hough, an Ohioan, spent nearly all his adult life as an Ohio and Mississippi river merchant navigator.

Courtesy of The Cincinnati Historical Society

George Caleb Bingham's *Watching the Cargo* (1849)
Courtesy State Historical Society of Missouri

George Caleb Bingham's *The Jolly Flatboatmen* (1846)
Courtesy Manoogian Collection, on loan to the National Gallery of Art, Washington

tants are principally supported by selling liquor" to frontiersmen and boatmen. Ellicott himself had just "proceeded down river to get clear of [a] town where some of our men got intoxicated and behaved extremely ill."[44]

The boatmen did not require a tavern or inn to get drunk, for there was always plenty of whiskey on board. Like merchant seamen and soldiers, early boatmen received a "fillee," or ration of whiskey, usually three times daily. A Pennsylvania flatboat merchant noted this practice when he observed twenty keelboatmen "rowing up . . . singing and shouting at a wonderful rate, I suppose the effect of their morning dram, being informed each man gets three daily." A keelboat captain named Dubreuil rationed seven and a half gallons of whiskey to each member of his crew during a ten-week voyage from New Orleans to St. Louis in 1781, but amounts of liquor varied. During the 1790s, Spanish governor Gayoso retained the fillee system among Spanish army rivermen because he believed it to be a good example of moderate use of liquor, but most boatmen drank much more than their daily fillee. The water of the western rivers was of very poor quality, and drinking it caused diarrhea, or the "Mississippi complaint." Therefore, many boat crews freely substituted whiskey for water and drank hard liquor regularly with meals. Many flatboats carried cargoes of "Monongahela" corn whiskey, and it was a regular practice among boatmen to tap a keg for their own use, with or without the captain's approval. As a result, many boatmen were in a continual state of drunkenness, except perhaps when sleeping, and even then it was only a few hours until "the steersman's call invited them to the morning 'fillee.'"[45]

44. Samuel B. Judah, "A Journal of Travel from New York to Indiana in 1827," *Indiana Magazine of History*, XVII (December, 1921), 351; Drake, *Notices Concerning Cincinnati*, 30; Thomas Ashe, *Travels in America, Performed in the Year 1806* (London, 1809), 260; Sir Jack D. L. Holmes, "Spanish Regulation of Taverns and the Liquor Trade in the Mississippi Valley," in John Francis McDermott (ed.), *The Spanish in the Mississippi Valley, 1762-1804* (Urbana, 1974), 149-82; Yoder, *Taverns and Travelers*, 200; Adams, "Journal of the Barge Lovely Nan," October 21, 1807; Andrew Ellicott, *The Journal of Andrew Ellicott* (1803; rpr. Chicago, 1962), 7.

45. Holmes, "Spanish Regulation of Taverns," in McDermott (ed.), *Spanish in the Mississippi Valley*, 165; Cuming, *Tour to the Western Country*, in Thwaites (ed.), *Early Western Travels*, IV, 355; Faye, "Arkansas Post of Louisiana," 693; Miscellaneous Papers (MSS in William Henry Harrison Papers, Indiana Historical Society, Indianapolis), July 10, August 17, 1795; Arthur Moore, *Frontier Mind*, 119.

Observers complained continually of the boat hands "tak[ing] too much corn." In 1803 Captain Meriwether Lewis found two of his hands "so drunk they were unable to help themselves." John Woods hired "two very drunken and troublesome boatmen" in 1819, and the pair drank themselves into a stupor "whenever they could get liquor." John Stuart described one Kentucky flatboat crew in 1805 as "drinking swearing & kicking," captained by a man named Baker who was "half drunk, his breeches absolutely torn off his arse." In New Orleans, merchant navigator William Johnson partook of an oyster supper where "13 of us drank 27 bottles of long-cork claret," and claimed the next day to feel "tolerable well" *because* of it. "[T]wo hired Debauch-eers" on an Ohio flatboat in 1806 proved less refined, "carousing and riding each other up and down the Strand all night." Their captain complained the drunkards "are now tired and wish to take their rest" and would "consent to go" only after having "taken out their nap." The drunken behavior of William Adams' crewmates proved less amusing. His barge was continually plagued by boatmen "in a state of intoxication" who threatened and fought the other men. The patroon, Louis Bordon, seemed the worst of the lot, continually staggering into the cabin "in a state of intoxication" and abusing crew members. Fired for his drunkenness, Bordon uttered "curses & a challenge to fight" and left in a huff, never to return.[46]

Abuse of alcohol led naturally to fighting and other acts of violence, but drunk or sober, the early boatmen were a violent breed. A great deal of this violence has been glorified by the folklore that has grown up around it. Visions of a rough and tough riverman with a red feather in his cap uttering a fantastic boast and then gouging out the eyeballs of some unfortunate adversary are part and parcel of the myth of the Alligator Horse.[47] Christian Schultz actually witnessed such a

46. James Trimble to John Trimble, December 28, 1822, in Trimble Family Papers; "The Journals of Captain Meriwether Lewis and Sergeant John Ordway Kept on a Tour of Western Exploration, 1803–1806," *Publications of the State Historical Society of Wisconsin, Collections,* XXII (1916), 44; John Woods, *Two Years' Residence . . . in the Illinois Country,* in Thwaites (ed.), *Early Western Travels,* X, 261, 244–45; Stuart, "A Journal" (Typescript), 1, 3; "William Johnson's Journal," *Louisiana Historical Quarterly,* V (January, 1922), 37; "Journal of a Trip from Champaign County, Ohio," 30–31; Adams, "Journal of the Barge Lovely Nan," July 25, November 11, 12, September 21, 1807.

47. For example, Gould, *Fifty Years on the Mississippi,* 53; Wilkerson, "Early Recollections," 272–73; Hall, *Letters from the West,* 229. Elliot Gorn interprets similar ac-

fracas in Natchez in 1808, and it is probable that scores of subsequent accounts were drawn from his, for it is one of the only documented stories of an actual Alligator Horse.

> I heard some very warm words; which my men informed me proceeded from some drunken sailors [boatmen] who had a dispute respecting a *Choctaw lady*. . . . One said "I am a man; I am a horse; I am a team. I can whip any man *in all Kentucky*, by G——d." The other replied, "I am an alligator; half man, half horse; can whip any man *on the Mississippi* by G——d." The other, "I am a Mississippi snapping turtle; have bear's claws, alligator's teeth, and the devil's tail; can whip *any man*, by G——d." This was too much for the first, and at it they went like two bulls, and continued for half an hour, when the alligator was fairly vanquished by the horse.[48]

Schultz's story notwithstanding, it is highly doubtful that many boatmen were quite so articulate in describing their prowess while preparing to thrash each other. Then there is the question of just *how* these men fought. Although eye-gouging and nose-biting were not exactly unheard of in frontier brawls, contrary to popular belief—and to any number of literary descriptions—most boatmen relied on less spectacular but equally effective modes of combat.[49] Firsthand accounts usually describe simple fist fights, with some kicking, biting, and an occasional jab at the groin tossed in for variety. For example, on a southbound flat in 1817, "the steersman & one of the bowhands commenced fighting in the boat" and were separated only "after exchanging a few blows acrost the fire." One of Fountain Perry's hands "had a fracas with an impudent negro man," and two rivermen accompanying John Audubon, "Ned Kelly & his Companion Joe Seeg, having Drank rather freely of Grog . . . had a little Scrape," with Kelly emerging the victor. A bit more deserving of their Alligator Horse credentials, "[Jean?]Marie and Clark quarreled," wrote John F. Watson in 1804, "and the former after tearing him much with his teeth endeavoured to throw him overboard." Aboard the barge *Lovely Nan*,

---

counts literally in "'Gouge and Bite, Pull Hair and Scratch': The Social Significance of Fighting in the Southern Backcountry," *American Historical Review*, XC (February, 1985), 18–43.

48. Schultz, *Travels on an Inland Voyage*, II, 145–46.

49. Evans, *A Pedestrious Tour . . . 1818*, p. 388. For the exaggeration of "gouging" and "nose-biting" boatmen, see Oglesby, "Half Horse, Half Myth," 263.

"a continuous tension . . . between the French & American" boatmen erupted into several fistfights in 1807. Nor were would-be peacemakers much esteemed at such affairs: after witnessing "a battle royal" between drunken keelboatmen in the early 1800s, Fortescue Cuming "delivered them a long lecture about this shameful, unmanly, and inhuman practice, condemning it in such strong terms, as to almost provoke an attack against myself."[50]

When knives and guns came into play, frontier fights could turn far uglier. "An American was stab'd here today by a Spaniard," a Kentucky flatboatman wrote in New Orleans in 1805. Accused of stealing a dog in 1817, a riverman named Winn fired on some Mississippians who "lay in their canues & rowed hard [for] their lives [w]ere in danger." A quarrel aboard Duke Paul Wilhelm's keelboat caused him to believe "bloodshed would follow," but "the instigators became frightened . . . jumped from the boat and fled into the forest." In New Orleans in 1806, disputes between flatboatmen and merchant seamen "bred a Riot," one riverman remembered, and the club-wielding boatmen and sailors fought it out, making "a hidious noise of blows and yells." An "officer with fifty armed men" broke up the fray, but hard feelings lingered. Several days later a Kentucky flatboatman named McClure shot fellow riverman "Thos Spankins . . . through the breast" when he mistook him for one of the hostile merchant seamen. McClure was subsequently "tried and acquitted by the Court."[51]

One well-documented account of boatmen's violence concerns the 1819 stabbing of Banks Finch, a drunken, "overbearing, troublesome man" employed aboard the keelboat *Massac* under Captain I. D. Wilcox. Sailing above Ste. Geneviève, Finch became enraged when Wilcox curtailed his whiskey ration. Witnesses remembered that Finch "would frequently threaten to whip" members of the crew, "cursing and abusing all on board, the Captain, passengers, and hands." After a confrontation with Wilcox, Finch quit the boat but soon returned, quite

---

50. "Journey Down the Ohio and Mississippi," 10–11; Fountain Perry, "River Logs," entry for December 2, 18[?]; Audubon, *Journal of John James Audubon . . . 1820–1821*, p. 19; Jane Ross, "Flatters and Keelers on the Western Rivers," *Early American Life*, VIII (1977), 60; Adams, "Journal of the Barge Lovely Nan," July, 1807 *passim*, August 1, 1807; Cuming, *Tour to the Western Country*, 303.

51. Stuart, "A Journal" (Typescript), 23; "Journey Down the Ohio and Mississippi," 23; Wilhelm, *Travels in North America, 1822–1824*, 214–15; "Journal of a Trip from Champaign County, Ohio," 52–54.

drunk, and provoked a fight between two members of the crew. During the scuffle a shoving match broke out between Finch and Wilcox, and one "lieutenant Campbell" entered into the fray. He and Finch squared off, and "both appeared to be exerting themselves to injure each other." Soon "Finch fell and expired," having "been dirked in a number of places" by Campbell. This violent story is told in great detail in a Madison County, Illinois, court deposition to which several of Finch's fellow keelboatmen attached their marks, the illiterate man's **X**.[52]

The western boatmen were driven to gamble, drink, and fight by a number of complex, interwoven reasons. They worked hard and lived in a filthy and unhealthy environment. Many of them had never experienced the comforts of a family and a real home. Most were ignorant men, unable to reason out the inequities in their lives. They lived and worked in a lawless frontier society, and when they became frustrated, there was no one to stop them in their vulgar quest for gratification. Thus, they gambled, drank to excess, and did battle with one another.

One other factor bears consideration in this regard, and that is the womanless existence of these men. Consider the psyche of a man who had never enjoyed a loving relationship with a woman—an ignorant man who had lived for years without sex or with sex only in its coarsest forms. This was the plight of the common boatman for part or all of his life. Like most young men, the rivermen wanted to meet women, but their transience and lowly station in life rendered any permanent or meaningful relationship all but impossible. In such circumstances, the western boatmen nevertheless sought out women. Surely more than one group of flatboatmen occasionally rowed ashore "in hopes of finding some strumpet" in the rough society on the banks of the Ohio and Mississippi rivers. If they were lucky enough to tie up next to emigrant flats, a crew might find farm girls to court, and one Kentucky flatboatman's journal tells in cold and impersonal terms of a "drunken frolic," gang sex, and other sexual triumphs. Even so, girls or women willing to have sex in the holds of flatboats must have been rare finds indeed for the early rivermen. Undoubtedly, many if not most of their

52. Reprinted from the Franklin *Missouri Intelligencer,* September 24, 1819, in John Francis McDermott (ed.), *Before Mark Twain: A Sample of Old, Old Times on the Mississippi* (Carbondale, Ill., 1968), 20–25.

sexual encounters were with women who engaged in such pleasures on a more professional basis.[53]

There is no solidly documented history of prostitution in the ante-bellum Ohio and Mississippi valleys.[54] A handful of firsthand accounts depict early Mississippi Valley whorehouses, however, and from these few a brief description and some idea of the nature of the trade can be drawn. While some prostitutes no doubt conducted their business in small villages, aboard trading flats, and even in the wilderness, the existing accounts concern their operations in the river districts of Natchez and New Orleans. At Natchez-Under-the-Hill, travelers were accosted repeatedly by solicitors from a number of whorehouses of varying size and "quality." No city ordinance ever outlawed these "houses of ill fame," where, according to one boat captain, "debauchery is practiced in a manner degrading to the human species." Reboarding his keelboat in Natchez early one morning, Christian Schultz discovered three "copper-coloured" women "who it seems had undertaken to enliven the idle hours of our Canadian Crew." Further south, in a New Orleans river district known as "the Swamp," prostitution flourished on an even grander scale. Writing to David Rees in 1804, George Morgan asked, "How the Devil came you to run off in debt to your whore, she has been raising hell here saying you owed her 120 or 160 doll[ar]s." The woman had searched for Rees throughout the river district "up among the Kentucky Boats enquiring for an American who had set out that morning," and Morgan advised him "another time . . . to negotiate better with your girls." Although such accounts are sparse, it is reasonable to assume that not a few boatmen patronized houses of prostitution. From this practice they no doubt gained some little gratification and pleasure in their hard lives. Unfortunately, gratification was not the only result of these liaisons: as one traveler

53. "Journey Down the Ohio and Mississippi," 20; Stuart, "A Journal" (Typescript), 11.

54. The problems inherent in tracing the history of prostitution in the early trans-Appalachian West are discussed in David Kaser's excellent article "Nashville's Women of Pleasure in 1860," *Tennessee Historical Quarterly,* XXIII (December, 1964), 279–82. Vern Bullough's *The History of Prostitution* (New York, 1964) is a helpful but general survey, while Russell Levy, "Of Bards and Bawds: New Orleans Sporting Life Before and During the Storyville Era, 1897–1917" (M.A. thesis, Tulane University, 1967) is a flawed study of a later period with an introductory chapter addressing antebellum prostitution in New Orleans.

wrote in Natchez in 1806, venereal disease was a natural result of the "unrestrained intercourse" in which the frontiersmen engaged.[55]

There was more than sex to be had in the Swamp in New Orleans and in Natchez-Under-the-Hill. If smoking, swearing, gambling, drinking, fighting, and carousing with whores were the favorite pastimes of rivermen, then these two river districts must have seemed to them heaven on earth. Indeed, in the Swamp and Under-the-Hill, any of the above leisure activities could be pursued singly or in various combinations, depending on the finances and stamina of those seeking entertainment. Pittsburgh, Cincinnati, Louisville, and St. Louis all had their saloon and whorehouse districts during this early period of riverboating, and later Memphis' "Pinch Gut" and Vicksburg's infamous gambling dens under the bluff began to flourish. In the years 1763–1823, however, the Swamp and Natchez-Under-the-Hill easily claimed matching crowns as the twin capitals of this "spillway of sin."[56]

Located in a river district bounded by South Liberty, South Robertson, Julia, and Girod streets, the Swamp was the sleaziest of New Orleans' neighborhoods of vice. Its filthy streets and motley collection of run-down shacks were home to an ever-growing criminal underworld. Taverns such as the vicious House of Rest for Weary Boatmen catered to a large clientele made up mainly of merchant sailors and Kentucky boatmen—or, as the French called them, "Kaintocks." Indeed, it was the influx of flatboatmen and keelers to New Orleans in the late eighteenth and early nineteenth centuries that led to the growth of the Swamp's underworld and criminal population. The district offered liquor, gambling, and prostitutes in beer sties that often consisted mainly of a red lantern hanging from the door, a board across two barrels for a bar, and a lousy straw mattress thrown in the corner of an upstairs room. Here "the canaille of the city, sailors, Kentucky boatmen," and others amused themselves, much to the distress of

---

55. James, *Antebellum Natchez,* 260–61; Edith Wyatt Moore, *Natchez Under-the-Hill* (Natchez, Miss., 1958), 45; "Journal of a Trip from Champaign, County, Ohio," 37; Schultz, *Travels on an Inland Voyage,* II, 136; George Morgan to David Rees, June 19, 1804, in David Rees Papers, Tulane University, New Orleans; Ashe, *Travels in America,* 287.

56. John Scott Elder, Jr., "The Autobiography of an Old Steamboatman" (Typescript of the original, in Manuscript Department, Filson Club Library, Louisville, Ky.), 9; Findlay, *People of Chance,* 69; Gerald M. Capers, Jr., *The Biography of a River Town;*

genteel Louisianians and moralistic visitors. Civic officials tried to regulate the Swamp's vice through legislation and the organization of a police force, but they never actually tried to break up this district of criminals. The government's policy during the French, Spanish, and early American administrations seems to have been to isolate the sailors and rivermen to the Swamp and let them wallow in their excesses. Many boatmen were only too happy to comply, and the Swamp flourished. There, as historian Herbert Asbury wrote, "for a picayune (six cents) a boatman could get a drink, a woman, and a bed for the night—and the practical certainty of being robbed and perhaps murdered as soon as he fell asleep."[57]

Boatmen reveled on a somewhat lesser scale at Natchez-Under-the-Hill, but for some reason that district was touted as the supreme example of decadence and lawlessness on the river. Perhaps the town's close proximity to the wilderness and the legendary Natchez Trace enhanced its reputation. In any event, there certainly was nothing glamorous about Natchez-Under-the-Hill in the late eighteenth and early nineteenth centuries. The boredom and frustrations of the boatmen vented themselves in ugly fashion there. As with the Swamp, vice had accompanied the influx of American rivermen to Under-the-Hill. During the 1790s, Spanish governor Gayoso had isolated the river district by prohibiting boatmen atop the bluff. By 1820, the inhabitants of the crude society that had grown below "formed a medley," Audubon wrote, "which it is beyond my power to describe." Along Silver, Choctaw, Cherokee, Chickasaw, and Arkansas streets milled hundreds of flatboatmen, frontiersmen, immigrants, travelers, Europeans, Creoles, blacks, Spaniards, and Indians. Grog shops, card rooms, hotels, dance halls, and whorehouses flourished in clapboard

Memphis: Its Heroic Age (Chapel Hill, 1939), 62; H. S. Fulkerson, Random Recollections of Early Days in Mississippi (Vicksburg, Miss., 1885), 97.

57. Asbury, French Quarter, 94–101; Wood, "New Orleans in the Spanish Period," 671, 691, 696; Findlay, People of Chance, 61; Henry P. Dart, "Cabarets of New Orleans in the French Colonial Period," Louisiana Historical Quarterly, XIX (July, 1936), 582–83; "A Letter from the Attorney General to the Cabildo," February 7, 1800, in Morazán (ed. and trans.), "Letters, Petitions, and Decrees of the Cabildo of New Orleans," I, 39–53; Jack D. L. Holmes, "O'Reilly's Regulations on Booze, Boarding Houses, and Billiards," Louisiana History, VI (Summer, 1965), 293–300; Rousey, "New Orleans Police," 24.

shacks and abandoned flatboats. Profanity and music filled the air, the ground was covered with filth and excrement, and vultures "strode along the streets" and alleys in search of a bite to eat.[58]

There were at least twelve taverns in Under-the-Hill, including the infamous Kentucky Tavern. Here the rivermen gave "themselves up to drink with the greatest excess," which in turn gave "rise to disputes and fights which occasion great injuries." One old boatman remembered a night in Under-the-Hill when "a dead man was dragged out of a dance house . . . and laid on the sidewalk while the revelry went on at white heat as though nothing unusual had occurred." Gambling dens and whorehouses stood with doors ajar, and "Numbers of half-dressed, faded young girls lounged within the bar-room or at the doors." Travelers and the uninitiated were shocked by what Thomas Teas called "the most infamous place I ever saw," but the western boatmen liked Natchez-Under-the-Hill just fine. It was their kind of place. As a horrified traveler, Henry Ker, wrote in 1808, Natchez-Under-the-Hill "is well known to be the resort of dissipation. Here is the bold-faced strumpet, full of blasphemies, who looks upon the virtuous of her sex with contempt and hatred; every house is a grocery, containing gambling, music, and dancing, fornicators, etc; yes I have in that place seen 150 boats, loaded with produce, bound to New Orleans, delaying their time, and spending days in the lowest orders of dissipation."[59]

All of this analysis of the boatmen's vices leads naturally to the subject of their "character," but any such discussion begs for a disclaimer at the outset. It is fine for historians to write about character (it is undoubtedly good intellectual exercise), but this great unanswerable question should be approached with a degree of humility, to say the

58. The best scholarly account of Natchez-Under-the-Hill is James, *Antebellum Natchez*, 36, 168–69, 273. See also Virginia P. Matthias, "Natchez Under-the-Hill as It Developed Under the Influence of the Mississippi River and the Natchez Trace," *Journal of Mississippi History*, VII (October, 1945), 201–21; Moore, *Natchez Under-the-Hill, passim;* Sir Jack D. L. Holmes, *Gayoso: The Life of a Spanish Governor in the Mississippi Valley, 1789–1799* (Baton Rouge, 1965), 42, 62, 109–10, 112. This composite is drawn from John J. Audubon, *Delineations of American Scenery and Character* (New York, 1926), 332–33, and Matthias, "Natchez Under-the-Hill," 202, 214–15.

59. Francis Bouligny quoted in Holmes, *Gayoso*, 62; Esarey (ed.), "Memoirs of Noah J. Major," 404; William Gratton Tyrone Power quoted in Matthias, "Natchez Under-the-Hill," 214; Teas, "A Trading Trip to Natchez and New Orleans, 1822," 388–89; Henry Ker quoted in James, *Antebellum Natchez*, 169.

least. Having acknowledged the audacity of the pursuit, one can then ask, what *was* the character of the early boatmen? What sort of men were they?

Setting aside for a moment the opinions of travelers and other contemporaries, one can attempt to investigate the character of the boatmen in an objective manner. For example, what records exist of boatmen breaking laws not pertaining to gambling, drinking, and fighting? Did they violate other, less moralistic legal rules? Did they desert their vessels? Did they steal or engage in other dishonest practices? Not surprisingly, anyone studying these men will find that some of them did all of these things, sometimes with justifiable cause, sometimes with no reason except their own greed and lack of principle. At the less serious end of the spectrum of violations, New Orleans police records reveal many instances of rivermen breaking city wharf regulations, mooring their boats illegally, and abandoning or illegally dismantling flatboats in the wharf area. Also, early newspapers contain notices of seizures of rivermen's boats to satisfy their creditors. Missouri boat owners used territorial statutes to bring suit against recalcitrant boatmen. In 1812, for instance, John Hamilton of Ste. Genevieve complained that he had contracted two French keelboatmen—"Delente & Rivet"—to make a trip to Pittsburgh, but both "now refuse to embark." Breach of contract is a two-way street, of course, and there are a number of accounts of boatmen suing their employers for back pay. Thus, merchant navigator Robert Perry expressed concern in 1825 over several angry unpaid hands who "call about two or three times a weak and . . . have commenced soot against me." [60]

Similarly, accounts of boatmen deserters and thieves must be weighed objectively. The actions of some rivermen who deserted their

---

60. City of New Orleans, *Police Code* (New Orleans, 1808), 92; John G. Clark, *New Orleans, 1718–1812: An Economic History* (Baton Rouge, 1970), 315; *Louisiana Gazette* (New Orleans), May 4, 20, 1815; *Laws of a Public and General Nature of the District of Louisiana, of the Territory of Missouri, and of the State of Missouri, Up to the Year 1824* (Jefferson City, Mo., 1842, 53–54, 249–52; *N. Wilson for John Hamilton v. Keelboatmen* (Microfilm copy in Ste. Genevieve, Missouri, Archives, in Joint Collection, State Historical Society of Missouri, Columbia), folders 197, 611, and *Francis Rudolph, Oarsman, v. John Chosser, Boatmaster, ibid.*, folder 595; May Wilson McBee (ed.), *The Natchez Court Records, 1767–1805: Abstracts of Early Records*, (2 vols.; Greenwood, Miss., 1953), II, 274–75, 278, 304, 307; Robert Perry to Fountain Perry, March 16, 1825, in Fountain and Roderick Perry Papers.

flats and keels en route seem clearly irresponsible and immoral, but other cases are not so easily labeled. William Adams' crewmates, for instance, daily endured backbreaking toil and the abuse of a drunken patroon. Who can blame some of them for walking off? Evidently not their captain, for he hired three of them back—then bailed a fourth out of jail, rehiring him, too, after receiving a "promise of future good conduck." Outright thievery by boatmen is less easily dismissed, although it was usually petty. Boatmen were sometimes blamed for stealing paltry items on board and for tapping into the "sider barrel." Some hands aboard one flatboat went ashore to "make wild geese out of tame ones" for "a fine supper," and doubtless they were neither the first nor the last to hit upon this expedient. "You must never, on any account, advance money to your boatmen," warned Christian Schultz. Keelboat captain Thomas Forsyth paid several of his men "some money in advance" in 1819, and "they thought proper to go out of the way by which means I was detained" four days. There are other instances of petty deceits and thievery, but perhaps the most amusing was related in 1822 by the stuffy traveler James Flint. Flint complained bitterly that after he had accused some boatmen of stealing his traveling companion's knife, they made a big joke of the matter—and one "degraded wretch offered to buy the fork."[61]

Accounts of more serious thievery and fraud perpetrated by boatmen are less amusing. Settlers in the vicinity of Natchez, for example, complained regularly of boatmen who stole horses and cattle. Another common complaint concerned disreputable agent boatmen who would contract to take loads south, then either disappear with the goods or return home claiming (falsely) to have run aground and lost everything. Lexington merchant James Wier suspected this of an agent boatman he had hired, "a small man tolerable well looking about Thirty six years of age." Wier wrote his business partner in New Orleans, "I have learnt that [he] is a man of extreme bad character [and] I think it not unlikely that he may attempt to dispose of the cargo as his Own property." Court records from Mercer County, Kentucky, tell of an

61. McBee (ed.), *Natchez Court Records*, II, 274–75; Adams, "Journal of the Barge Lovely Nan," September 18, 19, 1807; "Journey Down the Ohio and Mississippi," 12, 19–20; Schultz, *Travels on an Inland Voyage*, I, 193–94; Forsyth, "Voyage from St. Louis," 1; James Flint, *Letters from America*, in Thwaites (ed.), *Early Western Travels*, IX, 113.

irresponsible flatboat pilot named Matthew Galt, who took one Allen Caldwell's flat to Natchez, sold the cargo, and lived off the proceeds, telling Caldwell that he had been robbed. According to one boatman witness, Galt had a high old time of it, spending his boss's profits "principally in Gambling" and frequenting a "house that was kept by some females for the purpose of Dancing."[62]

There are stories of boatmen hoodwinking greenhorns—hiring on to help them navigate a difficult stretch or to push them off ground, and then upping the price when the job was done. In 1818, William Faux complained of two crooked Kentucky rivermen who ferried him across the Ohio and charged an exorbitant rate, telling him he looked "as though he could afford to pay, and besides, he [Faux] is so slick with his tongue." Faux castigated these men but was answered with "sauciness and impudence," the boatmen suggesting that if he did not like their price he should "commence [to build] a bridge over the river." A year later, near Wolf Island on the Lower Mississippi, traveler Thomas Nuttall ran his boat into a sandbar and wrote bitterly of a "harbour of sharpers" who "like genuine Arabs" took advantage of his plight and charged an exorbitant price to push him off ground. But Nuttall hated all frontiersmen and, like Faux, may have brought out the worst in the character of the boatmen through his haughty manner. It is also worth noting that many travelers did not complain of any such dishonesty, and some told of rivermen enduring great hardships to help travelers and boatmen in distress. Finally, of course, there are accounts of naïve boatmen being swindled by shrewd landsmen.[63]

Travelers and other contemporaries were thus divided in their estimation of the character of the western boatmen. The majority described the rivermen as repulsive and lawless characters who "appear

62. Jack D. L. Holmes, "Livestock in Spanish Natchez," *Journal of Mississippi History,* XXIII (January, 1961), 23; Holmes, "Law and Order in Spanish Natchez, 1781–1798," *ibid.,* XXV (July, 1963), 192–93; John [?] to Shepherd Brown, April 21, 1805, in Shepherd Brown & Co. Papers; James Wier to Smith Morrison, May 23, 1811, in Draper Collection, State Historical Society of Wisconsin, Madison, 21CC, 49; Court Records from Mercer County, 1815 (MSS in Kentucky Counties Court Records, University of Kentucky Library, Lexington).

63. W. Faux, *Memorable Days in America,* in Thwaites (ed.), *Early Western Travels,* XII, 15; Nuttall, *Journal of Travels into the Arkansas Territory . . . 1819, ibid.,* XIII, 74–76, 97; Schultz, *Travels on an Inland Voyage,* II, 114–15; Evans, *Pedestrious Tour . . . 1818,* in Thwaites (ed.), *Early Western Travels,* VIII, 319–20.

to pride themselves on the roughness and rudeness of their manners—
'half horse, half alligator &c.'" Charles Sealsfield commented on their
"uncouth appearance" and "boisterous and fierce manners," and Pittsburgh glass merchant Thomas Pears wrote home that "of all the men
I've ever seen the boatmen are the worst." In his autobiography, John
Hutchins wrote that the formerly hospitable French Creoles living
along the banks of the Mississippi between Natchez and New Orleans
had become distrustful because of their bad experiences with the
"rough and uncultivated" flatboatmen who passed through their farms
and villages. These "Ohio and Kentucky . . . oarsmen . . . had treated
the people so badly, not only taking what was not their own, but
adding insult to injury; until at length these kind hearted [Creoles] became . . . as inhospitable as they were formerly kind." John Palmer,
writing in 1819, described the crew of his flatboat as "a rough set,
amongst each other [who when] passing other boats, are sure to black-
guard for amusement; the insulted boat's crew never fail retorting,
sometimes with interest [and] he that can silence the other by vulgar
wit is considered the conqueror." [64]

"[N]otwithstanding this rugged behavior," Palmer noted somewhat belatedly, "they [the boatmen] were civil to us, and luckily we
found ourselves cooking by turns." It is interesting that although most
contemporary accounts of rivermen are derogatory, asides and dis-
claimers such as Palmer's appear frequently. Moreover, not everyone
who dealt with the boatmen thought them scum. Christian Schultz
declared, "I am confirmed in the good opinion I had formed, that the
Kentucky sailors, in general, although a rough, yet are a more amiable
class of citizens, than they have been represented to be." E. P. Fordham agreed: "[T]here are no desperadoes more savage in their anger
than these men," he admitted, but, "Give them your hand . . . Accost
them with a bold air—taste their whiskey—and you win their hearts."
Andrew Ellicott praised the "quiet submission to unusual hardships"
of his boatmen in 1796, adding that it "does them much credit." Like

64. Matthew Carey quoted in Blair and Meine (eds.), *Half Horse, Half Alligator*, 23;
Sealsfield, *Americans as They Are*, 108–109; Thomas C. Pears III, "Sidelights on the His-
tory of Bakewell, Pears, & Company," *Western Pennsylvania Historical Magazine*, XXXI
(September–December, 1948), 68; "Autobiography of John Hutchins" (Typescript in
Breckinridge Family Papers [M–1311], Southern Historical Collection, Library of the
University of North Carolina at Chapel Hill); Palmer, *Journal of Travels in America . . .
1817*, p. 63.

Ellicott, merchant navigator Joseph Lovell wrote appreciatively about one of his hands, Reuben, who had been "as true to me as skill[ed]—he is really a Brave Boy." Finally, it seems significant that many observers made no comments at all about the western boatmen. Surely this indicates that some boatmen were rather nondescript fellows who simply did their jobs and minded their own business.[65]

It should not come as any great surprise that there were all kinds of boatmen. "Sometimes I met real gentlemen, and sometimes I fell in with the perfect boor," Estwick Evans wrote in 1818 of his travels on the western rivers.[66] No doubt. Yet the majority of observers characterized the western boatmen as uncouth beings with no redeeming qualities, and this generalization eventually came to be applied systematically to all boatmen. In the final analysis, I suppose this is no great injustice. As has been shown, most of the early boatmen smoked, swore, gambled, drank to excess, fought, and bought whores, and many of them were deserters, petty criminals, or worse. There are documented accounts of rivermen who did not in any way fit this description, but most did. In short, the reputation that the western boatmen gained during the late eighteenth and early nineteenth centuries is for the most part an accurate one. Before the question of "character" is put to rest, however, two more points should be considered.

First, the main problem with the traditional stereotype of the early western boatmen is that too many different value judgments are attached to it—judgments by the boatmen's contemporaries and by subsequent generations alike. Because the boatmen themselves were for the most part inarticulate, others have always defined their character—usually from some particular moral perspective. Early rivermen were depicted as scum and "bad guys" by more genteel contemporaries and then, somehow, as swashbuckling, adventurous "good guys" by a later generation that venerated the Alligator Horse in folklore and literature. Viewed in their proper historical milieu, the actual boatmen were neither.

65. Palmer, *Journal of Travels in America . . . 1817*, p. 63; Schultz quoted in Oglesby, "Half Horse, Half Myth," 265; Elias P. Fordham, *Personal Narrative of Travels . . . 1817–1818*, (Cleveland, 1906), 196; Ellicott quoted in Oglesby, "Half Horse, Half Myth," 265; Joseph Lovell to Nancy Lovell, December 24, 1818, in Joseph Lovell Collection.

66. Evans, *Pedestrious Tour . . . 1818*, in Thwaites (ed.), *Early Western Travels*, VIII, 259.

The early western boatmen were, above all, frontiersmen. They lived and worked on the rough edge of civilized American society, and behaved accordingly. They were extremely ignorant, and I do not use the term pejoratively. One need only survey the many X marks on legal documents and court cases involving boatmen to see that most of these men were illiterate. They lacked the knowledge of more refined society, and they lacked the means to learn. Nor did these facts cause them any great concern. Boating, wrote Audubon, was a life that "produces heavy sweats and strong Appetite, & Keeps the Imagination free from Worldly thoughts." Audubon understated the situation. A passage from Captain Thomas Forsyth's journal of a rugged keelboat journey on the Upper Mississippi illustrates the extent of the boatmen's ignorance and naïveté: "Tuesday [June] 22nd The men have been complaining daily of the length of the days, I told them that this was the longest day in the year and of course every day afterwards would be shorter, they said they were glad to hear such good news and wished to know how I knew this." Forsyth did not indicate whether he lectured his crew on the earth's relationship to the sun in the solar system, but we can assume that the conversation soon became less complex. Although some merchant navigators were literate and entertained thoughts about science, religion, and politics, the vast majority of boatmen were simply illiterate frontiersmen. It is no great wonder, then, that they lived and behaved as they did.[67]

The second point about the boatmen's "character" is centered, once again, on the Alligator Horse. The "half-horse, half-alligator" boatman of Jacksonian folklore and literature was a hard-drinking, fighting, gambling, river rowdy. As I have shown, most of the actual boatmen on the western rivers from 1763 to 1823 engaged in all of these raucous pursuits. Does this mean that the mythical Alligator Horse is equivalent to historical fact—that the boatmen of literature are simply dramatized depictions of actual rivermen? The answer is no. The Alligator Horse of folklore and literature was a romantic character, but there was absolutely *nothing* romantic about the lifestyle of the lonely, womanless, alcoholic drifters who worked the western waters during

67. McDermott (ed.), *Before Mark Twain*, 20–25; Moore, *Natchez Under-the-Hill*, 37; Audubon, *Journal of John James Audubon . . . 1820–1821*, p. 95; Forsyth, "Voyage from St. Louis," 4.

the preindustrial era. There exists no better example of their plight than Mike Fink himself.

As was pointed out earlier, no one today knows a great deal about the real Mike Fink. Perhaps the only thing that can be said about Mike for certain is that he bragged loud enough, shot straight enough, and drank and fought to such an extent that his reputation spread thousands of miles by word of mouth and he became a folk hero in his own time. This is quite an accomplishment, and in this sense Mike Fink cannot be used as an example of a "typical" boatman. Yet in the undramatic, everyday aspects of his life that one can piece together, as well as in his heavy drinking and violent ways, Mike was quite typical of the men with whom he worked the western rivers for thirty years.

Born in Pennsylvania around 1770, Mike Fink came of age on the trans-Appalachian frontier. He was supposedly an Indian fighter and scout, but there is no documented account of these activities. Evidently he was a remarkable shot and a fine hunter. He took up boating on the Ohio as a very young man, probably around 1785. He rose in the trade but never married or settled down for long. By 1810, Mike owned two keelboats and was headquartered near Wheeling, but he kept moving west. In 1818 he was living near Ste. Genevieve, Missouri, where he may have been the "Michael Fink" taken to court by one Nicholas Hartzel over a sixteen-dollar debt. Mike refused to pay, and the sheriff seized some property to settle the matter. The only other documented account of Mike Fink during this time concerns his shooting the heel off a black man's foot. Although the "heel trimming" story was embellished in subsequent retellings, it is probably true. The outrageousness of this story and of others like it tend to smokescreen a plain truth: by 1818, Mike Fink was a frustrated, aging, alcoholic riverman whose way of life was incompatible with the civilization then emerging in the Mississippi Valley.[68]

68. There is no record of Mike Fink in any of the early manuscript censuses, but Mary and Andrew Fink, who were possibly his parents (see Ella Chafant [ed.], *A Goodly Heritage: Earliest Wills on an American Frontier* [Pittsburgh, 1955], 146–47), are both counted in First U.S. Census, 1790, Pennsylvania, Allegheny County, Washington County portion, II, 15, and Third U.S. Census, 1810, Pennsylvania, Allegheny County, Fayette Township, I, 232. See also Keyes, *Pioneers of Scioto County*, 3–4; Howe, "Talk with a Veteran Boatman," 322; *Nicholas Hartzel* v. *Michael Fink* (Microfilm copy in Ste. Genevieve, Missouri, Archives, in Joint Collection, State Historical Society of Mis-

An advertisement in the March 20, 1822, St. Louis *Missouri Republican* must have seemed to Mike Fink to offer the perfect solution to his problems: "To enterprizing young men. The subscriber wishes to engage one hundred young men to ascend the Missouri river to its source, there to be employed for one, two, three years. For particulars enquire of Major Andrew Henry, near the lead mines, in the county of Washington, who will ascend with, and command, the party. [signed,] William H. Ashley." Mike was no young man, but he was still strong and savvy, and Ashley and Henry were probably pleased to secure such an experienced keelboat master for the long journey up the treacherous Missouri. Jedediah Smith and others make no mention of Mike in their accounts of the trek west, but Fink arrived at the confluence of the Yellowstone and Missouri rivers late in 1822, as did two men named Carpenter and Talbot. Major Henry led Fink, Carpenter, Talbot, and five others on a trapping expedition to the mouth of the Musselshell River. Because of freezing weather and the threat of Indian attack, the group had a miserable time of it. Tensions rose. By the time the party returned to Fort Henry, at the confluence of the Yellowstone and the Missouri, there was evidently bad blood between Mike Fink and Carpenter.[69]

There are about two dozen versions of what happened next, and it is pointless to try to sort them out. Most versions include a scenario revolving around "the shooting of the whiskey cup," à la William Tell, which lends the story romance. The outcome, however, was not romantic at all. The feud between Mike Fink and Carpenter, fueled by alcohol, erupted into violence. A Rocky Mountain Fur Company report contains the only solid documentation of the death of Mike Fink: "In 182[3] Mike Fink shot Carpenter—Talbot soon after shot Fink and not long after was himself drowned at the Tetons." Thus ended the "romantic" life of the King of the Alligator Horses.[70]

souri, Columbia), folder 460, p. 252, and folder 689; C. B. Spotts, "Mike Fink in Missouri," *Missouri Historical Review,* XXVIII (October, 1933), 5; *Missouri Republican* (St. Louis), July 16, 1823.

69. Hiram M. Chittenden, *The American Fur Trade of the Far West* (2 vols.; 1902; rpr. Stanford, 1954), I, 262; Dale L. Morgan, *The West of William H. Ashley . . . Diaries and Letters . . . 1822–1838* (Denver, 1964), 39–41, and *Jedediah Smith and the Opening of the West* (Indianapolis, 1953), 45–49.

70. Blair and Meine (eds.), *Half Horse, Half Alligator,* 257–59; Smith, Jackson, and Sublette, "A Brief Sketch of Accidents, Misfortunes, and Depredations . . . on the East

It is not surprising that we know so little about the death of Mike Fink. As Joshua Pilcher wrote General William Clark in 1831, many of the specifics of murders on the Upper Missouri during the 1820s escaped his memory because "murders and robberies [were] occurrences so common in the country in question as to leave but little impression on the minds of those who are not interested." By the time there was sufficient interest in the details of Fink's death, it was too late to find the truth, and besides, the mythmakers had provided versions that were much more interesting and entertaining. Meanwhile, Mike Fink's body lay buried at the mouth of the Yellowstone, and his grave became something of a frontier tourist attraction. No trace of it remains today on the Montana floodplain where he was laid to rest. Fittingly, the waters of the decades no doubt have scattered Mike Fink's bones far down the Missouri and Mississippi valleys.[71]

In the end, the real Mike Fink bears only an indirect relation to the Mike Fink of folklore and literature, except in one important regard: writers often referred to Mike as the Last of the Boatmen or the "last of a vanishing race," and in a practical, unromantic sense, they were quite correct. Mike Fink's death in 1823 occurred at a critical juncture in the history of western river transportation. With the arrival of the steamboat and the dawn of the industrial era, Ohio and Mississippi riverboating and rivermen underwent great changes. The western boatmen of the 1830s, 1840s, and 1850s were a far different breed from those of Mike Fink's generation.

& West Side of the Rocky Mountains" (Microfilm copy in William Clark Papers, Kansas Historical Society, Wichita) VI, 298. This account states that Mike died in 1822—when, in fact, he was en route to the mouth of the Yellowstone during that year. He died during the spring of 1823.

71. Joshua Pilcher to General William Clark, November 19, 1831, in William Clark Papers, VI, 381; *Senate Executive Documents,* 35th Cong., 2nd Sess., No. 1, p. 440; Roy V. McCluskey (Chief Interpreter, Fort Union Trading Post National Historic Site, North Dakota) to Michael Allen, August 11, 1983, in possession of Michael Allen.

FIVE

Flatboating in the Steamboat Age

Even since the introduction of steam-boats, which in great numbers now traverse this river and its branches . . . flat bottom boats (called in the western boatman's dialect, "broad horns,") annually float from a thousand places on the Ohio and other western streams, to Cincinnati, or Louisville, or New Orleans. I have often passed fifty of them in a day, rowing with their long sweeps, or else floating leisurely with the current—often two or three lashed or fastened close together, and thus allowing the hands and passengers to while away the hours in holding converse together on the extended roof, or in each other's cabins.

—Robert Baird, *View of the Valley of the Mississippi*

In 1809 a flatboat left Pittsburgh, embarking on the long voyage down the Ohio and Mississippi to New Orleans. Other boatmen spying the craft must have noted its size and uncommon elegance, its "comfortable bedroom, dining room, pantry and a room in front for the crew, with a fireplace where the cooking was done." Indeed, if the onlooking boatmen had heard of the mission of this fancy flatboat, they may have stared in outright disbelief. Nicholas J. Roosevelt, the flat's commander, was making the trip south to observe and plan the projected route for a new, steam-powered riverboat that he intended to launch. Two years later, in 1811, Roosevelt's steamboat *New Orleans* successfully commenced its maiden voyage. The Steamboat Age on western waters had arrived.[1]

At first, flatboatmen refused to take seriously these strange, new, steam-belching craft. Merchant flatboatman Joseph Hough noted that in 1816 pioneer steamboatman Henry Miller Shreve "was regarded as being insane on [the] subject" of upstream navigation, and Hough "declined taking passage with him," choosing instead to travel home by horse over the Natchez Trace. Soon, however, Shreve's and Roosevelt's successes turned disbelief into fear, and boatmen began to ex-

1. Mrs. Nicholas J. Roosevelt quoted in J. H. B. Latrobe, *The First Steamboat Voyage on the Western Waters* (Baltimore, 1871), 7.

press opposition to steamboats on the grounds that "by their introduction [the flatboatmen] would be thrown out of employment." Their fears proved unfounded. By the early 1820s, steamboats were plying the western rivers on a regular basis, and many flatboatmen and keelboatmen had become steamboat pilots and captains. Nor were those men still manning the flats "thrown out of employment." In fact, by providing flatboatmen with a dependable ride home and by fostering river improvements, steamboats caused a great boom in flatboating. During the steamboat era, from the early 1820s until approximately 1861, the flatboatmen experienced unprecedented prosperity.[2]

"We all cont[inued] out this morning about daylight," a Wabash River flatboatman wrote in 1848, "and are now thicker than three in a bed—the river is full of us." New Albany, Indiana, boatman W. S. Ward in 1839 "entered the Mississippi with a fleet of about 60 Flat Boats." During autumns in the 1830s and 1840s, the river fronts of Aurora and Lawrenceburg, Indiana, were lined at any given time with as many as forty or fifty flatboats loading cargoes and departing south. Near Shawneetown, Illinois, in May of 1835, traveler E. S. Thomas observed "the average number of flatboats that passed us in *day-light* each day was twenty-five—their average burthen from five to six hundred barrells." Three weeks later, in Memphis, Thomas counted sixty flats in a period of nine hours. Obviously, business was booming.[3]

In other ways as well, the Steamboat Age had changed dramatically the world the flatboatmen knew. It is true that the Ohio and Missis-

2. "A Brief Account of Mr. Hough's Life Written by Himself in 1852," *Bulletin of the Cincinnati Historical Society,* XIV (October, 1966), 311; Edmund Flagg, *The Far West,* in Reuben Gold Thwaites (ed.), *Early Western Travels* (32 vols.; Cleveland, 1904–1907), XXVI, 150. For flatboatmen and keelboatmen who became steamboatmen, see Emerson Gould, *Fifty Years on the Mississippi; or, Gould's History of River Navigation* (St. Louis, 1889), 623–25, 646, 653, 721–23; Obituaries of Pioneer Rivermen (Scrapbook in Fred A. Bill and Family Papers, Minnesota Historical Society, St. Paul), Box 7; Louis C. Hunter, *Steamboats on Western Rivers: An Economic and Technological History* (Cambridge, Mass., 1949), 243–44.

3. F. A. L., "Journal of a Trip to New Orleans on a *Broadhorn,*" in "Atalantian" (MS in Indiana Historical Society, Indianapolis), IV, entry for August 8, 1848; W. S. Ward, "Journal of a Trip from New Albany, Indiana to New Orleans on Board a Flat Boat . . . 1839" (MS in W. S. Ward Collection, Indiana Historical Society, Indianapolis), 14; Archibald Shaw (ed.), *History of Dearborn County, Indiana* (Indianapolis, 1915), 447; Ebeneezer Smith Thomas, *Reminiscences of the Last Sixty-five Years, Commencing with the Battle of Lexington; also, Sketches of His Own Life and Times* (2 vols.; Hartford, Conn., 1840), I, 291.

sippi valleys still contained what one riverman described as "almost boundless forest, dark, gloomy, and desolate." Flatboatman Miles Stacy remembered that in the 1850s,

> the valleys as well as the hills were heavily wooded and the forests along the winding ways of the Mississippi were full of game. We frequently saw bear and deer come down to the river to drink. Wild turkeys were plentiful in the woods, and the boys often got a mess of red squirrels. . . . There were plenty of fish and geese and ducks in and on the river to catch and vary our menu of salt pork, beans, and potatoes. And along the banks of the Ohio were hickory trees full of large nuts, and on the lower river the finest pecans I ever saw waiting for us to gather.

Stacy neglected to mention, however, the growing towns and cities, especially along the banks of the Upper Ohio, on the Mississippi near St. Louis, and downriver in the state of Mississippi. In 1846–1847, a period during which more flatboats worked the Ohio and Mississippi than ever before or since, the city of Pittsburgh boasted a population of 30,000 and contained "tall factory chimneys belching out coal smoke giving all the buildings a smoky sooty color." One riverman remembered "the levee [was] full of drays and freight," and six iron foundries had earned Pittsburgh the title of the Iron City. To the south, Cincinnati had grown to contain over 12,000 houses and 75,000 inhabitants. Louisville was home to a population of 30,000, and Madison and Evansville, Indiana—towns that had not even existed during the early days of boating—had become important commercial centers for the burgeoning civilization north of the Ohio River.[4]

On the Mississippi, George Forman, a lumber raftsman, flatboatman, and steamboatman who shipped out of St. Louis from 1849 to

4. F. A. L., "Journal of a Trip to New Orleans on a *Broadhorn,*" in "Atalantian," IV, entry for August 8, 1848; Miles A. Stacy, "Flatboating Down Old Man River, 1849–1869: Reminiscences of Captain Miles A. Stacy as Related to His Daughter Adelaide Frost Stacy, February, 1913. Rearranged and Typed by Her, April, 1945" (Typescript in Ohio Historical Society, Campus Martius, the Museum of the Northwest Territory, Marietta, Ohio), 11; Samuel Cummings, *The Western Pilot, Containing Charts of the Ohio River and of the Mississippi . . . Description of the Towns on Their Banks* (Cincinnati, 1847), 5–6, 40–42, 49, 50–51, 62; George Forman, "Biographical Sketch of the Life and Ancestry of Geo. Forman of Stratford-Ontario, Canada Written in 1875 and 1883 by Himself," ed. E. Luella Galliver (Typescript in Western History Research Center, University of Wyoming, Laramie), 104; R. B. Way, "Commerce on the Lower Mississippi in the Period 1830–1860," *Proceedings of the Mississippi Valley Historical Association,* X (1919–21), 58.

1851, remembered "Hundreds of Steamers at the Levee [in St. Louis], which was alive with Drays, Mules and Negro drivers yelling like mad, and Piles of freight, and everything bustle and excitement." Much freight was bound for the Upper Mississippi and new river towns in Iowa, Illinois, Wisconsin, and Minnesota. Forman remembered the Mississippi below St. Louis as being "all alive with Steamers loaded with Cotton Bales, going up and down" past "Memphis, Vicksburgh, Natchez, Baton Rouge, &c"—towns that had been little more than frontier outposts at the time of the Louisiana Purchase. Although still retaining some of its frontier aura, Memphis in 1840 had a population of 1,800 and a landing lined with flatboats. To the south lay Helena, Arkansas, and, near the Walnut Hills, Vicksburg, Mississippi, a town described in Samuel Cummings' 1847 *Western Pilot* as having 4,000 inhabitants, a great number of stores, lawyers, and physicians, and two newspapers. Natchez, with a booming commerce and "Great numbers of boats . . . always lying" Under-the-Hill, remained the largest town in the state of Mississippi. In Louisiana, Baton Rouge had grown, but New Orleans, with 102,198 inhabitants and 15,000 houses in 1847, remained the crown city of the Mississippi Valley. George Forman saw New Orleans for the first time in 1849, and he described its lively exotic flavor in his journal: "The broad levee was alive with negroes & White me[n], the negroes all talking French. [There were] Drays. Cotton Bales. Sugar hogsheads. Hundreds of Steamers going and coming at the Levee. Miles of Ocean Ships, the first I had seen. . . . [I saw] ships from all parts of the world and Ocean Steamers to and from Panama or Chargres. Piles and Piles of Bananas, Oranges, and other tropical fruits on the Levee [and] Negro women with red turbans working among the men."[5]

In addition to this urban growth, river society witnessed other important alterations during the Steamboat Age. Flatboat commercial patterns changed dramatically, as did the kinds of cargoes, navigation conditions, and the size, quantity, and quality of boats. Generally speaking, boating became a more stable occupation and an easier way to make a living. Most of the proud flatboatmen would not have admitted it, but their improved skills had combined with state and fed-

5. Forman, "Biographical Sketch," 105, 107–109; Gerald M. Capers, Jr., *The Biography of a River Town; Memphis: Its Heroic Age* (Chapel Hill, 1939), 72–73; Cummings, *Western Pilot,* 110, 113–14, 121, 126–27.

eral river improvements to lessen their burden and foster easier and safer river navigation. To be sure, there were still dangers on the river, and robbers and other criminals still lurked on the shore. In this new era, however, flatboatmen who sailed the Ohio and Mississippi to New Orleans in four or five weeks could return home to their wives and families aboard a steamboat. These were far different men from the drifters who had walked the Natchez Trace in the early 1800s. The western boatmen had become civilized.

Some broad generalizations can be made about Ohio and Mississippi river flatboat commerce during the Steamboat Age.[6] Flatboatmen flourished during most of the 1823–1861 period, controlling approximately 20 percent of the total inland river commerce. The flatboat trade experienced considerable fluctuation and erratic economic behavior, but it remained profitable and competitive vis-à-vis steamboats and canal boats for many reasons. Declining costs (overhead) led to a long-run decline in freight rates. Also important were the ready availability of flatboats and their fitness for winter travel and low-water navigation not feasible for steamers and canal boats. These advantages were augmented by the increasing skills of flatboatmen, by federal and state river improvements, and by the availability of cheap passage home for flatboat hands on the decks of steamers. Keelboatmen, unlike flatboatmen, were unable to compete with steamers (because steamboats moved upstream more efficiently), and eventually the keelboat trade languished. Finally, after 1847, the erratic, fluctuating nature of flatboat economics began to take its toll, and the flatboatmen, too, began to lose out slowly to the more efficient steamboats, canal boats, and—ultimately—the railroads. Flatboating did not die easily, however, and on the Upper Mississippi, Upper Ohio, and many tributary streams, flatboatmen continued to work until well after the Civil War.[7]

6. The following discussion is based on Harry N. Scheiber, "The Ohio-Mississippi Flatboat Trade: Some Reconsiderations," in David M. Ellis (ed.), *The Frontier in American Development: Essays in Honor of Paul Wallace Gates* (Ithaca, 1970), 277–98; Hunter, *Steamboats on Western Rivers;* and Erik F. Haites, James Mak, and Gary M. Walton, *Western River Transportation* (Baltimore, 1975).

7. For summaries see Scheiber, "Ohio-Mississippi Flatboat Trade," in Ellis (ed.), *Frontier in American Development,* 298; Erik F. Haites and James Mak, "Ohio and Mississippi River Transportation, 1810–1860," *Explorations in Economic History,* VIII (Winter, 1970), 179–80.

It is ironic that the Steamboat Age nurtured so primitive and preindustrial a craft as the flatboat, but the fact is indisputable. Although the years 1815–1861 are known for the "transportation revolution," it is important to remember that this revolution occurred in stages, and that steamboats, canal boats, and railroads did not instantly replace cruder, preindustrial modes of transport. The impact of the railroads was not really felt in the Ohio Valley until the 1850s. In the meantime, flatboatmen provided an essential service. Because the all-important pork-packing season in the Ohio Valley occurred during the winter months, when ice and low water brought steamboat and canal traffic to a standstill, flatboatmen dominated the pork trade. They competed successfully in other markets as well.[8]

Thus, in the volatile, freewheeling economy of Jacksonian America, there was plenty of room for the flatboat entrepreneur. In 1816, before the steamers held sway, 1,287 flats arrived in New Orleans; the number had more than doubled, to 2,792, in the November-to-June shipping season of 1846–1847. Since a great many flatboats stopped short of New Orleans or in other ways remained uncounted, one can estimate that there were at least 4,000 flats operating annually during the 1840s, carrying some 160,000 tons of produce, and manned by more than 20,000 boatmen. The trade began to decline in the 1850s, but quantitative studies of antebellum river commerce show that throughout the 1823–1847 period, flatboating was profitable, competitive, and provided a viable alternative to downstream steamboat shipment.[9]

Besides competing successfully for trade on the main Ohio-Mississippi route well into the 1840s, flatboatmen achieved even greater success on the Upper Ohio, Upper Mississippi, and tributary streams. The heavy emphasis on the role of New Orleans, Natchez, and the South in general in the folklore of the western boatmen obscures the fact that flatboating was very much an Ohio Valley phenomenon. Most flatboatmen during the steamboat era hailed from the Ohio Val-

8. James Mak and Gary M. Walton, "The Persistence of Old Technologies: The Case of Flatboats," *Journal of Economic History*, XXXIII (June, 1973), 444–51; Scheiber, "Ohio-Mississippi Flatboat Trade," in Ellis (ed.), *Frontier in American Development*, 277, 286–87; George Rogers Taylor, *The Transportation Revolution, 1815–1860* (New York, 1951), 64–65.

9. Mak and Walton, "Persistence of Old Technologies," 444–45, 448; Scheiber, "Ohio-Mississippi Flatboat Trade," in Ellis (ed.), *Frontier in American Development*, 288–90; Haites and Mak, "Ohio and Mississippi River Transportation," 155, 163–64, 170, *passim*.

ley states, especially the Old Northwest—Ohio, Indiana, and Illinois—and 95 percent of the flatboats landing in New Orleans from 1845 to 1857 originated on the Ohio or a tributary thereof. By the same token, a great many Ohio Valley flatboats never even entered the Mississippi. In the commercial year 1852–1853 in Cincinnati, for example, an estimated 5,000 flatboats landed at the city wharf, and many of them traveled no farther. About half that number arrived in Pittsburgh from the Allegheny and Monongahela rivers. When one factors in the continuous local traffic on the Muskingum, Scioto, Kentucky, Green, Tennessee, Cumberland, and Wabash rivers, the great magnitude of the non-Mississippi trade becomes apparent.[10]

With the settlement of the Mississippi Valley and admission of new states into the Union, flatboating also increased on the Lower Missouri River, the Arkansas and Yazoo, the Illinois River, and on the Upper Mississippi. Flatboats were not so crucial to the growth of the upper Midwest as to that of the Ohio Valley, yet much of the lead from the mining regions of northwest Illinois (near Galena) and Wisconsin was first transported by flats and keels. Because of the treacherous Upper and Lower Rapids and continual low water on the Upper Mississippi River, Minnesota and Wisconsin farmers preferred flatboats to steamers when they started exporting their first agricultural surpluses in the late 1850s. A reporter for the St. Paul *Daily Minnesotan* observed several flatboats at the city's wharf in 1859, "freighted with corn, wheat, oats, potatoes, and other staples" and "destined for St. Louis, Memphis, Vicksburg, Natches, and New Orleans." The St. Paul *Pioneer Democrat Daily* enthusiastically recommended "these cheap modes of conveyance," predicting that they would soon "become a favorite means of transport to the Southern markets."[11]

The keelboatmen's retreat up the tributaries represented a less successful response to the Steamboat Age than that of the ubiquitous flatboatmen. Always a marginal mode of transport, keels could not begin to compete with the more efficient steamboats for upstream business

10. Hunter, *Steamboats on Western Rivers*, 55, 57; Scheiber, "Ohio-Mississippi Flatboat Trade," in Ellis (ed.), *Frontier in American Development*, 288–89.

11. Moses Meeker, "Early History of the Lead Region of Wisconsin," *Wisconsin Historical Collections*, VI (1872), 276; William J. Peterson, "The Lead Traffic on the Upper Mississippi, 1823–1848," *Mississippi Valley Historical Review*, XVII (June, 1930), 74; *Daily Minnesotan* (St. Paul), October 22, 1859; *Pioneer Democrat Daily* (St. Paul), November 9, 1859.

on the main Ohio-Mississippi route. Their upstream services did prove to be of some value on shallow portions of the Upper Ohio and Upper Mississippi and tributary rivers and streams, and there are a few accounts of keelboat transportation on these waterways as late as the postbellum years. The oil industry on the Upper Allegheny in the 1860s, for instance, relied heavily on keelboats during low water, and many Upper Mississippi steamboats hired keelboats as "lighters," onto which cargo was transferred to lighten the larger craft's load so that it could navigate rapids and shallow stretches of the river. If these chores seemed a bit degrading to the once lordly keelboatmen, they were only a portent of things to come. By the 1850s, one traveler noted, the keelboats of New Orleans had been demoted to service "as oyster barges." Even on the Minnesota River in 1852, the usefulness of these once-noble craft was dismissed by one journalist, who concluded, "Now that we have a regular packet steamer on this river, the keel[boatmen] will hang up the fiddle and the pole, gracefully surrendering to the democracy of steam."[12]

As for the flatboats, their types of cargoes and patterns of commerce grew increasingly complex during the boom years. Flatboatmen still hauled a great many staples: flour, tobacco, corn, whiskey, and hardy produce were common loads, and salted, barreled pork was carried on thousands of flatboats on the western rivers. Dealers in human flesh continued to use flats to ship slaves from the older slave states to the newer ones. Soon, however, cargoes entirely new to river commerce were drifting south. Hay, baled with willow "hoop poles," was shipped in great quantities. Many flats carrying penned cattle, hogs, sheep, and horses made their way south; one riverman delivered sixty milk cows to New Orleans in 1835, noting that "they were right glad to get onto land again." Cordwood for steamboat furnaces was a common load, fostering woodyards and a new addition to the boating

12. Haites and Mak, "Ohio and Mississippi River Transportation," 171; Hunter, *Steamboats on Western Rivers*, 53–54; River Transportation Bills, 1846–62 (MSS in Historical Society of Western Pennsylvania, Pittsburgh); John Flick, "A Round Trip by Raft and Keelboat from Dunville to Nelson's and Reed's Landing in the Late Forties" (Typescript in State Historical Society of Wisconsin, Madison); Samuel T. Covington, "Pioneer Transportation of the Ohio River," *Indiana Magazine of History*, IV (March, 1908), 129–32. William J. Peterson, *Steamboating on the Upper Mississippi* (Iowa City, 1968), 222–24; S. S. Prentiss, *A Memoir of S. S. Prentiss, edited by his brother* (2 vols.; New York, 1855), I, 183; *Minnesota Democrat* (St. Paul), July 14, 1852.

clan, the Ohio and Mississippi woodboatmen. In New Orleans, wood-boatmen would load forty or fifty cords into a used flatboat and sell the whole outfit to a passing steamer.[13]

A demand for logs and sawed lumber throughout the Ohio and Mississippi valleys gave rise to yet another important class of rivermen: the raftsmen. During the post-1823 era, raftsmen shipped billions of board feet of lumber down western rivers to Cincinnati, Louisville, St. Louis, and New Orleans.[14] Rafting became especially important on the Allegheny, Cumberland, Wisconsin, Yazoo, and Ouachita rivers and tributaries, and there are scores of accounts of lumber and log raftsmen piloting these huge craft. At St. Louis and New Orleans, raft crews of thirty men landed craft over 100 feet wide and 600 feet long. Despite the growth and importance of log and lumber rafting, however, the humble flatboats remained preeminent among the nonsteam river vessels.[15]

13. Logan Esarey (ed.), "The Pioneers of Morgan County: Memoirs of Noah J. Major," *Indiana Historical Society Publications,* V (1915), 400–401; Margaret Welsh, *The Rise of the Midwestern Meat Packing Industry* (Lexington, Ky., 1982); Scheiber, "Ohio-Mississippi Flatboat Trade," in Ellis (ed.), *The Frontier in American Development,* 286; Chester Haring to Fountain Perry, July 24, 1825, in Fountain and Roderick Perry Papers, Special Collections and Archives, University of Kentucky Library, Lexington; Peter W. Williams Collection (MSS in Indiana Historical Society, Indianapolis), *passim;* C. F. Clarkson, "Our First Flat-Boat Trip," in *Iowa State Register* (Des Moines), December 28, 1883; William E. Smith and Ophia D. Smith (eds.), *Colonel A. W. Gilbert, Citizen-Soldier of Cincinnati* (Cincinnati, 1934), 23–24; Stacy "Reminiscences of Captain Miles Stacy," 13.

14. William G. Rector, *Log Transportation in the Lakes States Lumber Industry, 1840–1918* (Glendale, Cal., 1953); Hunter, *Steamboats on Western Rivers,* 58–59; Thomas R. Cox, "Transition in the Woods: Log Drives, Raftsmen, and the Emergence of Modern Lumbering in Pennsylvania," *Pennsylvania Magazine of History and Biography,* CIV (July, 1980), 346–64.

15. George B. Engberg, "Who Were the Lumberjacks?" in Harry N. Scheiber (ed.), *The Old Northwest: Studies in Regional History, 1787–1910* (Lincoln, Neb., 1969), 270–79. For Upper Mississippi raftsmen, see Gustave A. Giese, "The Rafting and Running of Lumber Down the Wisconsin and Mississippi Rivers to the Southern Lumber Markets in Bygone Days" (Typescript in State Historical Society of Wisconsin, Madison); Stephen R. Bentley, "An Account of Wisconsin River Lumber Rafting Days" (MS in State Historical Society of Wisconsin, Madison); St. Paul *Weekly Minnesotan,* June 18, 1853; and Forman, "Biographical Sketch," *passim.* For Ohio Valley rafting, see Henry Baxter, "Rafting on the Allegheny and Ohio, 1844," *Pennsylvania Magazine of History and Biography,* LI (1927), 27–78, 143–71, 207–43; and Theodore Putnam, "A Rafting Journal of 1859—from Warren, Pa., to Louisville, Ky.," ed. Ernest Miller, *Western*

Many products of the emerging industrial society found their way aboard the inherently preindustrial flatboats. Coal was shipped almost exclusively in huge flatboats known in the trade as "coal flats" or "coalboats." Boatman T. C. Collins of Little Hocking, Ohio, built and captained a large coal flat that "carried between 12 and 20,000 bushels of coal." Pig iron, farm machinery, glass, and tools also moved south aboard flatboats. Riverman W. H. Jolly worked "on a couple of flat-boats loaded with boulders, going down to Evansville," and on the Upper Mississippi the Winona *Republican* reported "several ice barges" loaded with 375 tons of "Minnesota ice, seeking a Southern market." The prize for the most unique cargo would have to go to a boatman named Jamson, who kept a "bee boat" on the Ohio and Mississippi in the 1850s. "He would stay south through the winter," merchant navigator Miles Stacy of Marietta recalled, "then as the willows and other trees and flowers blossomed in the spring he would move up the river for fresh 'pastures' for his bees." [16]

Flatboatmen ran either "straight" or "mixed" loads. A straight load consisted of one product only and was much easier to load, unload, and maintain while en route. Pork, flour, hay, coal, or cordwood made good straight loads. If a boatman was lucky or maintained good business connections, he could run straight loads south with no stopovers, and sell out in one location to one buyer. This was very unusual, however; most boatmen ran mixed loads and stopped at several points before selling out. Flatboatman J. M. Readers, for example, hauled "lime, flour, pork, potatoes, Dried apples, lard, and Beef, Segars, some brooms, and some tobacco." Produce flatboatmen carried mixed loads of hardy fruits and vegetables, starting south about

Pennsylvania Historical Magazine, XL (Fall, 1957), 149–62. For Lower Mississippi rafting, see John Hebron Moore, "Simon Gray, Riverman: A Slave Who Was Almost Free," *Mississippi Valley Historical Review*, XLIX (December, 1962), 472–84.

16. Henry Howe, "A Talk with a Veteran Boatman," in *Historical Collections of Ohio* (2 vols.; Columbus, 1888) I, 321–22; Taylor, *Transportation Revolution*, 170; Herbert L. Roush, Sr., (ed.), *The Adventures of T. C. Collins—Boatman: Twenty-Four Years on the Western Waters, 1849–1873* (Baltimore, 1985), 60; City of New Orleans, Wharfinger Report, February and March, 1831 (MSS in Tulane University, New Orleans), *passim;* W. H. Jolly to Family, May 15, 1860 (Typescript in Charles Jolly Collection, Indiana Historical Society, Indianapolis); *Goodhue County Republican* (Red Wing, Minn.), May 25, 1860; Stacy, "Reminiscences of Captain Miles Stacy," 12–13.

the middle of November. Miles Stacy worked at produce flatboating throughout the 1850s, but he carried many other items in his mixed loads.

[My] flatboats would carry five tiers of barrels all the way through and six [tiers] through the center, but I always left a place in the bow to pack the pork, for I usually butchered 60 or 70 hogs and packed the pork there. For the rest of my mixed load I usually got about 100 bbls. of apples and placed them on the bottom of the boat where it was the coolest and they kept best; next some 600 bbls. of potatoes, 20 or 25 bbls. of Kraut, 10 or 15 bbls. of onions; 20 bbls. of beans, also I'd buy 15 or 20 dozen brooms and at the bucket factory in Harmar 8 or 10 dozen buckets. . . . On top of this load I'd place about 100 bbls. flour . . . some tobacco, cigars, and star-candles—that was before the time of Kerosene oil. I also got a few boxes of candy—the colored folks always wanted to buy candy.[17]

Stacy's huge loads were typical in their variety. He and thousands of merchant flatboatmen were engaged in what was called "coasting." Archibald Shaw remembered the coasting voyages of his father, a Scotsman who settled along the Ohio.

Father, when married, spent the winter months in [flatboating along "the coast"]. . . . The Coast was . . . that portion of the lower Mississippi where sugar cane [and cotton were] grown. . . . It was a rich country and the planters had about them negro slaves in great numbers . . . [and were] counted very rich. The two staples were about all they tried to grow and they became accustomed to depending upon these upriver boatmen to bring them most of other necessities such as fruit, potatoes, and even stock for butchering. It was a tempting market until after the Civil War when railways began to be built that brought this produce to the market down in the cotton and cane country, regardless of ice in the rivers or sandbars with shallow river crossings.

These Ohio Valley coasting flats, some flying calico flags to denote their status, worked the Lower Mississippi throughout the antebellum period. Some boatmen made one or more trips annually and cultivated regular customers along the route. T. C. Collins remembered coasting as the "hardest boating I ever done." He and his crewmates landed

17. Stacy, "Reminiscences of Captain Miles Stacy," 2–3, 7, 10; J. M. Readers to Jacob Brandenburg, November 26, 1858, in John Brandenburg Collection, Indiana Historical Society, Indianapolis.

their unwieldy craft several times a day, and the "Captain would jump out on shore . . . and in a few minutes he would come back and say 'Boys, get out 2 barrel of Whisky—500 pounds of pork—50 bushel of corn, 4 kegs of lard etc. etc.'" When, with considerable effort, the men had "got the stuff all on shore, the Captain had [business] settled for and it was 'Boys, get ready and we will push out. I wish to make another landing by such a time.'" Collins complained that there was "not much rest, day or night."[18]

While the common hands complained of hard work, the merchant navigators voiced more pecuniary grievances. Flatboating during the Steamboat Age was a volatile, cutthroat business. The ease with which one could become a flatboat speculator brought to the trade an incredibly diverse selection of mankind, from city slickers to unassuming farmers. Some merchant navigators doubled as storekeepers and commodities speculators, dealing with eastern wholesalers as well as their own western customers. They either bought goods outright for shipment or took them on consignment pending sale. Some of these merchants became reluctant flatboatmen, finding themselves with bartered produce on their hands and no ready market except downstream. Shrewder merchant navigators engaged agents or middlemen in Cincinnati, St. Louis, Natchez, and New Orleans to advise them and assist in the sales of their cargoes. Ideally, if one retained reliable agents, one could retire from the river altogether and hire out the work. Even so, there was always uncertainty and fear of competition. Currency exchange and credit were especially difficult to arrange, and if these problems baffled experienced urban businessmen, imagine their effect on the unsophisticated farmer flatboatmen. The fear of hitting a snag or sandbar began to pale compared with the fear of fluctuating prices and glutted markets, reports of which the nervous merchant navigator could study in his latest issue of *New Orleans Prices-Current*.[19]

18. Archibald Shaw, "The Autobiography of Archibald Shaw" (Typescript in Archibald Shaw Collection, Indiana State Library, Indianapolis), 15–16; Joseph Aricoin [?] to George Kapp, January 27, 1860, in George Kapp Collection, Indiana Historical Society, Indianapolis; Roush (ed.), *T. C. Collins—Boatman*, 87–88.

19. Scheiber, "Ohio-Mississippi Flatboat Trade," in Ellis (ed.), *Frontier in American Development*, 290–91; "Account of Mr. Hough's Life Written by Himself," 308–309; Lewis E. Atherton, "John McDonogh and the Mississippi River Trade," *Louisiana Historical Quarterly*, XXVI (January, 1943), 37–43. For examples of the volatile nature of

The letters and diaries of merchant navigators reflect this constant anxiety over business affairs. John Patton of Vevay, Indiana, complained in 1847 that his voyage had taken too long and "knocked me behind every market that I came to . . . 3 days sooner in Lafayette and we would have sold oats at $40 and hay at $22 per ton instead of $16.50." At the other end of the chain of commerce, "Our d——d farmers are to[o] d——d independent," Indiana flatboat speculator Alfred F. Howes complained to his partner, Peter W. Williams, in 1851. "I am willing they should take their produce to hell or any other market they choose in preference to begging them to sell as we had to last year." Two years later, learning that hay was in short supply in New Orleans, Howes wrote Williams, "I hope they will get entirely out [of hay in New Orleans] and have to pay some of us poor devil[-] dominated hay traders 4 prices for their winter's supply." Memphis merchant Louis Trezvant suffered greatly when a "spontaneous rot" ruined his flatboat load of turnips and pumpkins in the 1840s. The substantial correspondence of Wabash River flatboatman William P. Dole is replete with similar stories and constant agonizing over business matters. Dole nevertheless assured his wife that he possessed "to[o] much spirit to go down untill the Last hope is Lost. . . . I am one whose hope is pretty strongly developed."[20]

Captain Miles Stacy took the offensive when he found himself stranded in a glutted Memphis market in 1857 with two hundred barrels of potatoes. Reading in *Prices-Current* that in Cincinnati (from which he had departed just three weeks earlier) the price of potatoes was $2.25 higher than in Memphis, Stacy arranged to ship his flatboat cargo back to Ohio aboard a steamer. "I never heard of any other flatboatman shipping potatoes north," he later wrote. "I never did it

flatboat marketing, see Joseph Malin to U. P. Schenck, January 11, 1844, in "Flatboat Letters of Switzerland County, Indiana" (Typescript in Harold Brown Adkinson Collection, Indiana Division, Indiana State Library, Indianapolis); Jacob Weaver to Johannis Weaver, July 24, 1823, in Jacob Weaver Collection, Indiana Historical Society, Indianapolis; and Clarkson, "Our First Flat-Boat Trip."

20. John Patton to U. P. Schenck, November 12, 1847, in "Flatboat Letters of Switzerland County, Indiana"; Alfred F. Howes to Peter W. Williams, May 7, December 31, 1853, both in Peter W. Williams Collection; James Dick Davis, *The History of the City of Memphis . . . [and] the "Old Times Papers"* (Memphis, 1873), 288–90; Donald F. Carmony (ed.), "William P. Dole: Wabash Valley Merchant and Flatboatman," *Indiana Magazine of History*, LXVII (December, 1971), 361–62.

but this once but it paid me well." Equally resourceful was Indianan C. F. Clarkson. Sailing to New Orleans in a fleet of more than fifty hay flatboats in 1841, Clarkson and his men learned that there was absolutely no hay in the New Orleans market "and five thousand horses starving." This news "raised a fever heat" among the boatmen, he wrote, so the flotilla held a mass meeting and voted to band together, sell only at an agreed price, and thus command the market. Feigning agreement, Clarkson and his crew decided to "circumvent the crowd . . . and reach the market in advance of them." They did just that, arriving in New Orleans after a harrowing journey and selling out at top dollar just ahead of the rest of the fleet. Clarkson and his men immediately departed for home "on one of the best steamers on the river," suspecting that upon arrival of the other hay boats in New Orleans, "the climate might be too hot for a Hoosier."[21]

Changing commercial patterns were accompanied by other advances in flatboating. Although at first glance boatbuilding techniques do not appear to have changed drastically between 1823 and 1861, further investigation reveals important alterations in the state of the art. To be sure, flatboats looked much the same as in the early days—they retained the identical shape and superstructure and were built from the same materials as in the presteamboat era. The main differences lay in quality and size. After fifty years of experience, western Americans had become excellent flatboat builders. Farmers building flats alongside creeks and tributary streams benefited from the knowledge of the thousands of boatbuilders who had preceded them. Moreover, in professional boatbuilding centers like Pittsburgh, Cincinnati, Jeffersonville (Indiana), and St. Louis, master carpenters and craftsmen built huge flatboats of excellent quality, equipped with the latest in nautical gear.[22]

Improvements in navigation skills and in maintaining the river channels enabled rivermen to use larger boats, and boat size and capac-

21. Stacy, "Reminiscences of Captain Miles Stacy," 15; C. F. Clarkson, "Our First Flat-Boat Trip."

22. Donald F. Carmony (ed.), "Flatboat Building on Little Raccoon Creek, Parke County, Indiana," *Indiana Magazine of History,* LX (December, 1964), 305–22; Roush (ed.), *T. C. Collins—Boatman,* 11–13; Otto M. Knoblock, "Early Navigation on the Saint Joseph River," *Indiana Historical Society Publications,* VIII (1925), 188–90; Scheiber, "Ohio-Mississippi Flatboat Trade," in Ellis (ed.), *Frontier in American Development,* 279; Mak and Walton, "Persistence of Old Technologies," 446.

ity increased dramatically during the Steamboat Age. Early flatboats averaged 60 feet in length, carried 30 tons of produce, and cost about $75. By the 1850s, boatmen worked 100-foot-long flats carrying an average of 150 tons and costing $150. These were fine boats, too— excellently caulked and equipped with leather pumps, solid capstans, and factory-made check lines. Cabins were built for comfort: as one boatman remembered, they included "a stove . . . to heat and cook. A hinged table hung from the wall, and at either end was usually upper and lower bunks." Such accommodations were a far cry from the early boats with their sandbox cooking pits and a bedroom under the stars. No wonder some merchant navigators during the post-1823 decades discontinued the practice of dismantling and selling flats in New Orleans. Having invested in such solid, comfortable craft, rivermen engaged steamers to tow their flats north, sometimes loaded with a new cargo. As the Civil War approached, this practice of using flatboats and keelboats as auxiliary storage craft and "lighters" attached to steamers increased, and in it we see the very tender beginnings of modern-day barge commerce. At the same time, in naming their flatboats, some merchant navigators of this new era evinced the cold efficiency of the emerging industrial America: wharf registers and business correspondence show an increasing number of flatboats identified simply as "Boat No. 22" or "No. 4" or "Number 11."[23]

Because of the steamboat, flatboatmen now worked several trips a year, and they naturally became more skilled and proficient. To supplement their growing knowledge of the river, boatmen consulted the detailed and accurate maps and notes of Samuel Cummings' *Western Pilot* and other guidebooks. Boatmen perfected loading techniques, distributing the cargo evenly "to forstall twisting and consequent leaks" and more serious structural damage. Crew size nearly doubled— the largest flatboats carried ten hands. Rivermen adopted a more regu-

23. Mak and Walton, "Persistence of Old Technologies," 446; Haites and Mak, "Ohio and Mississippi River Transportation," 162; Alfred F. Howes to Peter W. Williams, February 10, 1852, in Peter W. Williams Collection; Roush (ed.), *T. C. Collins— Boatman*, 13; Scheiber, "Ohio-Mississippi Flatboat Trade," in Ellis (ed.), *Frontier in American Development*, 296; Milo M. Quaife (ed.), *The Early Days of Rock Island and Davenport: The Narratives of J. W. Spencer and J. M. D. Burrows* (Chicago, 1942), 176–77, 180; S. Martin to U. P. Schenck and Sons, October 6, 1858, in "Flatboat Letters of Switzerland County, Indiana"; John Duffield Hay to Griggs Wild Co., June 5, 1835, in John Duffield Hay Collection, Indiana Historical Society, Indianapolis.

lar watch system, working six hours and resting six. Of course, there were still problems. Boatmen complained of the drudgery in loading and unloading their huge cargoes, "tramp, tramp, tramp, up and down the steep bank all day long." And some captains did not maintain a regular watch, but put all hands on "dog watch," waking them up at all hours of the night and day with the call, "To oars!" T. C. Collins complained that "a great many people . . . have no idea about the river and how hard a boatman makes his money." Although in many ways he was right, the plight of the common boatmen had improved considerably from the days when everyone stood "dog watch," walked the Natchez Trace, and feared robbers and Indian attacks.[24]

No amount of technical improvements could prevent inclement weather, of course, and the fact that produce flatboatmen always departed in November or December meant that they continued to suffer from the elements. One of the greatest threats to flatboatmen during the Steamboat Age, however, bore no relationship to these natural phenomena. This danger was the steamboat itself. The classic scenes of Huck Finn and Mike Fink being run over by awesome, steam-spewing riverboats in *The Adventures of Huckleberry Finn* and "The Last of the Boatmen" were drawn from tragic, real-life encounters on the western rivers. One riverman in the 1840s worked in a flatboat fleet that carried "signal lights" to "ward off steamers" but nevertheless floated into the path of a paddle wheeler: it "struck our crafts about the middle and nearly ran over them, sinking them so water was three or four feet deep in the boats." Another flatboatman recalled an incident during the 1850s in which "a steamboat ran into a lime boat in . . . a fog" near Lake Providence, Louisiana. "[W]e could hear the men on the lime boat shouting," he remembered, but the steamboatmen did not hear them and "smashed into the lime boat and sunk it." As the Ohio and Mississippi became more and more congested with boat traffic, these accidents increased, and it was the flatboatmen

24. Mak and Walton, "Persistence of Old Technologies," 446 n. 11; Louisville *Courier Journal,* April 9, 1939; Haites and Mak, "Ohio and Mississippi River Transportation," 162, table 2. The average flatboat in 1810–1819 carried five men, those of 1840–1849 carried seven, and those of 1850–1859, ten boatmen. See also Manasseh Barney Slawson, "Life of M. B. Slawson" (Typescript in Indiana Historical Society, Indianapolis); Roush (ed.), *T. C. Collins—Boatman,* 48–49, 72; W. H. Jolly to Family, May 15, 1860, in Charles Jolly Collection.

who inevitably suffered most. This caused hard feelings and cemented the natural rivalry between steamboatmen and flatboatmen. Their mutual animosity is shown in a story told by T. C. Collins:

> As we were floating along, we met a steam boat and the Captain waved his hand and said, "Row that boat out of my way, or I will run over you." I answered, "The River is large and you can keep out of [m]y way with your steamboat." He got mad, jerked off his hat and said, "If you are not careful you will get run over and sunk." "I know marine law, Sir [Collins answered], and I dare you or any other steam boat to run over a floating boat. If you do, the boat will be well sold." He said no more and passed on.[25]

Collisions and foul weather notwithstanding, the industrial age was one of relative ease for the downstream men—although one would never suspect it from their correspondence. Flatboatmen continued to complain (as all workingmen do) and sometimes to exaggerate the dangers of their work so as to present it in a more romantic or dramatic light. "I cannot begin to tell you all the difficulties we encountered nor all the dangers we met up with, especially on the lower Ohio and the Mississippi," the old flatboatman Miles Stacy reminisced in 1913. "In the 1850s the Ohio was not cleared for navigation as it is today," he reminded the soft postpioneer generation. In fact, snag-pulling and dredging, the construction of wing dams, the engineering of the Louisville Lock and Canal (bypassing the Falls of the Ohio), and other important river improvements had been under way since the 1820s. River improvements, like everything else, are relative. Looking back as Stacy did from 1913 and the advent of the Army Corps of Engineers, numerous locks and dams, buoyed river channels, extensive dredging, and fog lights, one might very well assess the 1840s and 1850s as a period of rough-and-tumble river navigation. From the perspective of the pre-1823 era, however, river improvements by mid-century had progressed rapidly and broadly, revolutionizing the flatboatmen's work. Indeed, between 1823 and 1861 improvements re-

---

25. Clarkson, "Our First Flat-Boat Trip"; Stacy, "Reminiscences of Captain Miles Stacy," 9; Insurance claim, in Peter W. Williams Collection, Box 2, folder 8; "Excerpts from the Stone Diary" (Typescript in Ohio Historical Society, Campus Martius, the Museum of the Northwest Territory, Marietta, Ohio), 3 (the original of the diary is in possession of the Ross County Historical Society, Chillicothe, Ohio); Roush (ed.), *T. C. Collins—Boatman,* 149.

duced the average passage time of downstream flats by approximately 30 to 50 percent. With the additional time saved by taking deck passage home aboard steamboats, flatboatmen were making round trips in only one-quarter the time of the presteam era.[26]

River improvements were pioneered on a limited scale by the French and Spanish, who built levees on the Lower Mississippi in the eighteenth century and began some minor dredging and clearing of rivers and swamps. After the United States took charge of the region, westerners began to complain loudly to their state and national governments, requesting aid in making the western rivers more navigable. This issue fitted perfectly into the political context of the era: National Republicans and, later, Whigs and Republicans called for "internal improvements" subsidized by the federal government; Old Republicans and, later, Jacksonian Democrats balked at such measures. Meanwhile, the West demanded action. "Every boat that is snagged, every one that gets fast on a sand bar, every article that is lost, and every life that is sacrificed," cried the Cincinnati *Gazette* in 1846 after President Polk's veto of a river improvements bill, "will forcibly remind us of this destructive blow aimed by a Locofoco President against our Prosperity." Soon even states' rights advocate John C. Calhoun agreed that river improvements were necessary for the South to compete with the Erie Canal and maintain the Ohio Valley–New Orleans trade connection so vital to southern commerce and politics. In this combative political milieu began the first era of western river improvements.[27]

Between 1823 and 1861, the federal government spent over $3,000,000 in improving the western rivers. Although this figure is small when compared with expenditures after the Civil War, the early improvements established important precedents. They led to the development of effective river-clearing techniques and technology, and

26. William Buckner McGroarty (ed.), "Diary of Phillip Johnson Buckner, M.D.," *William and Mary Quarterly,* 2nd ser., XXIII (January, 1943), 83; Achilles E. Fretageot, "Flatboat Trip, New Harmony to New Orleans, December 1833–January 1834" (Typescript in Indiana Historical Society, Indianapolis), 8; Stacy, "Reminiscences of Captain Miles Stacy," 1–2; Hunter, *Steamboats on Western Rivers,* 181–215; Isaac Lippincott, "A History of River Improvement," *Journal of Political Economy,* XXII (July, 1914), 630–60; Mak and Walton, "Persistence of Old Technologies," 448–49.

27. Gould, *Fifty Years on the Mississippi,* 285, 309–311, 332; Hunter, *Steamboats on Western Rivers,* 190–93; Lippincott, "History of River Improvement," 637, 642–48; Cincinnati *Gazette* quoted in Hunter, *Steamboats on Western Rivers,* 191.

established the army engineers as the federal arm whose mission it was to maintain the western rivers. Congress first appropriated money in 1819, granting funds to survey and map the Ohio and Mississippi valleys "for the purpose of facilitating and ascertaining the most practicable mode of improving the navigation of these rivers." In 1824 Congress funded actual improvements on the western waters, and the Department of War contracted the first snag-removal and sandbar dredging operations. Congress appropriated more money in the late 1820s and 1830s, and state and local governments began to fund their own river improvements.[28]

President John Quincy Adams' appointment of Captain Henry Miller Shreve as "Superintendent of Western River Improvements" in 1827 proved to be a brilliant choice. Shreve, the keelboat entrepreneur turned steamboatman, developed a steam-powered snag-pulling apparatus that, mounted to his snag boat *Heliopolis,* became famous throughout the West as "Uncle Sam's Tooth-Puller." Shreve's snag-clearing and dredging operations on the Ohio and Mississippi in the late 1820s and the 1830s were paralleled by the long-awaited construction of a canal bypassing the Great Falls of the Ohio. Several groups had launched earlier, unsuccessful attempts to build a canal around this great bottleneck of the western rivers. Finally, in 1825, the state of Kentucky incorporated the Louisville and Portland Canal Company, a joint public and private venture that aimed to bypass the Falls. Completed in 1830, the Louisville Canal recorded 578 flatboat and keelboat passages in 1839. The increasing size of steamboats soon rendered the canal obsolete for their passage, however, and the reluctance of flatboatmen to pay a stiff user's fee clouded the accomplishment of this great engineering feat. Many flatboatmen continued to risk navigating the Falls, and not until a complete federal takeover in the post–Civil War decades did the Louisville Canal realize its full potential as a western river improvement.[29]

28. Lippincott, "History of River Improvement," 634–35, 648; Hunter, *Steamboats on Western Rivers,* 190–91; *Indiana Journal* (Indianapolis), November 9, 1839; Carmony (ed.), "Dole: Wabash Valley Merchant and Flatboatman," 335.

29. Caroline S. Pfaff, "Henry Miller Shreve: A Biography," *Louisiana Historical Quarterly,* X (January, 1927), 205–207; Edith McCall, *Conquering the Rivers: Henry Miller Shreve and the Navigation of America's Inland Waterways* (Baton Rouge, 1983), *passim;* Robert Baird, *View of the Valley of the Mississippi* (Philadelphia, 1832), 238–39. For the Louisville Canal see Hunter, *Steamboats on Western Rivers,* 182–86; Paul B. Trescott,

Meanwhile, rivermen along the tributary streams and upper reaches of the Ohio and Mississippi also began to enjoy some of the benefits of river engineering. Congress allotted funds for snag pulling on the Cumberland and Tennessee rivers, and state governments conducted limited improvement operations along the Wabash and other tributaries of the Ohio. On the Upper Mississippi, the army engineers attempted to widen and deepen the channel at the treacherous Lower Rapids near Keokuk, Iowa, and the Upper Rapids near Davenport, Iowa. Under the supervision of a young lieutenant named Robert E. Lee, the army engineers in the late 1830s drilled and blasted river rock on the Lower Rapids, but they made little progress. After an expenditure of some $335,000, the army decided to dig a canal, but this project was not completed until well after the Civil War. The same story can be told for the hazardous Muscle Shoals stretch of the Tennessee River, which continued to plague rivermen and defy the army engineers during the antebellum period. On the Lower Missouri and Red rivers, the army was more successful. Indeed, Shreve's breaking up in 1838 of a 150-mile-long stretch of log jam known infamously as the "Red River Raft" is one of the great achievements in the history of antebellum western river engineering.[30]

From approximately 1839 to 1861, the drive to improve the western rivers lost momentum. The ascension of anti-improvement presidents such as Tyler and Polk, the shifting of national attention to the Mexican War, the growth of the trans-Mississippi West, and the looming sectional crisis all served to stifle the push for river improvements. At the same time, some rivermen objected to wharf taxes used for the improvement and regulation of dock facilities in Memphis, Vicksburg, Natchez, and New Orleans. One group of old-time rivermen objected to river improvements for different reasons: according to one contemporary, these boatmen feared that improvements would "open the

"The Louisville and Portland Canal Company, 1825–1874," *Mississippi Valley Historical Review,* XLIV (March, 1958), 686–708; Heber P. Walker, "Louisville and Portland Canal," *Indiana Magazine of History,* XXVIII (March, 1932), 21–30; Roscoe Carlyle Buley, *The Old Northwest, Pioneer Period, 1815–1840* (Indianapolis, 1950), 435–36; Stacy, "Reminiscences of Captain Miles Stacy," 8–9; Roush (ed.), *T. C. Collins—Boatman,* 68.

30. Hunter, *Steamboats on Western Rivers,* 192, 186–89; 196–98; *Indiana Journal* (Indianapolis), November 9, 1839; Carmony (ed.), "Dole: Wabash Valley Merchant and Flatboatman," 335; Lippincott, "History of River Improvement," 640; Basil Hall, *Travels in North America in the Years 1827 and 1828* (3 vols.; Edinburgh, 1830), III, 382–83.

river to the prudent, timid, and unskilled, thereby reducing the monopoly" and changing the nature of the trade.[31]

These veteran boatmen were correct. River improvements, in combination with other factors, did open up the trade to a vast number of "prudent" (though not necessarily "unskilled") flatboatmen who otherwise might never have made the trip south. Because of river improvements begun in the 1823–1861 period, flatboating ceased to be a perilous adventure. Not only did flatboatmen complete their trips much more quickly than before, but flatboats often could be seen "running day and night" during the Steamboat Age. "There were instances," an Indiana pioneer remembered, "where the cables were never tied between the mouth of the Wabash and the landing at the City [of New Orleans]." During the early days of boating, most rivermen would have considered this practice of running all night sheer madness. The fact that it was standard procedure during the steamboat era is a powerful argument for the impact of river improvements on flatboating.[32]

A brief look at the marine insurance business on western rivers is indicative of some of the changes that have been discussed here. During the presteamboat era, insurance for flatboats was expensive and difficult to obtain. In the 1820s this situation began to change, although gradually. By the 1840s, there existed a number of marine insurance companies selling policies to flatboatmen for one-third to one-half the cost of insurance in the 1820s. True, flatboats were considered a greater risk than steamboats, and flatboatmen were sometimes unable to buy insurance during the hazardous winter months. For the most part, however, flatboatmen could buy insurance when they wanted it. Indeed, marine insurance—undoubtedly a luxury to pre-1823 flatboatmen—was a standard business expense to many rivermen of the steamboat era. This insurability must be attributed both to the increasing skills and professionalism of the boatmen and to

31. Lippincott, "History of River Improvement," 641; Hunter, *Steamboats on Western Rivers*, 196–98; New Orleans Municipal Papers (MSS in Tulane University, New Orleans), Box 15, folder 12; City of Vicksburg, *Revised Ordinances . . . 1839,* in Old Courthouse Museum, Vicksburg, 90–95; Davis, *History of the City of Memphis*, 195–96.

32. Esarey (ed.), "Memoirs of Noah J. Major," 397; Theodore Armitage, "Floating on the Wabash—A Diary of 1847," *Indiana Magazine of History,* IX (December, 1913), 272–75; Mak and Walton, "Persistence of Old Technologies," 448.

the improvement of navigation conditions on the western rivers. The army engineers still had a long way to go, but they already had altered drastically the lifestyle of the western boatmen. In 1848 a young Indiana flatboatman could write from the once-treacherous Lower Ohio that "we had nothing at all to do & were not obliged to wet an oar, from the time we unmoored in the morning until we ran into the Mississippi, a distance of a hundred miles."[33]

Flatboatmen of the Steamboat Age still faced dangers, but the situation had changed greatly since the days of drownings, Indian attacks, and wilderness robberies. Despite occasional accounts of rivermen getting lost or battling wild animals in the forests and swamps of the Lower Mississippi, the hazards of boating had become in general less dramatic. For instance, one persistent problem for flatboatmen appears to have been fires, especially chimney fires. There are many accounts of rivermen whose "wooden fireplace and chimney caught fire and was all in a blaze." The fact that chimney fires were a direct result of improved living conditions aboard flatboats (i.e., the increase in the number of stoves for heating and cooking) says a great deal about the nature of hazards during the steamboat days. Hardship and danger had a more modern face. Wilderness crime was replaced by urban crime, and the perils of travel on the Natchez Trace were replaced by an uncomfortable passage home on the crowded and filthy deck of a steamboat.[34]

Boatmen still feared robbers. One flatboatman noted that the populous "German Coast" of Louisiana was infamous because of "the thieving propensities of the negroes . . . the most accomplished and

33. Mak and Walton, "Persistence of Old Technologies," 448; Scheiber, "Ohio-Mississippi Flatboat Trade," in Ellis (ed.), Frontier in American Development, 295; Erik F. Haites and James Mak, "Social Savings Due to Western River Steamboats," Research in Economic History, III (1978), 294; Haites and Mak, "Ohio and Mississippi River Transportation," 164; Patton to Schenck, November 12, 1847, in "Flatboat Letters of Switzerland County, Indiana"; Pioneer Democrat Daily (St. Paul), October 31, 1860; Insurance policies and claims, in Peter W. Williams Collection, passim, especially Box 2, folder 8; F. A. L., "Journal of a Trip to New Orleans on a Broadhorn," in "Atalantian," IV, entry for July 10, 1848.

34. "Excerpts from the Stone Diary," 3; Slawson, "Life of M. B. Slawson"; Roush (ed.), T. C. Collins—Boatman, 36; McGroarty (ed.), "Diary of Phillip Johnson Buckner, M.D.," 76; F. A. L., "Journal of a Trip to New Orleans on a Broadhorn," in "Atalantian," IV, entry for July 10, 1848; Stacy, "Reminiscences of Captain Miles Stacy," 9–10.

daring sett of thieves to be found in the Country." A young Indiana flatboatman named Abraham Lincoln was attacked at night by a gang of blacks in this part of the country in 1828, but managed to hold his own. To the north, an 1854 Natchez police investigation "of negroes on the *Esperance* plantation of Mr. Lennox Surget" was reported to have resulted "in the recovery of a considerable quantity of goods belonging to [two murdered flatboatmen] and a confession on the part of the negroes of murder having been committed to obtain" the goods. The Natchez *Daily Courier* claimed the slaves "got aboard the boat, murdered the men, threw their bodies overboard, robbed the boat of its goods, and turned it adrift." Thirteen blacks "were committed to jail to be tried as principals and accessories."[35]

There are many other stories of "boat[s] robbed . . . Traces of blood," and "murdered bodies . . . thrown into the river," but the historian must exercise considerable caution in assessing these tales. For example, any account of crimes by free blacks or slaves published in antebellum southern newspapers should be weighed most carefully. Equally to the point, one should remember that the Jacksonian Age produced scores of robber folktales in oral and literary form. Sifting through them, one finds many similarities and patterns that are repeated in nonliterary, "factual" newspaper accounts of flatboat robberies. These "true" robber stories in newspapers of the post-1823 period skipped from locale to locale, satisfying the particular whims of the journalists who related them. This is obviously the case with one much-told story, based on an actual incident, involving river pirates, counterfeiters, and murderers near the mouth of the White River in Arkansas around 1841. The story describes a vigilante action against the pirates and their subsequent punishment by hanging or shooting, but the details as to the exact mode of punishment, the date, and the extent of the crimes vary greatly depending upon which version one consults. What is interesting is that the same story appears in a number of forms and that a vigilante action against a "desperate and extensive gang of river pirates" on the Upper Mississippi fifteen years after the original sounds suspiciously similar.[36]

35. F. A. L., "Journal of a Trip to New Orleans on a *Broadhorn*," in "Atalantian," IV, entries for August 28 and September 18, 1848; Abraham Lincoln, "Short Autobiography," in John G. Nicolay and John Hay (eds.), *Complete Works of Abraham Lincoln* (12 vols.; New York, 1905), VI, 28; *Daily Courier* (Natchez), April 19, 1854.

36. Edith Wyatt Moore, *Natchez Under-the-Hill* (Natchez, 1958), 87–88; Roush

Flatboat robbers simply did not pose as great a threat to Steamboat Age rivermen as they had to an earlier generation. Further, the abandonment of the Natchez Trace deprived murderers and highwaymen of one of their favorite haunts. After the invention of the steamboat, many Ohio and Mississippi valley criminals gave up the wilderness for more urban abodes—but in the cities they encountered policemen as well as potential victims.

While rendering the Natchez Trace obsolete, steamboat deck passage simultaneously revolutionized the boating profession. Deck passage (accommodation below the first-class cabins of a steamer, in the open cargo hold) had its own drawbacks and dangers, but it was a vast improvement over walking home on the Trace. Some early boatmen distrusted the steamers or could not afford to pay the hefty fare and continued to return home afoot or on horseback. Between 1825 and 1855, however, deck passage rates dropped from ten to three dollars, and flatboatmen flocked aboard. During the 1840s, an average of seventy-one deck passengers accompanied each upstream steamer. Among countless foreign immigrants and settlers traveling on deck were thousands of flatboatmen headed for home. Harriet Martineau, a tourist taking cabin passage aboard a northbound steamer in 1838, observed on deck "a multitude of Kentuckians and other western men . . . who had come down the river in flatboats with produce, who were to work their way up again by carrying wood at the wooding places, morning and evening, to supply the engine fire." As one such boatman noted, "I always traveled on deck when I boated," as "it would [have] took all [my wages] . . . to pay for a cabin passage." [37]

(ed.), *T. C. Collins—Boatman,* 71. For robber folktales, see H. Didimus [Edward Durrell], *New Orleans as I Found It* (New York, 1845), 7–14; Ben Casseday, *The History of Louisville from Its Earliest Settlement to the Year 1852* (Louisville, Ky., 1852), 67–71; and James Hall, *The Harpe's Head: A Legend of Kentucky* (Philadelphia, 1833), and *Legends of the West* (Cincinnati, 1852). For the actual incident upon which this paragraph is based and its folkloric dimensions, see Larry D. Ball, "Murrell in Arkansas: An Outlaw Gang in History and Tradition," *Mid-South Folklore,* VI (Winter, 1978), 65–75. The versions of the White River story I used are in Ball, "Murrell in Arkansas," 67 n. 8; *Jeffersonian Republican* (Jefferson City, Mo.), August 28, 1841; *Liberty Weekly Tribune* ([?] Minnesota), May 21, 1858 (Typescripts in Annals of Minnesota, Works Project Administration, Minnesota, Papers, Minnesota Historical Society, St. Paul); and *Iowa State Register* (Des Moines), December 28, 1883, reprinted from the Lawrenceburg (Ind.) *Beacon* n.d.

37. The best social and economic history of steamboat deck passage is Hunter, *Steamboats on Western Rivers,* 419–41. See also "Account of Mr. Hough's Life Written by Himself," 311; Erik F. Haites and James Mak, "Steamboating on the Mississippi: A

Deck passage was no pleasure cruise. If a flatboatman chose to re-
duce his fare by helping to take on wood—and many did—then the
steamer's mate would disturb him ten to twenty times during the trip, at
all hours and in all kinds of weather, with the cry, "Wood-pile, wood-
pile, where are the wooders?" This was hard, fast-paced work, and it
could prove dangerous as well. Loaded down with cordwood, walking up a narrow plank on his way to the boiler room, a man could
easily slip and "tumble down . . . cawollop into the river" or, worse
yet, onto the bank below. George Forman found that he lacked the
stamina for this strenuous job. Others endured, and their efforts were,
according to the Englishwoman Frances Trollope, a sight to behold.

> We had a full complement of passengers on board. The deck, as is
> usual, was occupied by Kentucky flat-boatmen, returning home from
> New Orleans after having disposed of the boat and cargo which they
> had conveyed hither. . . . We had about two hundred of these men on
> board, but the part of the vessel occupied by them is so distinct from
> the cabins, that we never saw them except when we stopped to take in
> wood; and then they ran, or rather sprung and vaulted over each other's
> heads to the shore, whence they all assisted in carrying wood to supply
> the steam engine; the performance of this duty being a stipulated part of
> the payment of their passage.[38]

Mrs. Trollope described the boatmen's quarters as being "distinct,"
and indeed they were. As Louis C. Hunter writes in his classic history
of western steamboating: "Only a thin layer of planking separated the
gilt splendor and 'conspicuous waste' of the [steamboat] cabin from
the miserable squalor of the deck quarters below. Never was the contrast between well-to-do and poor thrown into sharper relief." Steamboatman John Habermehl remembered the deck room as "an open
comfortless place. . . . All bleak and bare, no stool, no table, no utensils of any kind, aside from a few dim lanterns, a long sheet iron stove
and bunks on the side, which reminds one of a horse stable." Since the

---

Purely Competitive Industry," *Business History Review*, XLV (Spring, 1971), 75–76,
tables A-4 and A-5; Harriet Martineau, *Retrospect of Western Travel* (3 vols.; 1838; rpr.
New York, 1969), II, 164; Samuel P. Judah, "A Journal of Travel from New York to
Indiana in 1827," *Indiana Magazine of History*, XVII (December, 1921), 351; Roush (ed.),
T. C. Collins—Boatman, 38.

38. Hunter, *Steamboats on Western Rivers*, 427; Roush (ed.), *T. C. Collins—Boatman*,
55, 131–32; Forman, "Biographical Sketch," 167; Frances Trollope, *Domestic Manners of
the Americans* (1832; rpr. New York, 1949), 17.

lice-ridden bunks were best avoided, deck passengers slept, according to one government report, "in such positions as they may best secure; and this is generally found to be upon those piles of freight which will be for the longest unmolested." One riverman complained that he could find no place to sleep for two or three days, and "would [have] given a dollar for a flat board to lay down on." Deck passengers lived in filth, for there was no sanitation to speak of. Toilet facilities are never mentioned, and one can only speculate as to how matters relating to them were accomplished. Food and its preparation were strictly personal responsibilities. According to Habermehl, "As a rule bologna, sausage, dried herring, water crackers, cheese and a bottle of whiskey constituted the bill of fare." If a deck passenger had no money or was caught unprepared, he had to fend for himself as best he could.[39]

If the weather was mild and the deck uncrowded, the upstream trip was not too great a hardship. Inclement weather, however, caused suffering and, in extreme cases, heatstroke, frostbite, and even death. Moreover, deck passengers were especially vulnerable to steamboat disasters such as boiler explosions, steam leaks, and fires, and to drownings as a result of sinking or simply falling overboard. Disease and epidemic struck the congested and filthy deck quarters especially hard. George Forman recalled that a "large number of [deck passengers] died of the cholera on the passage to St. Louis" during the epidemic of 1849, and there are many other accounts of tragic epidemic conditions among steamboat deck passengers. To top it all off, criminals sometimes traveled aboard steamboats, and deck passengers had to be wary of what one contemporary described as the "tainted gambler, the sneak thief and robber . . . and the 'scarlet' woman." No wonder T. C. Collins left the deck quarters in disgust one night, noting: "The deck room was full of hogs, and only about 4 or 5 deck passengers on board, and one of them had been robbed the night before. I did not care to mix up with hogs and robbers, so I stayed up on the boyler deck, and kept warm by the chimney."[40]

The hazards and discomforts of the deck were borne most heavily

<hr />

39. Hunter, *Steamboats on Western Rivers*, 419, 424–25; John Habermehl, *Life on the Western Rivers* (Pittsburgh, 1901), 30, 55–56; Roush (ed.), *T. C. Collins—Boatman*, 42; Peterson, *Steamboating on the Upper Mississippi*, 353–57, 359.

40. Hunter, *Steamboats on Western Rivers*, 428, 435–38; Forman, "Biographical Sketch," 109; Habermehl, *Life on the Western Rivers*, 430–34; Esarey (ed.), "Memoirs of Noah J. Major," 403–404; Roush (ed.), *T. C. Collins—Boatman*, 93.

by passengers other than flatboatmen. It was the weak and uninitiated—for example, the women and children of German, Irish, and
Scandinavian immigrant families—who suffered most aboard upriver
steamboats. To the strong young flatboatmen, deck passage usually
entailed at worst several sleepless nights in filthy quarters and keeping
up one's guard against thieves and other rascals. To most Steamboat
Age boatmen, it was just part of the job—a necessary evil, and certainly better than walking the Trace. Deck passage enabled flatboatmen to make several trips a season, leading to the development of a
more affluent and truly professional class of rivermen. No wonder the
flatboatmen crowded the northbound steamers, dangers and discomforts notwithstanding.[41]

Besides advances in technology, skills, and comforts, there was a
final "modern" aspect of the lifestyle of the flatboatmen of the Steamboat Age: the urban specter. To farm boys and rural Ohio Valley
rivermen, the booming river towns of Pittsburgh, Cincinnati, St.
Louis, and New Orleans must have proved awe-inspiring. The initial
reaction of some men was elation. Finding themselves in a big city for
the first time in their lives, they began immediately to explore, "see
the sights," and spend their pay. There were shops, theaters, and
amusements, and, of course, taverns, dance halls, and whorehouses.
On the other hand, many flatboatmen and their families feared the big
cities and considered them dangerous places. "[B]e verry carefull how
you speak and transact business," John Brandenburg counseled his
New Orleans–bound son Jacob in 1858, imploring him to "be on your
guard for you don't know who you are amongst—only that you are
amongst Strangers." A friend advised young Brandenburg to "keep
your eyes open" for counterfeiters and to "be on the lookout that you
do not get Robbed or killed." Such warnings were not always rural
paranoia. Court records show that the city could be a dangerous place
to the unwary boatmen. The New Orleans *Picayune* reported boat
thieves absconding in rowboats with "thousands of dollars worth of
produce" in 1852, and one flatboatman in New Orleans wrote in his
journal: "[Today] a man [was] . . . overpowered on the street and his

41. Hunter, *Steamboats on Western Rivers*, 419, 438–39; Mak and Walton, "Persistence of Old Technologies," 449; Haites and Mak, "Social Savings Due to Western River
Steamboats," 284.

money taken from him. Such cases are heard of every day and one must be careful."[42]

The urban specter involved economic hardship as much as crime. George Forman remembered his stay in New Orleans in the winter of 1849–1850 as "the black time in my life before or since." Forman wrote: "The city was full of workingmen from the North, Sailors and Steamboatmen & flat boatmen, and not enough work for one quarter of them. I was young and not overly strong, without friends, and in the fierce struggle for work and a living I was pushed to the wall. . . . The 'Struggle for existence' in these centres of the United States is fearful." The farm boy turned boatman continued: "I can't and durst relate all I went through and suffered for two months in Orleans that winter. I did nothing wrong or criminal. I simply suffered. . . . I never would advise any young man to go to any of these centres of Business in the United States without any friends, the crush is fearful and few come out of them alive or uncontaminated. . . . I *did* come out of [New Orleans] uncontaminated." Forman's grim account is perhaps overdramatized, but it nevertheless depicts the impersonal, urban side of flatboating during the Steamboat Age. Many flatboatmen shared Forman's fear of "these centres of Business" but were in a better position to take a quick look and then make a hasty retreat to a more rural setting. Tens of thousands of flatboatmen returned home aboard steamers to their families and farms in the Ohio Valley during the 1823–1861 period. These boatmen had "seen the elephant" and returned home to tell about it.[43]

George Forman's account provides a compelling view of the urban specter in flatboating during the Steamboat Age, but it also hints at a far broader problem. Note that Forman refers to the winter of 1849–

---

42. John Brandenburg to Jacob Brandenburg, December 4, 1858, J. M. Readers to John Brandenburg, November 26, 1858, both in John Brandenburg Collection; City of New Orleans, Decisions of the Mayor in Criminal Court Cases, 1823–27 (MSS in Louisiana Division, New Orleans Public Library); City of New Orleans, Police Department Reports, Second Municipality, 1844–45 (MSS in Louisiana Division, New Orleans Public Library); Dennis Charles Rousey, "The New Orleans Police, 1805–1889: A Social History" (Ph.D. dissertation, Cornell University, 1978); *Daily Picayune* (New Orleans), April 16, 1852; J. G. Flugel, "Pages from a Journal of a Voyage Down the Mississippi in 1817," ed. Felix Flugel, *Louisiana Historical Quarterly,* VII (July, 1924), 427.

43. Forman, "Biographical Sketch," 115–16.

1850 as a bad economic time for rivermen. Flatboatman Manasseh Barney Slawson also wrote about this economic slump, saying that the end of the Mexican War had led to "very dull" times for flatboatmen. More scientific data substantiates these accounts. After the peak season of 1846–1847, flatboat trade declined slowly, never regaining its former strength. The decline is easily explained: shippers switched from flats to steamboats because of cheaper freight and insurance rates. By 1847, steamboat technology had evolved to the point that flats could no longer compete. This point would have been reached sooner or later, of course, but the fact that the demise of flatboating on the Lower Ohio and Mississippi came as early as it did can be blamed largely on the flatboating industry itself—or, more precisely, on the great numbers of merchant flatboatmen who had become involved in the trade. The ease with which one could enter into flatboating rendered the business overly competitive, chaotic, and, ultimately, vulnerable. Flatboats survived on the western rivers through the 1850s and well into the post–Civil War decades, but the contest long since had been decided: the steamboat had conquered its primitive predecessor.[44]

Ironically, steamboats met the same fate as the flats. By the 1830s and 1840s the canal craze in Ohio, Indiana, and Illinois was beginning to divert commerce from the rivers to the Great Lakes and then east via New York's splendid Erie Canal. This eastern flow of goods was catapulted by the rise of the railroads in the 1850s. By 1853, Cincinnati boasted direct rail connections with the East, and its river trade suffered acutely. Steamboats continued to churn the western rivers, with far greater success than flats—but the Steamboat Age was also over. The railroads revolutionized American transportation, supplanting the old Ohio-Mississippi route and changing forever the course of American commerce.[45]

Ohio flatboat merchant navigator Joseph Hough witnessed all of these changes during his years as a boatman. Looking back at his forty-six-year career on the western rivers, Hough reminisced in 1852:

44. Slawson, "Life of M. B. Slawson"; Haites and Mak, "Ohio and Mississippi River Transportation," 175–80; Scheiber, "Ohio-Mississippi Flatboat Trade," in Ellis (ed.), *Frontier in American Development*, 285, 296–97.

45. Taylor, *Transportation Revolution*, 45–48, 32–36, 102–103; Way, "Commerce on the Lower Mississippi," 59–65; Scheiber, "Ohio-Mississippi Flatboat Trade," in Ellis (ed.), *Frontier in American Development*, 289–90.

Now Steam Boats of the first class are plying to & from every point on the Ohio & Mississippi rivers; Railroad cars, stage coaches, & private Carriages are constantly in requisition to convey you from almost every prominent point in the country, to any other point you may desire to reach. The country is provided with Hotels and other suitable accommodations for travellers, and when far from home & friends, you may communicate with your family [via telegraph], advise them of your whereabouts and your condition, and learn from them their situation, in almost the twinkling of an eye.

Hough expressed amazement that these "great changes . . . have taken place in forty-six years!" As a flatboatman who had worked during both the presteamboat and steamboat eras, Joseph Hough had just cause for exclamation. Boating had changed considerably and would continue to do so. Had Hough lived another eight years, he would have seen the Civil War all but eradicate the world the boatmen knew.[46]

To the flatboatmen of the prosperous 1846–1847 season, however, the transportation revolution could be ignored, at least for another decade. Flatboating had reached its golden zenith. Even the bad years that followed must have seemed only a temporary aberration. Not until after the Civil War did it become apparent to western boatmen that their flats were headed for extinction. In the meantime, flatboatmen enjoyed their profits, accomplishments, and—especially—the mystique they had somehow acquired as Alligator Horses. Flatboat commerce was booming, cargoes were more diverse than ever, boats were bigger and more comfortable, river improvements rendered navigation faster and safer, and the steamboat provided a quick, inexpensive ride home for returning flatboatmen. Flatboating had undergone a revolution—and so had the flatboatmen.

46. "Account of Mr. Hough's Life Written by Himself," 312.

SIX

The New Flatboatmen

The instance of a young man of enterprize and standing, as a merchant, trader, planter, or even farmer, who has not made at least one [flatboat] trip to New Orleans is uncommon. . . . Every principal farmer along the great water courses builds and sends to New Orleans the produce of his farm in a flat boat. Thus a great proportion of the males of the West . . . have made this passage to New Orleans. . . . They have experienced that expansion of mind which cannot fail to be produced by traversing long distances of country, and viewing different forms of nature and society. Every boat, that has descended from Pittsburgh, or the Missouri, to New Orleans, could publish a journal of no inconsiderable interest.

—The Reverend Timothy Flint

Speaking to a campaign audience in New Haven, Connecticut, in 1860, presidential candidate Abraham Lincoln declared, "I am not ashamed to confess that twenty-five years ago I was a hired laborer, mauling rails, at work on a flatboat—just what might happen to any poor man's son." Although Lincoln's image as a rail splitter has endured to this day, his flatboating trips were just as important to mid-nineteenth-century Americans' vision of him as a westerner and "poor man's son" who aspired to greatness. Lincoln's claim to the title of western boatman was well founded. He had worked as a wood-boatman and ferryman on the Ohio, and in 1828 made his first flatboat trip to New Orleans as a hired hand on a boat belonging to James Gentry. The New Orleans trip opened the eyes of the nineteen-year-old Indiana farm boy. Although folklore depicts Lincoln viewing a slave auction in New Orleans and vowing to "hit it hard" if he ever got the chance, his experiences with southern blacks were in fact less inspiring. In Louisiana, Lincoln and young Allen Gentry "were attacked by seven negroes with intent to kill and rob them." Evidently this experience did not frighten Lincoln too badly, as he returned to New Orleans in 1831, piloting a flatboat he had helped to build, "getting the timber out of the trees and building a boat at Old Sangamon town on the Sangamon River" in his newly adopted state of Illinois. Returning home on the deck of a steamboat, the twenty-one-year-old Lincoln decided to give up boating and pursue a more stable occupation, and he soon began to study law.[1]

Other government and community leaders pointed with pride to their riverboating experiences. Andrew Jackson captained keels on the Cumberland and Ohio rivers, and presidential contender Henry Clay included flatboating in his claim to the title Harry of the West. During the Indiana constitutional convention of 1850–1851, Robert Dale Owen, son of the utopian reformer, alluded to the fact that about a dozen of his fellow delegates had worked as flatboatmen on the Ohio and Mississippi. Indiana Whig Congressman and Commissioner of Indian Affairs William P. Dole worked as a Wabash River merchant navigator, and one chronicler referred to scores of men who worked "at the oar and setting pole at fifty cents per day and came up to be men of wealth and standing" in their communities.[2]

That so many noted westerners served stints as rivermen underscores the fact that more than 200,000 men, common and uncommon alike, worked the flatboats of the western rivers during the Steamboat Age. Flatboating was simply an occupation that many westerners pursued during the period from 1823 to 1861—the work came with the territory. By the same token, the flatboatmen of this period were not rough and tough frontier rivermen like their predecessors. They were hardy enough, but their lifestyle was not so primitive and dangerous as that of the presteamboat rivermen. The new boatmen were family men or, like Lincoln, farm boys looking for some adventure and a few dollars in their pockets. Flatboatmen were no longer misfits escaping civilized ways, and flatboating was no longer so dangerous a pursuit.

1. Abraham Lincoln, "New Haven Speech (1860)," in John G. Nicolay and John Hay (eds.), *Complete Works of Abraham Lincoln* (12 vols.; New York, 1905), V, 361; Lincoln, "Short Autobiography," *ibid.*, VI, 28–30. The best secondary accounts of Lincoln's flatboat trips are Benjamin P. Thomas, *Abraham Lincoln: A Biography* (New York, 1967), 16–18, 23–24; Stephen B. Oates, *With Malice Towards None: The Life of Abraham Lincoln* (New York, 1977), 14–17; and Louis A. Warren, *Lincoln's Youth: Indiana Years, Seven to Twenty-One, 1816–1830* (Indianapolis, 1959), 145–46, 175–86.

2. J. S. Bassett (ed.), *Correspondence of Andrew Jackson* (7 vols.; Washington, D.C., 1926–35), I, 15, 94–95; Charles Henry Ambler, *A History of Transportation in the Ohio Valley* (Glendale, Calif., 1931), 49; Donald F. Carmony to Michael Allen, July 26, 1983, in possession of Michael Allen; Donald F. Carmony (ed.), "William P. Dole: Wabash Valley Merchant and Flatboatman," *Indiana Magazine of History*, LXVII (December, 1971), 335–63; Emerson Gould, *Fifty Years on the Mississippi; or, Gould's History of River Navigation* (St. Louis, 1889), 373.

John Ingle, "fixing and loading a flat Boat or ark with Oats & Corn for the Orleans market" in 1844, could assure relatives back East that his eighteen-year-old son Edward, who was to accompany the boat, would be perfectly safe.

> Edward is going with three hir'd hands, a helmsman and two to pull at the oars. you will likely think it a great risk to send a boy of eighteen a thousand miles to market. I can assure you [I have] every confidence in his fitness for the undertaking. he is a remarkable business like fellow for his age. and of very steady turn. The person who steers the boat is well acquainted with the river and capable of giving any advice that may be needed and withal a [reliable] man. . . . It will probably take them from four to five weeks to go down. [The] boat is then to be disposed of and all hands hire their passage back in a steamboat. . . . I certainly do not feel troubled as I expected to do about him.[3]

The "average" flatboatman of this period was a white, British-descended Ohio Valley male in his mid-twenties. Since 95 percent of the flats arriving in New Orleans listed Ohio Valley states as their point of origin, it is apparent that most flatboatmen hailed from the Old Northwest, especially Ohio, Indiana, and Illinois.[4] There is considerable evidence that common hands were mostly in their late teens and early twenties, while pilots and captains were generally in their late twenties, thirties, or forties. A number of firsthand accounts describe flatboat hands as "boys" and "young men." Indiana county histories corroborate this, noting, for example, that "No young man could count himself among the elite young bucks of the community without having made at least one trip" aboard a flatboat. Census data provide some concrete figures: a group of Indiana flatboat hands in 1850 averaged twenty years of age, their pilots forty-eight. Marietta, Ohio, deckhands working for William Devol in the 1860s averaged twenty-two years, and the pilots and captains thirty-four. Vicksburg raftsmen in the 1850 and 1860 censuses were not differentiated as pilots

---

3. John Ingle to Family, December 21, 1844, in John Ingle Collection, Indiana Historical Society, Indianapolis.

4. Louis C. Hunter, *Steamboats on Western Rivers: An Economic and Technological History* (Cambridge, Mass., 1949), 57; City of New Orleans, Wharfinger Report, February and March, 1831 (MSS in Tulane University, New Orleans).

or common hands, but the average age of two hundred of these rivermen was twenty-seven and one-half years.[5]

Increasing stability in river life enabled more boatmen to marry. The steamboat made a family life possible, for flatboatmen could return home from a voyage in a week to ten days. Many younger deckhands, of course, were bachelors, but most captains, pilots, and older hands were family men. Noah J. Major, a native of Morgan County, Indiana, noted that in the heyday of flatboating, "bachelors were in the minority" among the rivermen of his community. "On the eve of the departure of a boat," he remembered, "the wives and children of the crew assembled on the bank for the farewell word" and often wept "as the cable was being cut and the bow of the boat was turned for the Crescent City." His evidence is corroborated by census data from one river town showing a marked decrease, during the 1850–1860 period, of the number of rivermen residing in taverns, hotels, and rooming houses—many boatmen had moved into their own abodes and settled down to family life. Not only that, but quite a few of these boatmen were acquiring thrifty habits, even going so far as to establish savings accounts in banking institutions.[6]

5. Miles A. Stacy, "Flatboating Down Old Man River, 1849–1869: Reminiscences of Captain Miles A. Stacy as Related to His Daughter Adelaide Frost Stacy, February, 1913. Rearranged and Typed by Her, April, 1945" (Typescript in Ohio Historical Society, Campus Martius, the Museum of the Northwest Territory, Marietta, Ohio), 1; Felix Renick to William McNeill, March 15, 1823, in McNeill Papers, West Virginia and Regional History Collection, West Virginia University Library, Morgantown; Harold L. O'Donnell, *Newport and Vermillion Township: The First Hundred Years,* (Cayuga, Ind., 1969), 37; Archibald Shaw, *History of Dearborn County, Indiana* (Indianapolis, 1915), 448; Seventh United States Census, 1850, Indiana, Dearborn and Ohio Counties; Peter W. Williams Collection (MSS in Indiana Historical Society, Indianapolis); Robert Leslie Jones (ed.), "Flatboating Down the Ohio and Mississippi, 1867–1873: Correspondence and Diaries of the William Devol Family of Marietta, Ohio," *Ohio State Archeological and Historical Quarterly,* LIX (July and October, 1950), 296; Ninth United States Census, 1870, Ohio, Washington County; Seventh and Eighth United States Censuses, 1850 and 1860, Mississippi, Warren County (Typescript in Old Courthouse Museum, Vicksburg).

6. Logan Esarey (ed.), "The Pioneers of Morgan County: Memoirs of Noah J. Major," *Indiana Historical Society Publications,* V (1915), 408; Seventh and Eighth United States Censuses, 1850 and 1860, Mississippi, Warren County; Boatmen's Bank of St. Louis, *Semi-Centennial Souvenir of the Boatmen's Bank* (St. Louis, 1897), W. G. Rule, *The Means of Wealth, Peace, and Happiness: The Story of the Oldest Bank West of the Mississippi, 1847–1947, the Boatmen's National Bank of St. Louis* (St. Louis, 1947), 15, 24.

The fact that many flatboatmen were married, family men is best documented in their correspondence. Unlike the pre-1823 period, the steamboat era is replete with boatmen's letters bearing references to home, family, and loved ones. "I hope you . . . will try & reconcile yourself to our separation for a short time yet," a Terre Haute flatboat merchant navigator wrote his wife in 1842. She had earlier written him that "during a period of your absence I cannot partake of any real enjoyment because all I do is alloyd by the knowledg of k[n]owing my heart beloved cannot enjoy it with me." One married flatboatman returned from New Orleans to find "that we had increased one in family wich was a son and we called his Name Henry." John T. Campbell of Parke County, Indiana, remembered the poignant return of his boatman father to their own newly increased family "from his 'down river' trip" in the 1840s.

> It was getting twilight when he entered the house, and he had on [a] palm (chalk white) hat . . . and a nice suit of black cloth. Mother was sweeping the room and was near the door. He came in unexpectedly, put his arms around her and caressed her tenderly . . . then came on in to us children who were romping on the floor. . . . I was busting to tell him the news that a new baby had been found and brought to the family while he was gone, and told him to look in the cradle. He rose, took a stride or two and took up [the baby and] . . . asked mother "when was the baby born?" She answered, three weeks next [Sunday].[7]

Also new to the ranks of the flatboat crews were a few women, foreigners, and ethnic minorities. Women sometimes were hired as cooks on commercial flatboats after the average crew size doubled and boatmen began demanding full-time, professional kitchen help. Some rivermen protested this new presence. Pilot James Martin complained in 1847 of a woman cook "so fat she lies in bed all the time and eats apples," and boatman T. C. Collins opposed letting any women at all on board his flatboats (like many rivermen, Collins believed women to be bad luck on a boat). Other rivermen, however, welcomed the skills of women cooks—especially on the huge lumber rafts, whose thirty-

---

7. Carmony (ed.), "Dole: Wabash Valley Merchant and Flatboatman," 356–57, 361; Jacob Weaver to Johannis Weaver, July 24, 1823, in Jacob Weaver Collection, Indiana Historical Society, Indianapolis; John T. Campbell, "Reminiscence" (MS in John T. Campbell Collection, Indiana Division, Indiana State Library, Indianapolis).

to forty-man crews required expert kitchen workers. Minorities aboard flatboats included a number of foreign-born hands—"new European emigrants, hired for low wages, and often for a free passage." A few Indians and mixed bloods also worked the western rivers, but the largest minority group of rivermen was undoubtedly the black boatmen.[8]

Free black rivermen worked aboard Ohio and Mississippi river flatboats during the 1823–1861 period, but evidently not in great numbers. The majority of black boatmen were slaves who worked the flatboats and rafts of the cypress lumber industry of the Yazoo basin and Lower Mississippi. These slave rivermen worked alongside white employees, and some blacks even rose to supervisory positions and captained their own boats and rafts. Jim Matthews, a slave belonging to a Natchez lumber firm, commanded rafting crews on the Lower Mississippi in the 1840s, paying expenses and salaries, keeping records, and earning extra money by salvaging logs during his time off. William Thompson was a literate black riverman who forged a travel permit and escaped to freedom in Canada. But the best existing account of a black flatboatman concerns Simon Gray, a slave whose skills on the river enabled him to lead an extraordinary life in antebellum Mississippi.[9]

Simon Gray was a Natchez slave hired out to the firm of Andrew Brown and Company to work in its lumbering and construction operations in 1835. Gray soon gained the respect of his employers, and by 1838 he was directing rafting crews and handling large sums of

8. James Martin to I. Roberts, November 5, 1847, in "Flatboat Letters of Switzerland County, Indiana" (Typescript in Harold Brown Adkinson Collection, Indiana Division, Indiana State Library, Indianapolis); Herbert L. Roush, Sr. (ed.), *The Adventures of T. C. Collins—Boatman: Twenty-Four Years on the Western Waters, 1849–1873* (Baltimore, 1985), 212–13; Robert Carlton, *The New Purchase; or, Seven and a Half Years in the Far West* (2 vols.; New York 1843), I, 51; William Cooper Howells, *Recollections of Life in Ohio from 1813 to 1840* (1895; rpr. Gainesville, Fla., 1963), 84–85; Henry Baxter, "Rafting on the Allegheny and Ohio, 1844," *Pennsylvania Magazine of History and Biography,* LI (February, 1927), 28–29; Maximilian, Prince of Wied, *Travels in the Interior of North America,* in Reuben Gold Thwaites (ed.), *Early Western Travels, 1748–1846,* (32 vols.; Cleveland, 1904–1907), XXII, 151.

9. William Ranson Hogan and Edwin Adams Davis (eds.), *William Johnson's Natchez: The Antebellum Diary of a Free Negro* (Baton Rouge, 1951), 94; John Hebron Moore, "Simon Gray, Riverman: A Slave Who Was Almost Free," *Mississippi Valley Historical Review,* LXIX (December, 1962), 483.

money. In the 1840s, Brown promoted Simon Gray to flatboat captain and assigned him to coast lumber between Natchez and New Orleans. "Simon manage[s] the boats very well. . . . He is a first-rate fellow & can be as careful as anyone when he likes," Andrew Brown, Jr., noted in a business letter. From 1845 to 1862, Gray worked as the company's chief boatman, commanding his own crews and engaging in his own private speculative ventures. He lived with his wife and children in a company house in Natchez. With the Union victory, Simon Gray's name disappears from the records of Brown and Company, but his story may qualify certain preconceptions concerning southern slavery, even as it provides a fascinating glimpse of the life of a black slave raftsman and flatboatman.[10]

The vast majority of flatboatmen, however, were white men, American-born, and of English, Scotch, Scotch-Irish, Irish, or German ancestry. The French-Canadian rivermen who had played such an important role during the presteamboat days had all but disappeared. Wharf records show a few French surnames amid a preponderance of English, Scotch, and Scotch-Irish surnames, but even the English- and Scotch-descended rivermen had suffered a bit of a decline since their reign during the early nineteenth century. New waves of European immigration were beginning to make an impact on riverboating; by the 1840s and 1850s, Irish and German surnames appear on flatboat manifests in sizable and growing numbers. There were even a few Scandinavians, Slavs, and Jews manning the flats of the Ohio and Mississippi.[11]

The categories of merchant navigator, farmer flatboatman, agent boatman, and common boatman still serve quite well in classifying the flatboatmen of the post-1823 period. The only exceptions would be specialized merchant navigators and farmer flatboatmen belonging to such subgroups as peddler boatmen, coasters, blacksmith flatboat-

10. Moore, "Simon Gray, Riverman," 472–84.
11. The generalizations in this paragraph are based on a reading of City of New Orleans, Wharfinger Report, February and March, 1831; *ibid.*, 1846–47 (MSS in Louisiana Division, New Orleans Public Library); Works Progress Administration, "Returns of Seamen for Marine Hospital Tax, Port of New Orleans, 1805 to 1833" (Typescript in Louisiana Historical Center, Louisiana State Museum, New Orleans); Peter W. Williams Collection (MSS in Indiana Historical Society, Indianapolis); and "Flatboat Letters of Switzerland County, Indiana," *passim.*

men, dairy flatboatmen, and even theatrical and entertainer flatboatmen. These groups arose naturally in the increasingly complex
boating trade. Rather than try to enumerate every possible mutation
of flatboating, however, it is less confusing—and sufficiently accurate,
I think—to retain the four broad classifications that were used to discuss the pre-1823 boatmen.[12]

The merchant navigator of the 1823–1861 period was, as one of
them explained succinctly, the "builder, owner, Captain, and, for the
most part of the way down the rivers . . . also pilot" of his own flatboat. Of the 20,000 to 25,000 men who annually worked aboard flats,
probably 2,000 to 3,000 were merchant navigators. Many were men
like Jared Warner. Born in Canfield, Ohio, in 1812, Warner became
known in his community as a successful business entrepreneur, merchant navigator, lumberman, and farmer. He ran flatboats and rafts on
the Ohio and Mississippi during the late 1820s and 1830s, then moved
to the Wisconsin territory in 1838, where he was reportedly "early
identified with the Liberal movement of the West." Typical also was
Captain Henry A. Jones of Cincinnati, who "was his own captain and
supercargo" in the flatboat trade of the 1830s before becoming a steamboat pilot in 1838. A cautious man, Jones distrusted the banking institutions of his day so much that he "always carried his money either
in his pocket or in a belt buckled around his body" when returning
home aboard steamers. James Stowe, a farmer and family man from
Marietta, Ohio, engaged in flatboating for thirty years in the mid-
nineteenth century. "Every planter along the river knew . . . Stowe,"
a local historian wrote. "He had the reputation of being a sharp but
honest dealer." Living downstream a few miles from Stowe was T. C.
Collins, a native Virginian who spent one-third of his seventy-five
years in flatboating and wrote a four-volume memoir of his experiences. Collins early adopted the motto, "Root hog, or die!" He summarized his philosophy as a merchant navigator as follows: "Boatmen
make as much calculation on bad luck as good and, when they have
bad luck are not disappointed. . . . The whole business is a thing of
chance. When he strikes anything good, and makes money, it seems

12. Harry N. Scheiber, "The Ohio-Mississippi Flatboat Trade: Some Reconsiderations," in David M. Ellis (ed.), *The Frontier in American Development: Essays in Honor of
Paul Wallace Gates* (Ithaca, 1970), 291–93.

like clear gain. But when he loses all, 'Well, it's no more than I expected.'"[13]

Surveying the extensive narratives of these men, one is impressed by the great variety of characters who engaged in this risky business.[14] A few generalizations can be drawn, however. The merchant navigators tended toward middle age. A few were in their late twenties, but the large majority were in their thirties or forties. Most were married and raising families. Merchant navigators generally resided in towns and enjoyed a certain degree of respect, but they were not yet the pillars of society that many of them would become following their stints as rivermen: their lives were still too transient and unstable for such distinction, and their chosen occupation too lacking in status. The merchant navigators aimed to remedy these deficiencies as quickly as possible by the simple expedient of making money. They were ambitious, striving capitalists—businessmen with an eye on the main chance.

This same characterization applies, to a somewhat lesser degree, to farmer flatboatmen. As in the pre-1823 period, flatboating provided a prime means by which a farmer could supplement his income. River improvements and crop surpluses served to make an annual flatboat trip even more tempting. "After the crops are got in," an observer wrote of Ohio Valley farmers, "they have several months of leisure, during which time there is little to be done on their farms, so they can afford to combine both business and pleasure by navigating their own unwieldy crafts down to New Orleans." Judge Ephraim Cutler, writing in 1837, described the rural inhabitants of his native Washington County, Ohio, as an industrious people whose "situation is such that

13. Stacy, "Reminiscences of Captain Miles Stacy," 4; Obituary, in Jared Warner Papers, Wisconsin Room, University of Wisconsin–Platteville; Gould, *Fifty Years on the Mississippi,* 623–25; H. Z. Williams and Brother, *History of Washington County, Ohio* (Cleveland, 1881), 620–21; Roush (ed.), *T. C. Collins—Boatman,* 7, 217–18.

14. For example, see Edmund L. Starling, *History of Henderson, Kentucky* (Henderson, 1887), 678; Paul R. Coppock, "Not Bad for a Kid Off a Flatboat," *Commercial Appeal* (Memphis), December 2, 1979; Daniel Harmon Brush, *Growing Up with Southern Illinois, 1820 to 1861: From the Memoirs of Daniel Harmon Brush,* ed. Milo M. Quaife (Chicago, 1944), 85–86; William Buckner McGroarty (ed.), "Diary of Phillip Johnson Buckner, M.D.," *William and Mary Quarterly,* 2nd ser., XXIII (January, 1943), 70; John A. Quarles to James T. Quarles, August 14, 1838, in Mark Twain Research Foundation, Incorporated, Perry, Mo.; Captain Donald McDonald, "Diary," in *Indiana Historical Society Publications,* XIV (1942), 281.

almost every Farmer . . . can build . . . a boat which will waft away
from 50 to 100 tons of Produce & if he has not raised enough on his
own Farm the Mineral Kingdom or the Forest will Furnish abundance
to eke out his Load. Then himself or Son are tempted, almost com-
pell'd, to push a-Float and try Markets which extend nearly 2000
Miles."[15]

Joseph Ingraham described "the primitive navies of Indiana, Ohio,
and the adjoining states" in 1835, "manned by . . . 'real Kentucks'—
'Buck eyes'—'Hooshers'—and 'Snorters.'" Indianan Archibald Shaw
recalled that his father, a native Scot, made an annual coasting voyage
south to make money to improve his farm and support his growing
family. S. S. Prentiss passed a farmer flatboatman about 1850, "a
middle-aged stout yeoman in a long-tailed blue jean coat and snuff-
colored trousers . . . standing bareheaded at the long paddle which
served as helm, shading his eyes with his hair as he stared at our passing boat." The farmer boatmen, like their more urbane merchant
navigator counterparts, were mostly middle-aged family men out to
improve their lot in life. Unlike the merchant navigators, however, the
farmer boatmen lacked capital. A little bad luck or a glutted market
could ruin them. Moreover, their farming work at home limited them
to one flatboat trip a year. Thus, the most a farmer flatboatman could
hope for was enough extra cash to make a land payment or finance a
few improvements on his farm. In the volatile world of post-1823 flatboat entrepreneurs, farmer flatboatmen constituted the populous but
vulnerable lower rungs of the business ladder.[16]

For the agent boatmen of the steamboat era, flatboating was not a
speculative venture or a get-rich-quick opportunity. Boating to them
was just a way to make a living, and a pretty good living at that. Improved navigation conditions and speedy return passage aboard steamboats fostered a growing class of professional flatboat pilots. The 50
percent decrease in flatboat insurance rates between 1820 and 1840 was

15. Mrs. Houstoun, *Hesperos; or, Travels in the West* (2 vols.; London, 1850), II, 31;
Cutler quoted in Josephine E. Phillips, "Flatboating on the Great Thoroughfare," *Cincinnati Historical Society Bulletin*, V (June, 1947), 19.

16. Joseph Holt Ingraham, *The South-West: By a Yankee* (2 vols.; New York, 1835),
I, 105–107; Archibald Shaw, "The Autobiography of Archibald Shaw" (Typescript in
Archibald Shaw Collection, Indiana Historical Society, Indianapolis), 15–16; S. S. Prentiss, *A Memoir of S. S. Prentiss, Edited by His Brother* (2 vols.; New York, 1855), I,
181–82.

due in great part to this "set of Hardy, Interprizing young men who, by a few Voyages, become Masters of the down River Trade." Merchant Daniel Brush engaged a professional boatman "who knew the Mississippi well, to be chief pilot" of his flatboat fleet in 1846. Brush "put him in charge of the most valuable boat, loaded with the costliest articles, and he was to lead the convoy." The correspondence of Indiana speculators and hay traders Peter W. Williams and Alfred F. Howes is filled with references to agent boatmen. "Caldwell . . . is a man that does most of the steering himself," Howes advised Williams in 1851, adding that Caldwell worked "all of the night and half of the day as all pilots ought but few do. Daniels is one of the same sort." Howes paid one agent boatman $100 per trip in 1851 and counted it a good investment: "He is to my notion the safest man we can get." [17]

Some agent boatmen owned their own boats; others merely sold their services. Most of them do not appear to have engaged regularly in speculative ventures, being content simply to draw a salary. These rivermen were, by and large, stable family men who enjoyed a certain degree of respect in their communities. One longtime flatboat pilot, Philip Hetzer, "was an old religious man" and very strict: "When he came on board, he laid down his rules. He said, 'Well boys, my rules are to have no stealing, no swearing, no Sabbath breaking, no whisky drinking, and no card playing.'" Not many agent boatmen were so devout, and there were undoubtedly some derelicts and ne'er-do-wells among them. Agent boatmen who desired regular work, however, were out of necessity sober, prudent, industrious, and, most important, skilled and knowledgeable rivermen. As one Indiana pioneer remembered, "There were steersmen in those days who made so many trips that they knew the way to the gulf as well as the average man knows the way to Indianapolis." [18]

The account of the devout old pilot Philip Hetzer is also valuable

---

17. James Mak and Gary M. Walton, "The Persistence of Old Technologies: The Case of Flatboats," *Journal of Economic History,* XXXIII (June, 1973), 446; Scheiber, "Ohio-Mississippi Flatboat Trade," in Ellis (ed.), *Frontier in American Development,* 294; Brush, *Growing Up with Southern Illinois,* 151–52; Alfred F. Howes to Peter W. Williams, April 13, April 8, 1851, both in Peter W. Williams Collection.

18. "Flatboat Letters of Switzerland County, Indiana," *passim;* Gould, *Fifty Years on the Mississippi,* 374, 623–25, 646–47, 653, 721–23, 726; Obituaries of Pioneer Rivermen, in Fred A. Bill and Family Papers, Minnesota Historical Society, St. Paul, Box 7; Roush (ed.), *T. C. Collins—Boatman,* 35; Esarey (ed.), "Memoirs of Noah J. Major," 402, 406–407.

for what it tells us about common boatmen. One of Hetzer's crewmen was T. C. Collins, a sober, industrious man who, during a twenty-four-year career on the western rivers, advanced from common hand to pilot and, eventually, merchant navigator. But Collins' crewmates on his trip with Hetzer were not quite so upstanding—at least, that is not the image they had of themselves. Indeed, during Hetzer's lecture against drinking, gambling, stealing, swearing, and Sabbath breaking, Collins noted that Mark Boler, a deckhand, had a "2 gallon jug of whisky behind the chimney," and "Bill Collins had a deck of cards in his pocket. Mark Boler was a regular riverman and pretty tough. When Hetzer was out, Mark would haul out the jug, take a 'swig' and hand it around, and Bill Collins would watch his chance when Hetzer was at the steering oar, and haul out the cards and have a game with some of the crew." [19]

This is not to say that common hands during the 1823–1861 period were all rough characters. These young rivermen of the Steamboat Age would not have fared too well among the tough boat hands of the preindustrial era. The post-1823 common boatmen were, above all, just boys. They were naïve, yet adventurous enough to look for some new experiences and a chance to see some of the world outside their rural Ohio Valley homes. For many of them, the flatboat trip to New Orleans would be one of the most exciting events of their lives. They were a little wild, but more accurately (and significantly) they *perceived themselves* as wild. They had discovered the mystique of the western boatmen and claimed it as their own.

George Forman's story of his two-year stint as a flatboatman, lumber raftsman, and steamboat deckhand documents several of these generalizations. The nineteen-year-old Forman left his native Canada in 1849, bound for the gold fields of California. He never arrived in the Golden State, but he did find work as a riverman. Forman wrote lucidly of his experiences on the Upper and Lower Mississippi, Illinois, Missouri, and Ohio rivers from 1849 to 1851. The life he depicted was not always an easy one, and he was deeply ambivalent about the rafting and boating profession. As will be seen later, Forman destroyed the myth of "the jolly flatboatman" even while evincing a deep romanticism about his boating days. [20]

19. Roush (ed.), *T. C. Collins—Boatman,* 35.
20. George Forman, "Biographical Sketch of the Life and Ancestry of Geo. Forman

Few flatboatmen were as articulate as George Forman, but there are nevertheless many accounts of and by these common boat hands. Some rivermen were known only by nicknames. "Everybody was 'Jack' or something else," Forman wrote in 1849. "No one cared for ones true name." Peter Williams and Alfred Howes hired many young hands to man their hay boats in the 1850s. Howes wrote Williams in 1852 of "Irish John Allman . . . a trusty fellow & industrious man [who] is awkward but always on duty when needed." Another of Howes's flatboats was crewed by "5 hands and a good chunk of a Boy to cook & help pull when needed." Howes apparently had a fine eye for a man's usefulness. "I hired Jack because he is one of the most faithful fellows to attend to the pumps I ever saw," he wrote in February, 1852. "The other hand with the Hulk is named Tom Francis, a devilish, dirty, stupid fellow, but he can be managed." Similarly, pilot John F. Patton of Vevay, Indiana, wrote his boss in 1846 mentioning a hand named "Welsh [who] I give $12 per month" and "another boy with me by the name of Wales. He is sort of a half fool. I pay him nothing but his passage up on deck for his services. He answers my purposes very well, however, as he has not sense enough to do wrong."[21]

Manasseh Barney Slawson took his first flatboat trip in 1843. Safely back home, he gave up boating to get married, but his wife died soon thereafter. "Then I was left alone," he wrote, "and did not know what to do until the spring of 1846 [when I] hired to Barr and Willis to go down the river in a boat load of pork." In his reminiscence of Morgan County, Indiana, Noah J. Major listed more than twenty-five common boat hands, most of whom he says were married, family men. It appears that most of the "young bucks" were bachelors, however, at least during their stints as flatboatmen. During the long peace between 1815 and 1861, broken only briefly by the Mexican War, flatboating provided an outlet for the energies of young men who in another age might have joined the army. Flatboating became a rite of manhood for

of Stratford-Ontario, Canada, Written in 1875 and 1883 by Himself," ed. E. Luella Galliver (Typescript in Western History Research Center, University of Wyoming, Laramie), *passim*.

21. *Ibid.*, 111; Alfred F. Howes to Peter W. Williams, January 8, 1852, April 8, 1851, February 10, 1852, all in Peter W. Williams Collection; John F. Patton to U. P. Schenck, February 13, 1846, in "Flatboat Letters of Switzerland County, Indiana."

young Ohio Valley farm boys. A trip to New Orleans gave them a chance to "see the elephant." Thus, young flatboatman Gillis McCarty exhibited considerable pride (mixed with a bit of homesickness) in a letter home to Pennsylvania in 1848. After asking a friend to "tell me how their are all giting at home" and "how the girls is giting along or if any of them is Maried or not," McCarty spent much of his letter describing to his less worldly hometowners the wonders he had seen since becoming a boatman: "Tell my people that I am injoying the best of health the weather is very warm [and] the corn is 2 feet high down here this is the beautifulest country in the world along the co[a]st of the Mississippi you can see thousands of orrengs growing on the trees and the purttiest houses in [the] world along the co[a]st."[22]

As in the early days, boatmen's pay varied greatly, and there is a good deal of conflicting data relating to wages. The best quantitative study shows that during the 1840s, flatboat hands earned $40 and pilots $100 for a four- or five-week trip. Flatboatmen were earning about $1.40 per day, which compares favorably with the daily wages of other workingmen in river towns. The common boatman's average wages, however, did not increase at all between 1823 and 1861, while steamboat hands' wages rose 25 percent. The problems inherent in the boatmen's static wage scale were compounded by the erratic nature of their job. Because of inclement weather or dull markets, a hand could be laid off at a moment's notice, paid a portion of his salary, and left to his own resources anywhere along the western rivers. A boatman was paid only by the trip, and between trips he was on his own. His wages, therefore, had to be budgeted over his time off and did not amount to much. As in the early days, the practice of paying rivermen in one lump sum at trip's end created an illusion of prosperity, but the boat hands' wealth was almost invariably ephemeral. The story of Dyar Cobb, a young Indiana flatboatman, is typical. Having worked two flatboat trips to New Orleans in 1825, Cobb grew tired of boating and "engaged deck passage for home." It took him "fourteen days to come up to Lawrenceburg" where he "footed it home" nearly twenty miles.

22. Manasseh Barney Slawson, "Life of M. B. Slawson" (Typescript in Indiana Historical Society, Indianapolis); Esarey (ed.), "Memoirs of Noah J. Majors," 407–408; Gillis McCarty to Joseph Barrens, April 1, 1848, in Minnesota Historical Society, St. Paul.

He "got there about sundown, and had the sum of twenty-five cents in my pocket. 'A profitable trip,' I imagine you say. I had spent five months in 'sowing my wild oats.'"[23]

Flatboatmen of the 1823–1861 period at least slept more comfortably and ate better than before. For example, boatmen began to carry with them straw mattresses, and boat cabins were built now with comforts such as bunks, stoves for heating and cooking, and tables. Flatboat cabins provided something of a home, serving as what one boatman called "kitchen, dining-room, reception room, and bedroom, all in one." These accommodations were hardly luxurious, but they were clearly superior to those of the presteam days.[24]

Mealtimes were a far cry from the early boatmen's salt pork boiled over a sandbox fire and washed down with a slug of whiskey. New cooking stoves were complemented by more elaborate utensils—one Terre Haute, Indiana, riverman even boasted a dinner service of "all queensware & entirely new Cups & Saucers, plates, etc. etc. tinware being vanquished as only fit for the vulgar." Young boys and women hired on specifically as cooks, and the growing villages and towns along the banks made available a better quality and variety of foodstuffs. "[O]ur dinner was glorious," a Wabash riverman wrote in 1845. "[T]here was bread, wheat bread at that . . . then there was *fried ham—fried eggs* and to top all *hot coffee* . . . [and] homemade cake sugar to sweeten it." Another flatboatman reminisced in his memoirs, "We were hungry as wolves, and [had] such a supper!" The meal that inspired his rapture consisted of "fried squirrels, hot biscuit, pure white honey, hot coffee, *et cetera*." Indeed, one Kentucky flatboatman appears to have eaten a little *too* well. "Taylor overloaded his stomach

23. Erik F. Haites and James Mak, "Ohio and Mississippi River Transportation, 1810–1860," *Explorations in Economic History*, VIII (Winter, 1970), 159–62, table 2; Mak and Walton, "Persistence of Old Technologies," 446 n. 9; Timothy R. Mahoney, "River Towns in the Great West, 1835–1860" (Ph.D. dissertation, University of Chicago, 1982), 772, figure 76; Carmony (ed.), "Dole: Wabash Valley Merchant and Flatboatman," 349–51; Roush, Sr. (ed.), *T. C. Collins—Boatman*, 122; Dyar Cobb, "Reminiscences of Dyar Cobb . . . 1819–1830" (Typescript in Dyar Cobb Collection, Indiana Division, Indiana State Library, Indianapolis), 19–20. For raw data on flatboatmen's wages, see Esarey (ed.), "Memoirs of Noah J. Major," 403; Peter W. Williams Collection; and "Flatboat Letters of Switzerland County, Indiana."

24. "The Beauties of Flatboating; or, Journal of a Trip to New Orleans," in "Atalantian" (MS in Indiana Historical Society, Indianapolis), II, entry for July 28, 1848; Stacy, "Reminiscences of Captain Miles Stacy," 6.

[with] peach dumplings," his captain noted in a journal entry, "and in half an hour [he] disgorged the whole of his dinner."[25]

Improvements in at least one other area lagged. Writing home to his wife in 1840, William P. Dole alluded to sanitation procedures aboard his boat. "[W]e use [the] top of a chicken coop for a table & between them & the hogs we have no need of a smelling Bottle," he informed her. "I believe Allen has not forgotten but once to wash his hands before making Bread after cleaning out the hog pens so you see we are a cleanly set of fellows." Although Dole undoubtedly had tongue at least partly in cheek, it is quite safe to assume that flatboats were far from antiseptic. There does seem to have been much more interest in soap and water during the steamboat era than before, but sanitation procedures still left a great deal to be desired. Aboard flatboats one urinated in the time-honored fashion of all rivermen—taking care never to do so over the bow, for that was bad luck. Modes of defecation are not discussed. Body lice found flatboats much to their liking; T. C. Collins' description of one boatman afflicted with the vermin could scarcely be more graphic: "When he was taking off his cravet, he was standing close to me and I could see a row of big white lice, as large as the largest kind of hog louse, sitting on his cravet in a row with their heads all turned towards his neck, where they had eaten it so it was a scab and raw. The row of lice looked like a row of white, long beads on his black cravet."[26]

Lice and other problems notwithstanding, flatboat sanitation had in fact improved somewhat since the primitive early days of boating. Along with better diet, this advance meant that rivermen were healthier and death through illness less likely during the Steamboat Age. The great danger to flatboatmen was cholera: during the terrible epidemic of 1849–1852, rivermen suffered and died throughout the Mississippi Valley. Malaria also took its toll. In general, however, the healthier

25. F.A.L., "Journal of a Trip to New Orleans on a *Broadhorn*," in "Atalantian," IV, entry from June [?], 1848; Carlton, *New Purchase*, I, 51; Brush, *Growing up with Southern Illinois*, 150–51; "Beauties of Flatboating," in "Atalantian," II, entry for July 28, 1845; Milo M. Quaife (ed.), *The Early Days of Rock Island and Davenport: The Narratives of J. W. Spencer and J. M. D. Burrows* (Chicago, 1942), 115; Fountain Perry, "River Logs" (MSS in Fountain and Roderick Perry Papers, Special Collections and Archives, University of Kentucky Library, Lexington), n.d.

26. Carmony (ed.), "Dole: Wabash Valley Merchant and Flatboatman," 347; Roush (ed.), *T. C. Collins—Boatman*, 75–76, 85.

boatmen of the post-1823 generation were better able to resist disease. Further, those who did become ill found more doctors and marine hospitals in the growing towns and villages along the banks of the western rivers.[27]

Although inadequate in many respects, marine hospitals were an important element in the "civilizing" of the river towns during the nineteenth century. Earlier efforts to provide medical aid for sick boatmen were renewed in 1836 when Cincinnati physician Daniel Drake petitioned Congress on behalf of the General Assembly of Ohio, requesting "the establishment of Western commercial hospitals." Congress in 1837 responded by allocating money for the construction of eleven marine hospitals along the Ohio and Mississippi rivers. Characteristic delays and red tape plagued the system, but by 1861 the federal government had built marine hospitals in Pittsburgh, Cincinnati, Louisville, Evansville, and Paducah on the Ohio River, and in Galena, Burlington, St. Louis, Napoleon (Arkansas), Natchez, and New Orleans on the Mississippi.[28]

The outbreak of the Civil War temporarily ended government efforts in this direction. In 1870 the system was reformed, and Congress placed aid to sick rivermen and seamen on a strict contract basis with local hospitals. Critics of antebellum marine hospitals complained that unlicensed vessels such as flatboats did not pay marine hospital tax, and their crewmen were therefore unable to take advantage of the system as steamboatmen and merchant seamen did. This was not altogether true: many flatboatmen paid marine hospital tax in New Orleans and were eligible for benefits. Even those who did not pay the tax could secure aid in other public hospitals or in private, charity hospitals that emerged during the Steamboat Age. Medical care and health, like many aspects of this study, must be viewed in relative terms. From the perspective of the twentieth century, the diet, sanitation, health, and medical facilities of the flatboatmen may seem

27. Hugh Donnelly to John Roberts, January 22, 1849, in "Flatboat Letters of Switzerland County, Indiana"; Charles E. Rosenburg, *The Cholera Years: The United States in 1832, 1849, and 1866* (Chicago, 1962), 114, *passim;* D. Clayton James, *Antebellum Natchez* (Baton Rouge, 1968), 267; Henry J. Reynolds, "Journal, 1839–1840" (Typescript in Cincinnati Historical Society), 70.

28. The best summary of the post–1823 marine hospital system is in Hunter, *Steamboats on Western Rivers,* 463–65, and *Appleton's Annual Cyclopaedia, 1879* (New York, 1880), 788–98.

primitive. When one considers the conditions prior to the steamboat days, however, it is obvious that western boatmen of the 1823–1861 era were eating better, living in cleaner quarters, and enjoying better health and medical care than ever before. Their lives had improved considerably.[29]

The most common maladies of the Ohio and Mississippi flatboatmen during the dawning industrial era were not physical—they were psychological. "I was low spirited—did not care much what I did nor how things went," complained an Ohio flatboatman required to wait for a load in a strange town "a week or ten days. . . . I could scarcely put in the time at all." Another boatman wrote his family that he had not "ben ashore since we Left so you must supose I am getting tired of the Boat." At times this confinement in close quarters led to quarrels and feuds among crew members. Hay merchants U. P. Schenck and I. Roberts of Vevay, Indiana, received letters from both factions of "a fuss between the captain and Mr. Jessup" on a grounded flatboat near Memphis in 1847. The captain, James Martin, complained that Jessup "has ordered me to shore but I have not went yet . . . [and] I don't intend to until I find some one that has better authority than him." A hand complained to Schenck that "something ought to be done. . . . One man ought to have command." This dispute evidently started when Captain Martin refused to buy apples for the crew.[30]

Boatmen faced painful separations from their friends, wives, and families. Joseph McDowell wrote his boatman friend John Trimble in 1826, confessing, "I am anxious to [see you] return and hope you will not engage any longer in trading to Orleans." Pilot William Patton wrote his employer in 1845, "Tell my mother and sister I will write to them if I have to go further than Vickburg." Indiana boatmen F. Marion Teague and Jerry Plew wrote their boss asking him to tell their

29. Hunter, *Steamboats on Western Rivers*, 463–75 n. 74; Works Progress Administration, "Returns of Seamen, Marine Hospital Tax, 1805 to 1833." For public and private hospitals, see *The Louisville Directory for 1832* (Louisville, 1832), 143–44; Harvey Hall, *The Cincinnati Directory for 1825* (Cincinnati, 1825), 125–26; Thomas S. Teas, "A Trading Trip to Natchez and New Orleans, 1822: Diary of Thomas S. Teas," eds. Julia Ideson and Sanford W. Higginbotham, *Journal of Southern History*, VII (August, 1941), 388.

30. Roush (ed.), *T. C. Collins—Boatman*, 209–10; Carmony (ed.), "Dole: Wabash Valley Merchant and Flatboatman," 363; Henry Weaver to Mr. Roberts, n.d., James Martin to I. Roberts and U. P. Schenck, November 21, 1846, both in "Flatboat Letters of Switzerland County, Indiana."

wives that they were "well and hearty and will get home as soon" as possible. The correspondence of flatboatmen, especially pilots, often concerns family matters or requests for employers to "let me know how my family is" and to "let my family hear from me as soon as you get this."[31]

In some cases flatboating caused marital difficulties. "I think I have good reason to scold," Jane Dole wrote her husband William in 1842. "[I]t has been 3 weeks since I heard from you . . . [and] it has caused me a great uneasiness. . . . If I dont get a letter I Shall think you ar Sick or have forgotten me one or the other Shure. . . . I think you ar retalliateing." Husbands and wives alike feared infidelity and philandering. "An *onconstant* lover / Is worse nor a thief / An *onconstant* lover / Will bring you to your grave!" were the words of a popular boatmen's ballad. And one riverman sang, "Oh! It's love was the 'casion of my downfall / I wish I hadn't never lov'd none at all!"[32]

Thus, instead of fighting Indians and river pirates, the flatboatmen of the Steamboat Age fought "the blues" and homesickness. "Jake was in a terrible stew to get home," T. C. Collins wrote of a flatboat hand who left the boat in the middle of a trip. Another co-worker of Collins', a deckhand named Baxter, "took it in his head he must go home" and borrowed money from the captain to do so. One homesick Terre Haute, Indiana, flatboatman in the Deep South in 1845 wrote sadly in his journal, "I'll go on deck [tonight] & gaze at the moon & stars & think of those I've left a thousand miles behind." Three years later, another boatman expressed the same emotions: "It was the first time I believe that I ever felt homesick in the least upon leaving home. It isn't often that I can say anything of the kind, but I must confess that yesterday I had the blues, just a little. I was upon the point of making up my mind to leave the boat at Shawneetown & return, the only thing preventing me was the dislike I have of backing out of anything I

31. Joseph A. McDowell to John A. Trimble, March 24, 1826, in Trimble Family Papers, Ohio Historical Society, Columbus; William Patton to U. P. Schenck, September 25, 1845, F. Marion Teague to Messrs. U. P. Schenck & Son, December, 1858, Francis Pickett to Mssrs. Schenck & Son, November 9, 1857, C. Adlricks to U. P. Schenck, December 3, 1857, all in "Flatboat Letters of Switzerland County, Indiana."

32. Carmony (ed.), "Dole: Wabash Valley Merchant and Flatboatman," 359–60; James Hall, *Letters from the West* (1828; rpr. Gainesville, Fla., 1967), 93.

have undertaken. Perhaps also the fear of being ridiculed by my friends may have somewhat influenced my decision against doing so."[33]

To relieve the pressures of boredom, loneliness, and homesickness, the western boatmen of the steamboat era sought recreation. Although many of their leisure pursuits were the same as those of early rivermen, there were some important differences. Reading and letter writing, for example, became more popular leisure activities than ever before, indicating increasing literacy among rivermen. "I have Brother Joseph at the stearing oar," one Wabash River boatman wrote, "and shall finish my letter before Allen gets up that he may have a chance to write." Reading novels "gave me a high tone to my mind," George Forman remembered, "and as the mind improves and becomes stronger [novels] will lead on to and give a desire for stronger reading, as they did in my case." A windbound flatboatman in 1848 "spent [the morning] in reading some Tales that I purchased in Paducah," and Pennsylvania lumber raftsman Henry Baxter "went on shore" in 1844 to purchase "a Philadelphia Dollar newspaper and an Ohio Statesman. This gave us a fine recreation in reading the news." One of the humorous scenes in Twain's *Life on the Mississippi* is a true story of some steamboatmen who trick a flatboat crew into rowing hard across the river to fetch some "newspapers"—which turn out to be religious tracts. There were, no doubt, boatmen in this era who never opened a book or wrote a letter in their lives, but existing accounts show a significant and increasing interest in reading and writing aboard flatboats.[34]

Boatmen continued to sing, dance, and make music with fiddles and other instruments. Englishman James Flint, sailing on board an Ohio River flat on a Sunday, noted that one riverman "commenced a song" and, when reproached for singing on the Sabbath, "alleged he was in a 'land of liberty' and that no one had a right to interfere."

33. Roush (ed.), *T. C. Collins—Boatman,* 85, 185–86; "Beauties of Flatboating," in "Atalantian," II, entry for September 1, 1845; F. A. L., "Journal of a Trip to New Orleans on a *Broadhorn,*" in "Atalantian," IV, entry for June 19, 1848.

34. Carmony (ed.), "Dole: Wabash Valley Merchant and Flatboatman," 348; Forman, "Biographical Sketch," 117; F. A. L., "Journal of a Trip to New Orleans on a *Broadhorn,*" in "Atalantian," IV, entry for July 31, 1848; Baxter, "Rafting on the Allegheny and Ohio," 45; Samuel Clemens [Mark Twain], *Life on the Mississippi* (1874; rpr. New York, 1960), 54.

James Hall, who collected boatmen's songs, published in 1828 a tune he had heard concerning a boatman's infatuation with a lass who was "so neat a maid" that she carried her stockings and shoes in her "lilly white hands / For to keep them from the dews." Another popular song, "Woman in Our Town," concerned a promiscuous woman who "loved her husband dear-i-lee / But another man twyste as well." And traveler Robert Carlton noted in his journal a lively song written and sung by an Ohio River flatboatman to the tune of "Yankee Doodle":

> Get up good sirs, get up I say
> And rouse ye, all ye sleepers
> See! down upon us comes a thing
> To make us use our peepers!
> Yankee Doodle, etc.
>
> Yet what it is, I cannot tell
> But 'tis as big as thunder;
> Ah! if it hits our loving arks
> We'll soon be split asunder!
> Yankee Doodle etc.[35]

Less musically inclined rivermen found pleasure in baiting green-horns, and the practice of systematically harassing new hands prevailed aboard most flatboats. New men were often ordered to treat the crew to rounds of drinks as part of an initiation ritual or suffer the consequences. Men making their first trip aboard Captain Miles Stacy's flatboats were set "to work scouring or greasing the anchor," Stacy remembered, as the old hands "watched and grinned until the victim 'caught on.'" One Ohio flatboatman recalled ordering "green ones" to "Coon the Steering oar"—crawl out to the blade and then back, taking a cold swim in the Ohio River if they slipped and fell.[36]

Rivermen in passing flatboats often amused themselves by calling to one another, swearing back and forth, and howling like Indians and wolves at the top of their lungs. According to one Wabash River flat-

---

35. John Habermehl, *Life on the Western Rivers* (Pittsburgh, 1901), 57; Maud D. Brooks, "Rafting on the Allegheny," *New York Folklore Quarterly*, I (November, 1945), 225; James Flint, *Letters from America*, in Thwaites (ed.), *Early Western Travels*, IX, 109; James Hall, *Letters from the West*, 90–91; Clemens, *Life on the Mississippi*, 54; Carlton, *New Purchase*, I, 53.

36. Stacy, "Reminiscences of Captain Miles Stacy," 7; Roush (ed.), *T. C. Collins—Boatman*, 113.

boatman, "Such conversations are frequently carried on between boatmen, when either tries his wit against the other & make very witty and
laughable replies & equally witty and laughable questions." One favorite joke of boatmen was to answer frivolously any questions concerning their cargoes. North-of-the-Ohio flatboatmen reportedly
informed overly curious southerners that their cargo was "pitcoal, in-
digo, wooden nutmegs, straw baskets, and Yankee notions." Another
standing joke played on curious boatmen or landsmen in passing went
something like this:

> Hallo, the boat! [questioner]
> Hallo, the boat! [boatman]
> Where are you from?
> Redstone.
> What's your lading?
> Millstones.
> What's your captain's name?
> Whetstone.
> Where are you bound?
> To Limestone.[37]

For energetic flatboatmen there were foot races, rowing contests,
and hiking. Boatmen continued to hunt and, as in the early days,
seemed unable to resist the temptation of killing any wild animal that
swam into their paths. Some kept pets aboard their flatboats. One
boatman wrote fondly of a dog that "we had so much fun with . . .
all the way down," making him "climb the ladder about 10 times a
day, on average." Raftsman George Forman spent part of his "idle
time . . . tatooing with Indian ink on the men's arms." As in the presteam days, of course, flatboatmen spent many of their leisure hours
simply lounging around and talking with one another. The platform

---

37. Thomas Bolling Robertson, "Journal of a Tour Down the Ohio and Mississippi" (Typescript in Thomas Bolling Robertson Papers, Louisiana and Lower Mis-
sissippi Valley Collections, Louisiana State University Libraries, Baton Rouge); John
Palmer, *Journal of Travels in America . . . 1817* (London, 1818), 63; "Beauties of Flatboating," in "Atalantian," II, entry for September 1, 1845; Archer B. Hulbert, *Waterways of
Westward Expansion: The Ohio River and Its Tributaries* (Cleveland, 1903), 164; Thomas D.
Clark, *The Rampaging Frontier: Manners and Humors of Pioneer Days in the South and
Middle West* (Indianapolis, 1939), 94. Walter Blair informs me that English rivermen
were also known for their "river wit," yelling to landsmen: "Oars! Oars! Will you have
any oars!" Walter Blair to Michael Allen, June 20, 1986, in possession of Michael Allen.

on which the huge steering oar was mounted was called the "lazy board" because, according to one old flatboat captain, that is where "the oarsmen lounged when off duty." Atop the flatboat deck, another boatman remembered, "we often laid & whiled away the time lazily—laughing, talking, eating & drinking."[38]

Once ashore, the western boatmen at their leisure took on the character of tourists. "[E]very man took his own way, and was soon lost from each other," Henry Baxter wrote of his fellow raftsmen in Cincinnati in 1844. There were sights to see: "restaurants, bowling alleys, all kinds of gaming tables together with the theatres for the evening entertainment." According to one historian, boatmen landing in Cairo, Illinois, in the 1850s could enjoy circuses, menageries, museums, minstrel and variety troupes, tightrope walkers, magicians, phrenologists, and all types of musical programs. Flatboatmen became enthusiastic circus fans, and one crew attended a "circus in full blast, with its usual outside accompaniment of ragged boys & niggers—who with gaping mouths were wondering what was going on inside & wishing for a dime to see the show." A crew of lumber raftsmen in Cincinnati in 1844 "went to see the great European Magician, Herr Alexander [Alexander Hermann] perform at the National Theatre." In Cairo, rivermen could have seen "Fontelle, the great swimmer . . . [swim] from the point back of the old hotel to the bend of the Mississippi and back." Boatmen also attended "lecture[s] upon phrenology" and even dabbled in spiritualism and séances. In 1859, T. C. Collins traveled downstream with some "rappers"—spiritualists who claimed to summon knocking sounds from the world beyond—but "they began to think we were non-believers and would never perform any more on the way down."[39]

38. F. A. L., "Journal of a Trip to New Orleans on a *Broadhorn*," in "Atalantian," IV, entries for July 10, September 18, 1848; Achilles E. Fretageot, "Flatboat Trip, New Harmony to New Orleans, December 1833—January 1834" (Typescript in Indiana Historical Society, Indianapolis), 4; Roush (ed.), *T. C. Collins—Boatman,* 52; Forman, "Biographical Sketch," 123; Stacy, "Reminiscences of Captain Miles Stacy," 6; "Beauties of Flatboating," in "Atalantian," II, entry for August 18, 1845.

39. Baxter, "Rafting on the Allegheny and Ohio," 49–50, 163, 222; Harold E. Briggs, "Entertainment and Amusement in Cairo, 1848–1858," *Journal of the Illinois State Historical Society,* XLVII (Autumn, 1954), 231, 244–45; "Beauties of Flatboating," in "Atalantian," II, entry for August 18, 1845; Roush (ed.), *T. C. Collins—Boatman,* 145–46.

There was also the theater. Some flatboatmen were themselves dramatists, staging "flatboat shows" in the river towns of the West. Other rivermen attended theatricals on steam-powered "showboats" that featured "Ethiopian companies" of minstrels such as "Ned Davis' Ohio Minstrels." Ashore, boatmen frequented regular theaters and variety shows. In Memphis, Miles Stacy "went to see Joseph Jefferson play 'Rip Van Winkle.'" Henry Baxter saw Edwin Forrest, "the greatest tragedian in the world," play "Shakespeare's Richard the Third." Baxter and his fellow raftsmen were duly impressed with Forrest's performance, for "as he commenced 'Now is the Winter of our discontent' . . . it seemed as if his whole soul worked up in revolt at the proceedings which had taken place." Not all of the performances the boatmen witnessed were so polished. One traveler observed a flatboat show in which "Macbeth was performed, Duncan being got rid of by throwing him into the river instead of stabbing him."[40]

As for less wholesome entertainments, many rivermen continued to smoke, swear, drink, gamble, philander, and fight, but these vices played a less important role in their lives than during the presteamboat days. The boatmen's lifestyle had changed. Part of this change was voluntary—as family men who had a stake in life, many older boatmen were not as interested in wild escapades as their predecessors had been. But much of the change, especially among the younger and more reckless common hands, was involuntary. The river towns of the Ohio and Mississippi valleys were becoming "civilized" and, among other things, were cleaning up the rowdy river districts popular with boatmen. Tough new city ordinances, enforced by newly created professional police departments, made it much more difficult for rivermen to drink, gamble, fight, and carouse to excess. The flatboatmen of the Steamboat Age were not always model citizens, but they had learned some manners and given up quite a few of their former bad habits.

The civilizing influence had not washed the rivermen clean of all

40. Briggs, "Entertainment and Amusement in Cairo," 241–43, 245–46; Noah M. Ludlow, *Dramatic Life as I Found It: A Record of Personal Experience* (St. Louis, 1880), 237–38; Stacy, "Reminiscences of Captain Miles Stacy," 13; Baxter, "Rafting on the Allegheny and Ohio," 52; Alexander Mackay, *The Western World; or, Travels in the United States in 1846–1847* (3 vols.; London, 1849), III, 41.

their sins, however. One devout flatboatman was appalled at the "profane language" he heard in the river district of Louisville in 1839, declaring that it "would make the devils stand aghast and wonder." There also are reassuringly familiar accounts of boatmen scoundrels, deserters, and thieves in the new age—but in fact, rivermen by this time were probably no more inclined to criminal activity than their landsmen contemporaries. Although boatmen were reputed thieves and sharkers, New Orleans criminal records from a sampling of the steamboat era show that the rivermen were themselves often the victims of crime. The boatmen of the 1823–1861 period were not generally thieves, and those who did steal were at most only a minor nuisance. As one old boatman noted, "Deck hands . . . do not seem to want to steal anything of consequence, only something to eat or drink." [41]

Some boatmen gambled when the opportunity arose, but it appears that the thriftier, more stable men who worked the flats during the steamboat era found better uses for their pay than to paper the gaming table. Moreover, the once-popular gambling dens and card rooms no longer thrived along the western rivers. Beginning in the mid-1830s, a score of vigilance committees in river towns from Cincinnati to Natchez began to wage war on professional gamblers. This movement to purge gambling was part of an effort by family-oriented citizens to clean up their communities. In July of 1835, outraged local citizens in Vicksburg declared martial law and lynched five gamblers from a hastily erected gallows. The remainder of the professional sharpers fled to Natchez and set up shop in Under-the-Hill, but not for long. Natchez citizens organized the Adams County Anti-Gambling Society, and a committee of vigilance rounded up the gamblers and ran them out of town. Law-abiding Memphians acted similarly in 1835, sending their city's professional gamblers scurrying across the Mississippi to Arkansas. Similar campaigns against gamblers occurred frequently during

41. Reynolds, "Journal, 1839–1840," entry for September 29, 1839; Brush, *Growing Up with Southern Illinois*, 82; *Joseph McCormack v. Nathaniel Clark,* February 26, 1841 (MS in David F. Beem Collection, Indiana Historical Society, Indianapolis); City of New Orleans, Decisions of the Mayor in Criminal Court Cases, New Orleans, 1823–27 (MSS in Louisiana Division, New Orleans Public Library); City of New Orleans, Police Department Reports, Second Municipality, 1844–45 (MSS in Louisiana Division, New Orleans Public Library); Roush (ed.), *T. C. Collins—Boatman,* 22.

the 1830s and 1840s, until most of the river towns had rid themselves
of the gambling dens the boatmen of the early days so loved to frequent. The professional gambler was exiled to the mobile and as yet
unpoliced steamboats to practice his trade.[42]

Americans, rivermen included, were drinking less alcohol during
the post-1823 years than during the "national binge" of the early national period, but boatmen still were known as a hard-drinking class,
and there are many post-1823 accounts of alcoholic rivermen and
drunken brawls. One outraged observer noted that on board a Mississippi River steamboat, "*whiskey* was literally carried round to the
hands *in a bucket or pail,* once in *four hours,* and everyone was allowed
to help himself with a tin cup!" The same author, however, also observed that "temperance reform is making gradual progress" in the
West. Indeed, there are many examples of teetotaling rivermen, and
one group of Ohio River raftsmen in 1844 "found a Temperance
Pledge with about a hundred names attached to which we put ours,
one and all." Many other boatmen were no doubt less concerned
about the evils of alcohol; nevertheless, their increasing family and financial obligations must have decreased their affinity for drunkenness.
Then, too, the vigilante actions against the gambling dens also eliminated some of the worst of the river-town beer sties and saloons.[43]

Like gambling dens and beer sties, the whorehouses of the Ohio
and Mississippi valleys felt the encroachment of civilization. Some
prostitutes continued to ply their trade—and counted rivermen among
their best customers—but river-town prostitutes did not flourish in
complete freedom as they had during the presteamboat days. When

42. Samuel Chew Madden Notebook (Typescript in Indiana Historical Society, Indianapolis), 3; "Excerpts from the Stone Diary" (Typescript in Ohio Historical Society,
Campus Martius, the Museum of the Northwest Territory, Marietta, Ohio), 4–5 (the
original of the diary is in possession of the Ross County Historical Society, Chillicothe,
Ohio); John M. Findlay, *People of Chance: Gambling in American Society from Jamestown to
Las Vegas* (New York, 1986), 63–71; H. S. Fulkerson, *Random Recollections of Early Days
in Mississippi* (Vicksburg, 1885), 97; James, *Antebellum Natchez,* 259; Habermehl, *Life on
the Western Rivers,* 45.

43. W. J. Rorabaugh, *The Alcoholic Republic: An American Tradition* (New York,
1979), xi–xii; Roush (ed.), *T. C. Collins—Boatman,* 22, 66–67, 191; Robert Baird, *View
of the Valley of the Mississippi,* (Philadelphia, 1832), 326; F. A. L., "Journal of a Trip to
New Orleans on a *Broadhorn,*" in "Atalantian," IV, entry for July 10, 1848; Baxter,
"Rafting on the Allegheny and Ohio," 44; Ephraim Forman Papers (MSS in Old Courthouse Museum, Vicksburg).

irate citizens began to purge the professional gamblers in the 1830s, they also challenged the prostitutes who were part and parcel of the river district underworld. Vicksburg lawmakers imposed a $250 fine on any person operating a "gaming or disorderly house, or house of ill fame within the limits of the city" and indicted Ephraim Forman, owner of the Kangaroo, one of the sleaziest of Vicksburg's bawdy houses. City officials in Cape Girardeau and St. Louis, Missouri, in Fort Madison and Burlington, Iowa, and in Quincy, Illinois, all set stiff fines and punishments for the operators of river district whorehouses. In New Orleans, however, the main object of legislation was merely to confine the brothels to "the Swamp" and other river districts and to regulate their practices.[44]

While prostitutes continued to flourish in the Swamp, they were run out of many other river districts and, like the gamblers, retreated to the steamboats to practice their skills. On the Upper Mississippi, flatboat brothels known as "gunboats" appeared in increasing numbers. Several city councils followed the example of Fort Madison, Iowa, and outlawed "any flat boat, keelboat, or scow, or any other watercraft . . . used for the purpose of prostitution, lewdness, dancing, fiddling, and drinking." In at least one instance, however, the rivermen themselves saved the town fathers the trouble and expense of policing a floating whorehouse. Disgruntled at the quality of service they received on an Upper Mississippi gunboat near La Crosse, Wisconsin, a group of lumber raftsmen reboarded the craft, ran off the proprietor and "staff," drank up all the whiskey on board, and then burned the abandoned bordello to the waterline.[45]

Unfortunately, the boatmen of the Steamboat Age sometimes vented their anger and violence on one another or on more upright and law-abiding citizens. For example, a quantitative study of Galena, Illinois, court records for 1849–1851 shows that the highest number of

44. David Kaser, "Nashville's Women of Pleasure in 1860," *Tennessee Historical Quarterly,* XXIII (December, 1964), 379–82; Phillip D. Jordan, *Frontier Law and Order: Ten Essays* (Lincoln, Neb., 1970), 115–39; City of Vicksburg, *Revised Ordinances* (Vicksburg, 1855), 96–97; Ephraim Forman Papers; Gordon Cotton, "Citizen Kept Bawdy House, Jury Charged," Vicksburg *Sunday Post,* December 31, 1978; Semper Idem [pseud.], *The Blue Book: . . . The Guide Books to the Houses of Ill Fame in New Orleans* (N.p., 1936), 15–22.

45. Habermehl, *Life on the Western Rivers,* 36; Jordan, *Frontier Law and Order,* 78–79, 129.

arrests for drunk and disorderly conduct, "quarreling, fighting, and disturbing the peace and quiet of Main Street," and "fighting in the streets" always occurred in April and May—the peak of the spring steamboat, flatboat, and lumber raft navigation season. There are many instances of fistfights and scuffles aboard flatboats, and not a few of these altercations featured the brandishing of clubs, guns, or bottles.[46]

On the other hand, there is much evidence with which to rebut generalizations about rowdy, fighting rivermen. A nineteenth-century Washington County, Ohio, historian noted with considerable pride that Marietta merchant navigator James Stowe had "been down the Mississippi and up Red river and in the most dangerous parts of the south at dangerous times, and yet has never owned a revolver or carried a firearm." Indeed, as early as 1818, one traveler on the Mississippi argued that the "numerous stories, which have so often been circulated, and believed, respecting the cruel modes of fighting prevalent among the boatmen of the west are, generally speaking, untrue." He concluded that the "society of this part of the world is becoming less savage, and more refined," and he was quite right. By the 1830s and 1840s, most flatboatmen had improved their demeanor considerably, and those who had not were left to deal with a growing number of concerned citizens and law enforcement agencies in the Ohio and Mississippi valleys. Much of the confusion over boatmen's violence is due to the transitional nature of the 1823–1861 era and to the growing contemporary fascination with folkloric and literary accounts of violent "half horse, half alligator" boatmen. This problem is especially evident in the so-called flatboat wars—a series of conflicts that have been pointed to as examples of rivermen's violence, but which in fact symbolize the taming of the western boatmen.[47]

The flatboat wars were a series of protests, sometimes violent, over the passage of wharf regulations and taxes in the hitherto unregulated river towns of the Lower Mississippi. Many flatboatmen became angry

46. Mahoney, "River Towns of the Great West," 622; Blaine A. Guthrie and Mitchell R. Guthrie (eds.), "Catfish, Cornmeal, and the Broad Canopy of Heaven: The Journal of the Reverend Guerdon Gates," *Kentucky Historical Society Register,* LXVI (January, 1968), 14–15; William Oliver, *Eight Months in Illinois . . . with Information to Immigrants* (1843; rpr. Chicago, 1924), 44–47.

47. Williams, *History of Washington County, Ohio,* 621; Estwick Evans, *A Pedestrious Tour of . . . Western States . . . 1818,* in Thwaites (ed.), *Early Western Travels,* VIII, 344.

when the arm of government at last found its way to the wharfs, but there were in fact several legal precedents for the post-1823 wharf taxes and regulations. The Spanish governors had taxed flatboats during the eighteenth century, and American officials in early nineteenth-century New Orleans had continued the practice by passing "an ordinance continuing in force the Levee duty paid upon vessels, Flats, Boats, Barges, [and] Rafts." In 1807 the wharf fee for flatboats at New Orleans was set at six dollars, and a wharfmaster was appointed to collect the money and keep accurate records of boat arrivals. Boatmen grumbled, but paid up. One wrote a letter, signed "Martinus," to the *Louisiana Gazette* in 1806, charging that the wharf tax was "unconstitutional," but was chastised for his "consummate impudence" in a rebuttal from a local citizen. "Kentucky boatmen and bacon fellers may complain," the New Orleans resident scolded, "and *Martinus* may write," but the police of "the city of New Orleans stand unrivalled on the continent," and flatboatmen should therefore take heed.[48]

As it happened, New Orleans itself never did suffer a flatboatman's riot, even though the town fathers continued to pass stiff taxes and wharf regulations. The trouble started thirty years later, when civilization crept northward and the city governments in Natchez, Vicksburg, and Memphis passed similar legislation to raise revenues and regulate their crowded, troublesome wharf areas. In Vicksburg, for example, a wharf statute taxed flatboatmen two dollars for the first two days in port and fifty cents a day thereafter, with a ten-dollar fine for violators. In addition, retailers were to pay an ad valorem tax, buy licenses, fill out a number of forms, and pay a fifty-dollar fine if they failed to comply. All of this may smack of the inevitable to modern readers, but the freewheeling entrepreneurs of the 1830s and 1840s viewed the new regulations with contempt. Most of their hostility was vented against the wharfmaster, an 1830s Mississippi Valley type somewhat akin to the Stamp Tax collector of 1760s Massachusetts. This ignominious soul benefited from the boatmen's plight, garnering approximately 15 percent of the wharf taxes he collected.[49]

48. City of New Orleans, Municipal Papers (MSS in Tulane University, New Orleans), Box 15, folder 10; City of New Orleans, *Police Code* (New Orleans, 1808), 156; *Louisiana Gazette* (New Orleans), August 29, 1806.
49. City of Vicksburg, *Revised Ordinances*, 90–95.

There was bound to be conflict. The striking fact, however, is that the flatboat "wars" ended as quickly and with as little bloodshed as they did. Mississippi Valley residents of the 1830s and 1840s did not view crowds of angry boatmen in rational or relative terms. Rivertown citizens were intent on bringing stability and order (and a tax base) to their communities and told the flatboatmen to pay up or else. Some boatmen refused to pay, but usually not for long. The first confrontation occurred in Natchez–Under-the-Hill in November of 1837. A dramatic Natchez *Free Trader* news article entitled "Daring Resistance to the Law" recounted the story: When nine flatboat captains refused to pay a wharf and hospital tax of ten dollars per boat, Wharfmaster M. Wells issued a subpoena, confiscated their cargoes, and prepared to auction off everything to the highest bidder. The flatboatmen, shocked at being the first to feel the sting of law and order in Under-the-Hill, appeared in force at the auction "armed with bowie knives," and "threats of violence and death [were made] upon all who attempted to sell and buy their property." At length a local militia company appeared, and "the cold and sullen bayonets of the Guards were too hard meat for the Arkansas toothpicks. There was no fight." Natchez mayor Tooley put two rivermen into jail, and the affair ended without violence. The *Free Trader* denounced the flatboatmen and concluded: "We heartily rejoice that we have a city government that both knows its duty and fears not to do it. The law of the land will be maintained here . . . and mercenary ruffians will find threats of violence against the law to be as ineffectual as they have now proved to be." [50]

The following spring, in St. Francisville, Louisiana, the flatboat troubles were renewed when, according to Mayor Hinch, boatmen "began to revolt" against a heavy wharf tax. Hinch wrote his brother saying that he "had to use the utmost precaution in quelling the angry spirit that was engendering itself between our citizens and the flatboatmen." In Vicksburg in February, 1838, the city government defused a similarly volatile situation. According to one sensationalized account, the city had levied an outrageous wharf tax in order to "run the flatboats off." Mayor McGinty and Chief of Police Schofney soon found that the boatmen had "armed themselves with one or more ri-

---

50. Natchez *Free Trader*, n.d., reprinted in Vicksburg *Register*, November 29, 1837.

fles or shotguns on each boat and with heavy blugeons" and were reportedly "determined upon resistance by force, if necessary." As in Natchez, the militia appeared, and although "much quarreling and threatening" ensued, the mob dispersed and the troops marched back up the hill without firing a shot. In a resolution published in the Vicksburg *Register,* the boatmen used a moderate tone but vowed to obey only those laws "having the appearance of justice" and "executed in a peaceable and easy manner." This reasonable attitude resulted in a settlement that, in retrospect, drains much of the drama from the situation. Pooling their resources, the flatboatmen raised two thousand dollars, hired a lawyer, and took the city to court. They eventually won, and agreed to pay a wharf tax set at a much lower rate.[51]

To the north, the Memphis flatboat war of 1842 took on a more violent taint, but settled once and for all the question of sovereignty along the river-town flatboat wharfs. The Memphis troubles are the most famous of the flatboat wars, and rightly so. Although providing a dramatic depiction of boatmen's violence, the Memphis flatboat war also symbolizes the final, dying gasp of the reckless behavior that characterized early rivermen, but not the flatboatmen of the Steamboat Age. The stage was set in 1841, when Memphians elected to office a reform ticket pledged to clean up the city's flatboat wharfs—and fatten the city's coffers with new wharf taxes. Mayor Spickernagle instituted a law to that effect in 1841, appointing a new wharfmaster and granting him a generous 25 percent commission on all the fees he collected. A tough new constable, Colonel G. B. Locke, was appointed to back him up, but neither man found his job very pleasant. James Dick Davis, a former wharfmaster himself, claimed to have seen the wharfmaster "streaking it up the hill, with a dozen or more fellows after him, lashing at his heels with long cane poles, and from the way he wriggled, occasionally, it was evident that some of the licks took effect." Colonel Locke seemed intent on curtailing such abuse, and in May of 1842 he got his chance.[52]

51. A. Hinch to Benjamin Hinch, March 15, 1838, in Benjamin Hinch Papers, Illinois State Historical Library, quoted courtesy of Illinois State Historical Library, Springfield, folder 1; Fulkerson, *Random Recollections,* 97–99; Vicksburg *Register,* February 12, 1838. Fulkerson's lively account of "this hostility [which] came near culminating in a bloody war between the flatboatmen and citizens" should not be read too literally.

52. The most detailed description of the Memphis flatboat war is in James Dick

More than five hundred flatboats, most of them manned by "Hoosiers" from the Wabash Valley, were lying in port on the spring day that law and order came to Memphis. One of these flatboatmen, a man named Trester, thought the new wharf regulations "onconstitutional," refused to pay his wharf fee, and threatened to lick anyone who attempted to force him to do so. Confronted by the new wharfmaster, Trester brandished a heavy stick and "proposed to comb the Memphis Wharfmaster's head" with it. "I cut this on purpose for you," Trester supposedly taunted, "and I am going to use it on you if you ever show your face here while I remain." The wharfmaster prudently retreated, only to return with Constable Locke, a company of local militia, and a warrant for Trester's arrest. No longer feeling quite so bold, Trester quickly launched his boat into the current. He was pursued by Locke, Captain Ruth of the militia, and several soldiers who boarded the flatboat and began to struggle with Trester and his crew. When Trester knocked Captain Ruth to the ground and began to beat him severely with a club, someone (it is not clear who) commanded the men to "Fire! Fire!" Four soldiers obeyed. Trester was killed, and the rest of the flatboatmen surrendered quickly.[53]

The trouble was not over. Landing at the foot of Beale Street, Locke and Ruth found themselves standing face to face with scores of armed and angry flatboatmen. Luckily, another militia company appeared, reinforced by gun-carrying local citizens. When several of the belligerent boatmen advanced, Ruth called out, "Arrest those men!" A half-dozen boatmen found themselves in armed custody. For a few moments it had seemed as though there really would be war in Memphis, but sanity prevailed. The flatboatmen returned to their boats, the prisoners were released, and the situation defused. The mayor forbade local citizens the slightest display of triumph. Later, a board of magistrates investigated the proceedings, but none of the involved flatboatmen chose to return to Memphis to testify. The board exonerated

Davis, *The History of the City of Memphis . . . [and] the "Old Times Papers"* (Memphis, 1873), 96–103. Davis lived in Memphis most of his life and actually served a stint as wharfmaster. Unfortunately, his penchant for the dramatic makes his account an interesting blend of history and folklore. I have used Davis' account selectively and also relied on a reconstruction of the incident in the Memphis *Daily Appeal*, November 26, 1867, and Gerald D. Capers, *The Biography of a River Town; Memphis: Its Heroic Age* (Chapel Hill, 1939), 50, 73–74.

53. Davis, *History of Memphis*, 96–103; Capers, *Biography of a River Town*, 50, 73–74.

the city of any wrongdoing, the flatboatmen submitted to wharf fee collections, and river commerce in Memphis became more or less stable. The flatboat wars were over.[54]

In retrospect, even this most violent of the flatboat wars seems pretty tame when compared with other riots of the Jacksonian era.[55] In Memphis, Natchez, St. Francisville, and Vicksburg, the flatboat troubles now appear to have consisted of many threats by the boatmen, but not much action. Yet these "wars," exaggerated and romanticized by local historians, are very much a part of the mythology of the Alligator Horse as a violent, untamable threat to civilized society. The flatboat wars are thus important in both the historic and folkloric perspectives.

The image of a mob of belligerent boatmen storming a town and taking it for their own debauched pleasures is an integral part of the lore of the western boatmen. Much folklore is based on a grain of truth, of course, and in the early, presteam days of boating, many rivermen were indeed rowdy, drunken brawlers. This violent, rioting boatman soon found his way into the historical works and journalism of the post-1823 period, whether he belonged there or not. Writers told trumped-up stories of rivermen, "lawless and dissolute to a proverb," who "frequently stopped at the villages along their course and passed the night in scenes of wild revelry and merriment." As the nineteenth century advanced, these stories became bloodier and more farfetched, and the boatmen of the post-1823 generation gained a reputation for violence and mob action that is not supported by the historical evidence.[56]

For example, in an 1890 newspaper story, an "old timer" told a dubious tale of two hundred antebellum flatboatmen boarding a northbound steamboat, refusing to pay their fare, and taking possession of the entire steamboat deck. When the steamer's crew, "armed with clubs," accosted the flatboatmen, "the most terrible fight in the his-

54. Capers, *Biography of a River Town,* 74; Davis, *History of Memphis,* 101–103.

55. David Grimsted, "Rioting in Its Jacksonian Setting," *American Historical Review,* LXXVII (April, 1972), 361–97; Leonard Richards, *Gentlemen of Property and Standing: Anti-Abolition Mobs in Jacksonian America* (New York, 1970); Carl Prince, "The Great Riot Year: Jacksonian Democracy and Patterns of American Violence in 1834," *Journal of the Early Republic,* V (Spring, 1985), 1–19.

56. Edmund Flagg, *The Far West,* in Thwaites (ed.), *Early Western Travels,* XXVI, 61–62.

tory of the river took place." At last the flatboatmen met defeat, and those who did not agree to pay "were put ashore." Another dubious story of this dramatic genre appeared in the Indianapolis *News* in 1883. It told of a flatboat war in New Harmony, Indiana, in 1830. The cause of the trouble was not specified, but the author related in familiar terms the despicable conduct of about forty rivermen, who "went on a big spree and decided to 'take' the town. They shouldered their spiked poles, tying a red shirt to one for a banner, and marched up into the town, blowing tin horns and beating tin pans for drums. They rent the air with yells, vulgar epithets, and declarations that they would thrash the men and carry off the women. Fortunately for the town," the writer concluded, "a company of military volunteers" led by Captain Richard Owen joined with local citizens to quell the disturbance, and "New Harmony never again suffered insults from drunken boatmen."[57]

Like robber folktales, these stories of local flatboat wars permeate the literature of the western boatmen. The problem they present to the historian is not insurmountable. Firsthand witnesses and newspaper accounts prove that there *were* flatboat troubles over wharf fees in Natchez, St. Francisville, Vicksburg, Memphis, and other river towns during the 1830s and 1840s. These same accounts, however, also prove that the flatboat wars were not wars at all. The flatboatmen became very angry and talked a good fight, but when push came to shove they were always quite ready to bow to the forces of law and order. The more stable, married flatboat captains and pilots of the post-1823 era, and even their young crewmen, were not particularly anxious to challenge armed militiamen over a matter of principle. When all was said and done, these civilized flatboatmen of the Steamboat Age buckled under and obeyed the law.

In this perspective, the flatboat wars represent the final taming of the western boatmen. The Memphis episode showed that the last small vestiges of the wild, reckless behavior of early riverboating days had

57. Hutchinson (Kans.) *Daily News*, October 11, 1890, reprinted from the Indianapolis *News*, n.d.; Indianapolis *News*, December 27, 1883. I can find no firsthand account of the New Harmony incident, but there is a local legend about a "free-for-all" involving nonrivermen combatants, and the "Captain Owen" tale probably emerged from this. John and Josephine Elliott, New Harmony, Indiana, to Michael Allen, March 25, 1987, in possession of Michael Allen; Aline Cook (Librarian, New Harmony Workingmen's Institute) to Michael Allen, July 21, 1988, informs me that Richard Owen was not commissioned captain until April, 1847, during the Mexican War.

all but withered away by 1842. The once-wild river towns of the Ohio and Mississippi valleys had become more civilized, with churches, schools, and libraries replacing beer sties, gambling dens, and whore-houses. James Hall noted in 1828 that Shawneetown, Illinois, once presenting "the most barbarous scenes of outrage . . . is now a quiet place, exhibiting much of the activity of business, with but little dissi-pation, and still less out-breaking disorder." As I have shown, Mem-phis, Vicksburg, and Natchez banished their gamblers and cracked down on the brothels and saloons. Nature itself cleansed Natchez-Under-the-Hill of sinful elements in May of 1840 when, according to one old riverman, a great tornado "swept from sight nearly all the buildings and flatboats that had so long served as a rendezvous for the thousands of desperate and dissolute that congregated there." To the south, in Louisiana's growing river towns, citizens cleaned up their wharfs, replacing whorehouses with warehouses, and ordering va-grants to "give a correct account of themselves."[58]

Even New Orleans, always the capital city of this "spillway of sin," became more respectable. By the 1840s, New Orleans officials had perfected their strategy of isolating the town's vice and debauchery to specific districts and there regulating and taxing the criminals. As one Englishman visiting the Crescent City around 1840 reported, "New Orleans appears to be more orderly, or, at least, a far less disorderly, place than I had expected to find it." The New Orleans *Picayune* boasted that "our New Orleans loafers are not generally vicious fel-lows. . . . They are not taken up for assaulting ladies in the streets, for riots in houses of ill-fame, for pulling down dwellings and setting fire to property &c." Crime and violence persisted, but times were tame compared with the late eighteenth and early nineteenth centuries. So, too, were the flatboatmen who visited the city during the Steamboat Age. Accounts of their behavior sound very modern—almost like those of merchant seamen and towboatmen who visit the peep shows on Bourbon Street today. Receiving their pay, flatboatmen of the post-1823 era became New Orleans tourists who, according to one old Louisianian, "tarried with us only a few days." Having drunk a little too much and "see[n] all the 'sights,' the 'elephant' included," they

---

58. James Hall, *Letters from the West*, 231; Gould, *Fifty Years on the Mississippi*, 734; A. Hinch to Benjamin Hinch, June 17, 1838, in Benjamin Hinch Papers.

would depart for home on a northbound steamboat. "They had been to 'Orlins.'"[59]

As in the early days, considerable disagreement existed among Steamboat Age observers about the "character" of the western boatmen. The most widely read accounts on the subject were those written by European tourists who, after making a quick steamboat trip up or down the Mississippi, published their travel journals, claiming to be experts on the character and "domestic manners" of the Americans. These travelers seemed fascinated by flatboatmen, and an assessment of this exotic species became a standard ingredient of nearly all European travel diaries. Interestingly, these travelers' characterizations of boatmen all bear a suspicious resemblance to one another. Indeed, they form a literary genre of the Alligator Horse that has little relationship to the real flatboatmen of the West. Many of the accounts are borrowed or plagiarized, sometimes word for word, from an 1828 description of boatmen by the ubiquitous American traveler and chronicler the Reverend Timothy Flint. Although he did note some of the dangers and discomforts of river work, Flint suffused his portrait of the flatboatmen of the West with clouds of romance. The boatman appears as a dashing blade in a red shirt, sawing on a fiddle atop his flatboat roof, sounding a lingering note on his boatman's horn, sailing serenely along in warm spring weather, and calling to fair young girls and envious landsmen who line the banks to watch and wish secretly that they, too, could become flatboatmen.[60]

Using Flint's description as a basis, and adding their customary aversion to Americans in general and western Americans in particular, European travelers depicted a romantic yet violent Alligator Horse. For example, Edmund Flagg borrowed heaping portions of Flint's account but added some negative comments of his own concerning the boatmen's "lawless and dissolute" behavior and their constant quest

59. E. Merton Coulter (ed.), *The Other Half of New Orleans: Sketches of Characters and Incidents from the Recorder's Court in New Orleans in the Eighteen Forties as Reported in the "Picayune"* (Baton Rouge, 1939), 4; Harry C. Castellanos, *New Orleans as It Was: Episodes of Louisiana Life* (1896; rpr. Baton Rouge, 1979), 161–62.

60. Timothy Flint, *A Condensed Geography and History of the Western States, or the Mississippi Valley* (2 vols.; 1828; rpr. Gainesville, Fla., 1970), I, 232–33. It is possible that George Caleb Bingham used Flint's famous description as a basis for his *Jolly Flatboatmen* paintings of the 1840s and 1850s.

for "indolent gratification." While condemning flatboatmen as "a most disorderly set of persons, constantly gambling and wrangling, [and] very seldom sober," the upright Englishwoman Frances Trollope also pointed out that "these Kentuckians are a very noble-looking race of men . . . [and] extremely handsome." Another Englishwoman, Mrs. Houstoun, solved the problem of assessing the boatmen's character quite handily by plagiarizing the Flint account to make gods of the *presteam* Ohio boatmen—and then lambasting their successors. "Since that time [of the early rivermen] many changes have taken place," Mrs. Houstoun informed her readers: "[C]rime . . . Drunkenness" and other vices had transformed the upright and bold flatboatmen of the presteam era into a "swearing, murdering, and violent" race of men.[61]

Mrs. Houstoun's account is fascinating precisely because it is so inaccurate—in fact, the diametric opposite of the true situation—but the penchant to romanticize or demean or in other ways generalize about flatboatmen as Alligator Horses led to utter confusion among almost all travel writers (and their readership) as to the real character of the western boatmen. Robert Baird fared better than anyone else in his 1832 depiction of flatboatmen: "There is not on earth a class of men of a more peculiar and marked character, than the western boatmen. . . . They have, it is true, lost much of the lawless and outrageous spirit which they had in olden times, and before the introduction of steamboats upon the western waters. They have become less intemperate, [and] more civil in their intercourse with other men." Even Baird, however, could not resist adding that the flatboatmen of the steamboat era's "distinguishing traits of character remain—boldness, readiness to encounter almost any danger, recklessness to consequences, and indifference to the wants of the future, amid the enjoyment, the noise, whiskey, and fun of the present." The Alligator Horse was not easily put to rest.[62]

Setting aside for just a moment the comments of observers who did not know flatboatmen on a day-to-day basis, one can explore this question of character through the eyes of the boatmen themselves. As

61. Flagg, *Far West*, in Thwaites (ed.), *Early Western Travels*, XXVI, 61–62; Frances Trollope, *Domestic Manners of the Americans* (1832; rpr. New York, 1949), 17–18; Houstoun, *Hesperos*, II, 31–33.
62. Baird, *View of the Valley of the Mississippi*, 116.

might be expected, men who knew the river made no monolithic generalizations about their fellow boatmen, but rather offered disparate assessments of individuals—simply because there were all kinds of boatmen manning the flats of the post-1823 era. For example, the correspondence of flatboat hay trader U. P. Schenck of Vevay, Indiana, contains references to boatmen of good character, but it also mentions men who were "of no account here nor no where else." Pilot S. Martin complained to Schenck in 1858 of a steersman "you sent with me [who] knows nothing about the river," and one year later pilot Francis Pickett wrote, "I am sorry to say that I have two men that is not worth their grub." A Wabash River flatboatman who signed his diary simply "F.A.L." wrote harshly about some flatboatmen he encountered in 1848—"a low dirty set of Black guards . . . the crew of a Cincinnati boat. They make more noise than forty Indians, whooping & yelling & insulting every one they pass on shore." Near Memphis, the same writer expressed dismay at the behavior of some rivermen, "nearly all of them from near Terre Haute . . . the hardest set of cases I ever saw. . . . They were literally raw, backwoods flatboatmen and their greatest pleasure seemed to be who could drink the most whiskey and make the most noise. . . . I am heartily tired of such company and so much of it. Forty thousand Devils careening on the waters could not make more noise nor be more disagreeable than this portion of the unterrified democracy."[63]

Of course, F.A.L.'s final comment reveals *his* true character—he was an upright Whig, disgusted at the unrefined manners of his less advantaged fellow Hoosiers. "*Our* crew," he added with an air of superiority, "are a perfect set of gentlemen. . . . It is a great pity our Example is not more followed on the river!" It is highly debatable how many "perfect set[s] of gentlemen" manned the Ohio and Mississippi flatboats of the 1823–1861 period, but there were most certainly a great many honest and upstanding flatboatmen, and there are many accounts of these "A number 1" rivermen. Kentucky merchant navigator Fountain Perry made a practice of assisting grounded and other-

63. Francis Pickett to Messers [*sic*] Schenck & Son, December 15, 1857, S. Martin to Messers U. P. Schenck & Son, December 1, 1858, Francis Pickett to Messers Schenck & Son, January 4, 1859, all in "Flatboat Letters of Switzerland County, Indiana"; F.A.L., "Journey to New Orleans on a *Broadhorn*," in "Atalantian," IV, entries for August 8, 28, 1848.

wise distressed flatboatmen during the 1830s, with no thought of the trouble and expenses he incurred. Despite the prejudice and hostility shown toward him, black riverman Simon Gray handled large sums of his employer's money in an honest, businesslike manner for more than twenty years. T. C. Collins described one trustworthy boat hand in typical river fashion when he wrote, "I knew as soon as I saw him that he would do to tie to." Collins was himself a moral man, well-respected in his Ohio village of Little Hocking. "It is a singular fact," he remembered, "I never asked for credit at one of the banks that I was refused. Everyone seemed to trust me and, I can now say and tell the truth, I don't owe one cent to one of the many that was good enough to trust me. . . . Honesty is the best [policy] everywhere." Raftsman George Forman stressed his belief in a moral code of behavior even more emphatically: "I had a pride and self-respect, and romance in my character. . . . I did not commit a single criminal or immoral act during all my [time as a riverman]. . . . I did not drink a drop of liquor or even taste it then, and never learned or knew how to play a single game of cards, or have anything to do with prostitutes, although I was surrounded by Drinking, gambling, prostitution, and every form of vice. It disgusted and repelled me."[64]

Although not many rivermen were as devout as Forman, a number of these men were practicing Christians. The pietistic followers of George Rapp, for example, actively engaged in flatboating while residing along the Wabash and Ohio rivers, and many other Christian boatmen worked the western rivers during the Steamboat Age. John Brandenburg cautioned his New Orleans–bound son that "the same God sees the actions of men in that country that does in this, and you should reverance and serve Him and pray for His mercy." Raftsman Henry Baxter attended church regularly during his stint on the Ohio, and one boatman expressed shame that "we had lost [count of] the day of the week and we were running around town with our guns on our shoulders on Sunday." Some boatmen actually tied up to the shore on the Sabbath to observe a day of rest, and there exist many accounts of

64. F.A.L., "Journey to New Orleans on a *Broadhorn*," in "Atalantian," IV, entries for August 8, 28, 1848. Emphasis added. Francis Pickett to Messers Schenck and Sons, November 1, 1857, in "Flatboat Letters of Switzerland County, Indiana"; Fountain Perry, "River Logs," *passim;* Moore, "Simon Gray, Riverman," 477; Roush (ed.), *T. C. Collins—Boatman,* 115, 198; Forman, "Biographical Sketch," 117.

churchgoing boatmen. Simon Augustus Sherman, an Upper Mississippi raftsman, appears to have been a bit overzealous one Sunday when he went ashore and "attended the Baptist, Presbyterian, and Catholic churches," one after the other. He added, however, that "this was the second time I had heard a church bell since I left New England in 1848."[65]

It is apparent that the intellects of boatmen were improving. Flatboatmen were writing more letters, keeping journals, and, as shown, reading books, newspapers, and magazines on a regular basis. Some even took up the writing of verse. Ohio flatboatman Jared Warner wrote in his journal, "Loose, loose, every sail to the breeze / The course of the vessel improve / I've done with the toil of the seas / Ye sailors, I'm bound to my *love*." And a Marietta, Ohio, riverman, upon returning home, rhapsodized, "Twas not blind chance or Friendly star / Held fast the tiller of my struggling craft."[66]

Few rivermen were quite so poetic, and although their intellectual capacities had no doubt improved, boatmen were ultimately workingmen whose thoughts and perceptions did not escape the bounds of their class and prejudices. For instance, traveler and scientist Prince Maximilian of Wied complained in 1832 about his crewmen throwing overboard the "skins, skulls of animals, and the like" that he had been gathering into a "collection of natural history." Evidently these artifacts were cluttering up the men's deck space, so they simply got rid of them. Scientist Henry Rowe Schoolcraft earlier had voiced similar complaints about his Upper Mississippi boat hands' lack of appreciation for scientific endeavors. Leaving a rare rock specimen on deck for a few minutes, Schoolcraft returned and discovered, much to his dismay, that the rock had been knocked to pieces by one boatman—

65. McDonald, "Diary," 248; John Brandenburg to Jacob Brandenburg, December 4, 1858, in John Brandenburg Collection, Indiana Historical Society, Indianapolis; Baxter, "Rafting on the Allegheny and Ohio," 52–53; Roush (ed.), *T. C. Collins—Boatman*, 35, 147; "Memorandum of a Trip to New Orleans" (MS in Hawes Family Papers, Special Collections and Archives, University of Kentucky Library, Lexington), entry for January 1, 1843; Reynolds, "Journal, 1839–1840," 21; Fountain Perry, "On Religion" (MS in Fountain and Roderick Perry Papers, University of Kentucky Library, Lexington); Simon Augustus Sherman, "Lumber Rafting on the Wisconsin River," *Wisconsin Historical Society Proceedings*, X (1911), 180.

66. Jared Warner, "Flatboat Book Number 5," (MS in Jared Warner Papers, University of Wisconsin–Platteville), VIII; "Excerpts from the Stone Diary," 2.

"who acted probably," Schoolcraft wrote, "like the boy who broke the fiddle 'to get music out' of it." When Schoolcraft scolded the brawny riverman for destroying the rock specimen, the offender replied insolently, "There is more where this comes from," and stretching his huge frame and flexing his rocklike muscles, he taunted, "Help yourself!"[67]

There are other instances of ignorant and superstitious behavior, and of anti-Semitism and vulgar racist epithets as well, but in assessing the intellects of western boatmen during the post-1823 years, one must retain some sense of perspective. On the whole, these men were more intelligent than their crude frontier predecessors. There is perhaps no better example of this advancement than the fact that the flatboatmen of the Steamboat Age were gaining a *self-perception*—including an appreciation of the mystique they had acquired as Alligator Horses and "jolly flatboatmen." The flatboatmen of the 1823–1861 period, for the first time in the history of American riverboatmen, could afford the luxuries of self-glorification and romanticization, and many of them possessed the mental equipment to engage in such pursuits. Even their descriptions of the scenery reflect this changed awareness. "Imagine yourself on the roof of a flat boat, moving along on the bosom of a smooth though rapid and mighty river," Ohio flatboatman Henry R. Reynolds wrote in 1840. "It is one continued scene of beauty, order and splendor and scenery, as if art and nature had combined to render this part of creation lovely, most lovely." An Indiana flatboatman agreed: "Yesterday . . . we beheld the beauties of flatboating in bright colors with such a day & such scenery I did not wonder that boatmen love to be on the river. . . . At such times everything combines to make flat boating very romantic." The boatmen of the presteam days led much too hard a life and were much too ignorant for such romanticization. During the post-1823 decades, increasing ease of navigation combined with increasing literacy, enabling numerous boatmen to write fancifully about their trade. Thus, a Washington County, Ohio, flatboatman could declare, "I recall no experience of my subsequent life that furnished such enjoyment of physical and

67. Maximilian, Prince of Wied, *Travels in North America,* in Thwaites (ed.), *Early Western Travels,* XXIII, 58; Schoolcraft quoted in Jane Ross, "Flatters and Keelers of the Western Rivers," *Early American Life,* VIII (February, 1977), 21.

mental pleasure as filled my cup in the opening hours of a twenty-two hundred mile trip from Marietta to New Orleans."[68]

Another important example of the generally more-involved intellects of the new boatmen is the increasing number of political discussions that took place aboard flatboats. Political commentary almost never appears in early accounts of and by rivermen, but during the Jacksonian and pre–Civil War period, many flatboatmen became partisans in the important political debates and contests of their day. A September 9, 1840, article in the New Orleans *Picayune* described a fierce brawl between a Whig flatboatman and two of his Democratic colleagues. The fracas had begun as a debate over the presidential race between Whig William Henry Harrison and Democrat Martin Van Buren. Van Buren's two supporters won this match, at least, and "but for the interference of the police, Harrison might [have counted] with certainty on a negative gain of one at the November elections." When former Democratic vice-president Richard M. Johnson visited Memphis in 1844, he was "greeted . . . with a shout" by a huge gathering of flatboatmen along the wharf of the city. Pennsylvania riverman Henry Baxter was a dyed-in-the-wool Polk Democrat who, while rafting lumber on the Ohio in 1844, "had some quite severe political discussions" on an almost daily basis. Baxter hated the Whigs and "the God they worship (Henry Clay)." One day he attended a huge Ohio Democratic barbecue along with "two thousand . . . of the very bone and sinew of the country." After hearing various speakers discuss "the Tariff, the Texas question, Native Americanism, and Whiggery in general," the crowd sat down to eat. At this point, Baxter apparently suffered a mild disillusionment: he complained that some of his fellow Democrats "carried off enough to last them a week, and in consequence many did not get more than a taste."[69]

As the debate over slavery raged, western boatmen inevitably were

68. Stacy, "Reminiscences of Captain Miles Stacy," 10–11; Roush (ed.), *T. C. Collins—Boatman,* 114–15, 211; Reynolds, "Journal, 1839–1840," 93–94; F. A. L., "Journal of a Trip to New Orleans on a *Broadhorn,*" in "Atalantian," IV, entry for July 10, 1848; "Excerpts from the Stone Diary," 2. See also Stephen R. Bentley, "An Account of Wisconsin Lumber Rafting Days" (MS in State Historical Society of Wisconsin, Madison), 14; and Chapter 7 below.

69. Coulter (ed.), *Other Half of New Orleans,* 14–16; Davis, *History of Memphis,* 183–87; Baxter, "Rafting on the Allegheny and Ohio," 77–78, 146–47, 235.

drawn into it. George Forman wrote that in St. Louis in 1849, "Politics were high over the [proposed] repeal of the Missouri Compromise &c and I heard Thos. H. Benton U.S. Senator from Missouri deliver one of his great speeches in the Rotunda of the Court House [in] St. Louis against Calhoun, before an immense crowd." Many merchant navigators voted Whig, and merchant flatboatman William P. Dole served as a Whig congressman and Lincoln delegate to the Republican convention in Chicago in 1860. A few rivermen espoused abolitionism, calling for "publick opinion [to] be roused so that by one unanimous voice, slavery shall be pronounced as among the evils that have passed." On the other hand, the number of racial slurs found in flatboatmen's correspondence indicates that although many of these Ohio Valley rivermen opposed the South and slavery, they held no great love for the black man. Indeed, T. C. Collins, landing in Illinois after working for three years on the Lower Missouri River, wrote, "I jumped out on shore, got on top of the bank, turned around and looked back to old Missouri, flapping my wings and crowed, thanking God I had got on free soil once more after being shut up in niggerdom three years." [70]

By the mid-1850s, discussions of the slavery issue appeared with increasing frequency in the writings of flatboatmen. Captain Miles Stacy of Marietta, whose "boating was mostly in slavery days," wrote at length about the peculiar institution in his flatboating reminiscences. The "darkies would come down to the boat," he remembered. "We could usually tell by their looks whether they had a kind master." He also recalled that "down below Vicksburg was Jeff Davis' large plantation," adding, "I never tried to sell anything there for other boatmen told me that he bought everything at wholesale in New Orleans." At Grand Gulf, Mississippi, Captain Stacy once "saw an auction sale" of slaves: "A 'boy' and a 'gal'—as they were called—were in turn put upon a platform about four feet high and seven or eight feet square. The prospective purchaser would go up, open their mouths to

70. Forman, "Biographical Sketch," 114; Carmony (ed.), "Dole: Wabash Valley Merchant and Flatboatman," 336–38; Baxter, "Rafting on the Allegheny and Ohio," 215–16. "Journal of a Trip from Champaign County, Ohio, Down the Mississippi River to New Orleans with a Cargo of Flour (MS in Illinois State Historical Library, quoted courtesy of Illinois State Historical Library, Springfield), 9; Reynolds, "Journal, 1839–1840," 46–47; Roush (ed.) T. C. Collins—Boatman, 143.

look at their teeth, examine their backs to see if they had been whipped much, strip and feel them all over, as they would an animal. I watched while the man was being sold but left when the young woman was put up. I took my boat and went on and did not try to sell anything there." [71]

By 1859, Stacy continued, "the war feeling was running pretty high against the northerners, but I was well known and did not have any trouble." At one village, however, several men "tried to pick a fight" with Stacy and his crew and were "very insulting." T. C. Collins heard of Abraham Lincoln's election to the presidency while working aboard a flatboat near St. Louis. "I had no objections to it being that way," he remembered, "but I could not believe it at all." Soon he "saw the war coming" and began to work his way back to his Ohio home. Miles Stacy "was in New Orleans March 4, 1861, when Lincoln was first inaugurated. After that I went up and stopped at Lake Providence but I could tell it was time that I was getting home. . . . About two weeks after I got home all travel and transportation between the north and the south ended." Stacy enlisted in the 36th Ohio Volunteer Infantry, "served over [three] years in the Civil War," and "was honorably discharged Dec. 1, 1864." He "was commissioned Captain of Co. K. 36th O.V.I. April 28, 1864," Stacy stated proudly in the conclusion of his flatboating memoirs, and so had "the title [of captain] from the Civil War as well as a flatboat Captain." [72]

While Stacy and many other rivermen prepared to fight in the Civil War, a former boatman left his home in Illinois for Washington, D.C., where he was to serve as president of the United States. Twenty-eight years after he made his last flatboat trip down the Mississippi to New Orleans, Abraham Lincoln prepared to deal with the greatest crisis ever faced by an American president.

71. Stacy, "Reminiscences of Captain Miles Stacy," 16–17.
72. *Ibid.,* 17–18; Roush (ed.), *T. C. Collins—Boatman,* 143–44, 150.

SEVEN

Myths and Other Realities

About the winter of 1837 [I] took a [flatboat] trip to New Orleans with [my] brother.
- *It was the first [time I] was over twenty miles from home. . . . I was proud to get
home to tell the family what wonders I had seen, of all the big towns and the big steamboats and of all the negroes, I thought I had seen most of the world. Had to tell all the
girls in the neighborhood. I thought I was the biggest man in the neighborhood.*

—Manasseh Barney Slawson

Historian Frederick Jackson Turner often reminisced fondly of his
childhood on the vanishing Wisconsin frontier of the 1860s and 1870s,
and figuring importantly in his memories were the rivermen of the
Upper Mississippi and its tributary streams. A native of Portage, Turner remembered "my boyhood days, when the Wisconsin River rafts
came down and tied up at Portage, when the red-shirted, profane,
hard-drinking, and virile Irishmen came ashore and took possession.
Talk about he-men and red blood! They had it, 100%." Turner's memories of these "red-shirted Irish raftsmen" later figured in his work as a
historian when, in *The Rise of the New West,* he depicted the Ohio and
Mississippi boatmen as "a turbulent and reckless population, living on
the country through which they passed, fighting and drinking in true
'half-horse, half-alligator' style." Turner's depiction of Alligator Horse
boatmen was just one small facet of his theory of the significance of
the frontier in American history. In Turner's view, it was the frontier
lifestyle that molded boatmen into a rugged and independent group of
men. If, as Turner argued, the frontier experience produced a unique
American character, then the boatmen (along with other Westerners
such as trappers, yeoman farmers, scouts, and cowhands) were living
proof of the impact of the frontier on American society.[1]

1. Ray Allen Billington, "Young Fred Turner," *Wisconsin Magazine of History,* XLVI
(Autumn, 1962), 40–41, 44; Frederick Jackson Turner, *The Rise of the New West, 1819–*

As Ray Allen Billington has shown, however, Turner's memory "was as fallible as that of most humans, endowing the recalled scenes of his boyhood with a romance that they scarcely possessed." Turner's depiction of rivermen is just one example of his bent for artistic history, but the purpose here is not to criticize Turner. Frederick Jackson Turner was a great American historian and literary artist, and the Alligator Horse was just one of several tools he used to create his art—his grand vision of life on the American frontier.[2]

The men who actually worked the flats, keels, and rafts of early America bore only an indirect relationship to the Alligator Horse of Frederick Jackson Turner's America. The early, presteam rivermen were, it is true, hard-drinking, gambling, violent "he-men," but they were not, in the final analysis, Alligator Horses. Alligator Horses were romantic, swashbuckling, and compelling characters, whereas—to repeat a point I have emphasized throughout this work—there was absolutely nothing romantic, swashbuckling, or compelling about the poor, sick, womanless, alcoholic drifters who worked the Ohio and Mississippi rivers during the late eighteenth and early nineteenth centuries. With the advent of the Steamboat Age, the character of the western boatmen changed—but not in the direction of the Alligator Horse. The post-1823 rivermen became more civilized; many of them settled down to homes and families and were in most ways indistinguishable from their more sedentary countrymen. These rivermen became Alligator Horses only in their (or their countrymen's) wildest imaginations.

To students of American society and culture, the Alligator Horse is more important than his real-life counterpart, the western boatman. Like all folk heroes, the Alligator Horse served as a symbol for Americans—a fulfillment of their desires and fantasies. And although Americans in the nineteenth and twentieth centuries alike have identified with the Alligator Horse, it was Jacksonian and pre–Civil War America—from approximately 1828 to 1861—that really took this character to its heart. During that era, scores of Mike Fink stories appeared in newspapers and magazines, as did tales of other Alligator Horse river-

1829 (New York, 1906), 102–103; Turner, "The Significance of the Frontier in American History," ed. Harold P. Simonson (New York, 1966), 27–58.

2. Billington, "Young Fred Turner," 40; Harold P. Simonson, "Frontier History as Art," *Antioch Review,* XXIV (Summer, 1964), 201–11.

men. George Caleb Bingham's first painting entitled *The Jolly Flat-boatmen* appeared in 1846 and achieved a smashing success. Bingham soon put three more versions of *The Jolly Flatboatmen* on canvas and produced a score of popular river paintings that were imitated by many other artists. In "Our Old Feuillage," Walt Whitman sang the praises of boatmen "danc[ing] to the sound of the banjo or fiddle," and boatmen's songs were sung in theaters and minstrel shows. The Davy Crockett almanacs commanded a huge national audience and further fueled the Alligator Horse craze. Jacksonian society was infatuated with the Alligator Horse, and in this sense a study of the Alligator Horse is ultimately a study of the psyche of Jacksonian and pre–Civil War America.[3]

Beginning with Alexis de Tocqueville's analysis of American society in the 1830s, a number of observers and scholars have assessed the tensions and frustrations of the turbulent Jacksonian epoch. It is difficult for us today to fathom the stress Americans endured while undergoing the change from an agricultural to an industrial society, all the while bitterly debating the slavery question and the looming sectional crisis. There have been other critical junctures in American history, but this period surely ranks with the most important of them. An exciting and crucial time, it was also extremely confusing and unsettling—and it was in this milieu that Americans first became nostalgic for what seemed, to many of them, a simpler and more virtuous frontier past.[4]

3. Walter Blair and Franklin J. Meine (eds.), *Half Horse, Half Alligator: The Growth of the Mike Fink Legend* (Chicago, 1956), 19, 29. Blair and Meine charted the patterns of publication for existing Mike Fink stories as follows:

1828–1840	10 stories and reprints
1841–1850	24 stories and reprints
1851–1860	23 stories and reprints
1861–1870	1 story and reprint
1871–1880	4 stories and reprints
1881–1890	7 stories and reprints
1891–1900	3 stories and reprints

4. Alexis de Tocqueville, *Democracy in America* (2 vols.; 1835; rpr. New York, 1945); Marvin Meyers, *The Jacksonian Persuasion: Politics and Belief* (Stanford, 1957); John William Ward, *Andrew Jackson, Symbol for an Age* (New York, 1968). Although encompassing a far greater sweep of American history than these works, Henry Nash Smith's *Virgin Land: The American West as Symbol and Myth* (New York, 1950) has had an important influence on my own ideas concerning Jacksonian Americans' yearning for a frontier past.

The Jacksonian scene in many ways evinced this yearning for the vanishing agrarian Republic. The political spotlight was on Old Hickory, the Hero of New Orleans, and later Old Tip, the Hard Cider and Log Cabin candidate of 1840. Culturally, there flourished James Fenimore Cooper's *Leatherstocking Tales,* New England's Major Jack Downing, the Davy Crockett almanacs, and, of course, Mike Fink and his Alligator Horse brethren. In this context, it is no surprise that Mike was often labeled the Last of the Boatmen, for he symbolized the vanishing frontier. Mike was pitted against the steamboat, the symbol of industrial society, in much the same way that John Henry later challenged the steam-driven hammer. "The rifle won't make a man a living now—he must turn nigger and work," Mike laments to his crew before setting out for the Rockies. "If the forests continue to be used up, I may yet be smothered in the settlement. Boys, this 'ere life won't do." [5]

On a less symbolic level, Jacksonian Americans were envious of what they falsely perceived to be the advantages of working as a riverman. They imagined being boatmen in much the same way that some Americans today secretly fantasize about working as truck drivers or rodeo cowboys, and wave wistfully at the lone railroad engineer as he passes by. Why? Mobility is a key, I think. The western boatmen traveled—they were on the move, visiting new places, experiencing new adventures, and "seeing the elephant" on what seemed to be a daily basis. To those dissatisfied with their own sedentary, routine lives, this perpetual motion was (and is) very appealing. The boatmen were detached from the norms of society in both a literal and a symbolic sense: they drifted away from the banality of life on the bank every time they shipped aboard a southbound flat. Thus they appeared to be rebels, nonconformists, or—as Richard E. Oglesby has suggested—some of "America's first dropouts." [6]

A feeling of envy toward those one perceives to be free of the restrictions of the workaday world seems to me quite normal. People unhappy with their lives alleviate their regrets through fantasy and wish-fulfillment. When all is said and done, most people lack the

5. Thomas Bangs Thorpe, "The Disgraced Scalp-Lock," in Blair and Meine (eds.), *Half Horse, Half Alligator*, 30–31, 71.

6. Richard E. Oglesby, "The Western Boatman: Half Horse, Half Myth," in John Francis McDermott (ed.), *Travelers on the Western Waters* (Urbana, 1970), 253–55.

courage and, ultimately, the desire to abandon their "dull" lives, and so they continue to fantasize and wave at truck drivers and railroadmen. In the Jacksonian and pre–Civil War era, they waved at flatboatmen. "The flat boats we met . . . are so picturesque," Harriet Martineau, safely ensconced in her luxurious steamboat cabin, observed wistfully, "that some of us proposed building a flat boat on the Ohio, and floating down to New Orleans at our leisure." Ohioan William Cooper Howells "often watched [the flatboats] from the bank of the river with longing envy. To think of being always on the river where there was no confinement to close quarters, and where you could stand on the water's edge and fish, and watch the passing shore, with all its changes of scene, to me was enchantment." The Reverend Timothy Flint best summed up both the myth and the reality of flatboating in his classic account of 1828:

> All the toil, and danger, and exposure, and accidents of this long and perilous voyage, are hidden, however, from the inhabitants, who contemplate the boats floating by their dwellings on beautiful spring mornings. . . . At this time there is no visible danger, or call for labor. The boat takes care of itself; and little do the beholders imagine, how different a scene may be presented in half an hour. Meantime one of the hands scrapes a violin, and others dance. Greetings, or rude defiances, or trials of wit, or proffers of love to the girls on the shore, or saucy messages, are scattered between them and the spectators along the banks. The boat glides on, until it disappears behind the point of wood. . . . These scenes . . . have a charm for the imagination, which . . . present the image of a tempting and charming youthful existence, that almost inspires a wish, that we were boatmen.
>
> No wonder, that the young, along the banks of the great streams, should detest the labors of the field, and embrace every opportunity, either openly, or, if minors, covertly to escape, and devote themselves to the pernicious employment of boating.[7]

A less charming aspect of some Americans' attraction to the Alligator Horse also demands our scrutiny, however, and that is the fas-

---

7. Harriet Martineau, *Retrospect of Western Travel* (3 vols.; 1838; rpr. New York, 1969), II, 178; William Cooper Howells, *Recollections of Life in Ohio from 1813 to 1840* (1895; rpr. Gainesville, Fla., 1963), 85; Timothy Flint, *A Condensed Geography and History of the Western States, or the Mississippi Valley* (2 vols.; 1828; rpr. Gainesville, Fla., 1970), I, 232–33.

cination with violence. To the twentieth-century mind, the Alligator Horse often appears to be a crude and violent character. As I have shown, this mystique was based on a grain of truth: the rivermen of the presteamboat days were a tough, rowdy set, some of whom regularly got drunk on rotgut whiskey, made general nuisances of themselves, and beat the living daylights out of anyone who did not like it. As the Mississippi Valley became more civilized in the nineteenth century, this violent behavior of the early days declined considerably. Yet it was exactly at this time that stories of boatmen's violence became popular, and many of the tales were not very pretty. Today we can smile while reading about Mike Fink's misadventures with the hornets' nest and Deacon Smith's bull, or the image of him poling his keel up Third Street in Louisville. The tale of his covering his girlfriend with dry leaves and setting them on fire because she had smiled at another man, however, is distinctly less entertaining to most of us. The same applies to the story of his shooting a whiskey cup from between a woman's thighs to test her fidelity. Mike had some endearing qualities, but in the final analysis the Mike Fink of legend was the kind of fellow who amused himself by shooting the heel off a black man's foot, all the while basking in the adulation of his fellow Alligator Horses and the reading public.[8]

True, some contemporaries condemned this folkloric violence— Mike Fink and his Alligator Horse cronies were not without detractors. For most Americans during the Jacksonian and pre–Civil War periods, however, the Alligator Horse was a hero, not a villain. Interestingly, many upright admirers dealt with the Alligator Horse's failings through rationalization and managed somehow to have their cake and eat it too. In his "historical" 1855 article, "Remembrances of the Mississippi," Thomas Bangs Thorpe admitted that the western boatmen "committed, it is true, great excesses" and often defied the law, but he contended that the rivermen obeyed their *own* code, in which "fair play was a jewel," and that they "could be entrusted with uncounted sums of money" without fear of dishonesty. "In difficulties between persons," Thorpe informed his readers, the boatmen "invari-

8. Charles Cist, *The Cincinnati Miscelleny; or, Antiquities of the West* (Cincinnati, 1845), 156–57; Henry Howe, "A Talk with a Veteran Boatman," in *Historical Collections of Ohio* (2 vols.; Columbus, 1888), I, 322.

ably espoused the cause of the weaker party, and took up the quarrels of the aged, whether in the right or wrong." There are a number of such accounts rationalizing the boatmen's violence by arguing for their inherent honesty and virtue. Through a strange twist of mind, many Americans managed to perceive the Alligator Horse simultaneously as a "good guy" and a bad one. Mark Twain later enshrined this ambiguity when, in *Life on the Mississippi,* he described the boatmen as "rude, uneducated . . . heavy drinkers, coarse frolickers . . . [and] braggarts yet, in the main, honest, trustworthy, faithful to promises and duty and often picturesquely magnanimous."[9]

Many Americans, on the other hand, felt no compulsion whatsoever to rationalize the violence of the Alligator Horse; they looked upon his crude behavior with awe and admiration. In this sense the Alligator Horse became something of an alter ego, a darker side with which law-abiding citizens could secretly identify even while following the norms of civilized society. This kind of wish-fulfillment demonstrates, to my mind, that although antebellum Americans were incurably romantic, they were at the same time peculiarly romantic. They venerated the noble Daniel Boone and Leatherstocking, but simultaneously admired the crude Davy Crockett and Big Mike Fink. A flair for violence seems to have commanded their respect. The great irony, of course, is that most Americans of the Jacksonian era would not have fared too well among the men they chose to admire. Mike Fink was not a very pleasant fellow. Nor were his Alligator Horse brethren who, in Harden E. Taliaferro's *Fisher's River,* kept "their thumb-nails oiled and trimmed sharp as hawk's claws. Ask them why, they would reply, 'To feel fur a feller's eye-strings, and make him tell the news.'"[10]

9. For a scathing contemporary view see Blair and Meine (eds.), *Half Horse, Half Alligator,* 83. See also Thomas Bangs Thorpe, "Remembrances of the Mississippi," *Harper's New Monthly Magazine,* XII (December, 1855), 31; S. Wilkerson, "Early Recollections of the West," *American Pioneer,* II (June, 1843), 273; Emerson Gould, *Fifty Years on the Mississippi; or, Gould's History of River Navigation* (St. Louis, 1889), 54; James Hall, *Notes on the Western States* (Philadelphia, 1838), 220; James T. Lloyd, *Lloyd's Steamboat Directory* (Cincinnati, 1856), 35; Charles Cist, "Last of the Girty's," *Western Boatman,* I (June, 1848), 127–35; Constance Rourke, *American Humor: A Study of the National Character* (New York, 1959), 54; Richard M. Dorson, *America in Legend: Folklore from the Colonial Period to the Present* (New York, 1973), 92; Samuel Clemens [Mark Twain], *Life on the Mississippi* (1874; rpr. New York, 1960), 10.

10. Oglesby, "Half Horse, Half Myth," in McDermott (ed.), *Travelers on Western*

To Americans living in the increasingly complex and volatile Jacksonian era, the Alligator Horse provided a release, a wish-fulfillment through which they could realize their most farfetched fantasies. Some of these fantasies were violent, but some were not—the nice thing about the Alligator Horse was that he was such a versatile fellow. He could be a bad guy, or he could be a rustic "jolly flatboatman" à la Bingham, all at the same moment. His personality was as split as that of his admirers.

Among the biggest fans of the Alligator Horse were the rivermen themselves. It is ironic that the men who actively engaged in this trade should have embraced such an utter misrepresentation of their lifestyle, but like their fellow citizens, the boatmen needed to fantasize. Boating was not a particularly easy or remunerative occupation, but it did have one unrivaled fringe benefit—it had a mystique. Professional boatmen were all too familiar with the disadvantages of their calling, but they enjoyed the fact that the average American knew nothing at all about its drawbacks and rather wished that he, too, could become a riverman. Even though status and mystique did not fatten the paycheck, they helped to salve the ego. Flatboatmen were always objects of curiosity and envy in their villages and, upon their return, held court at the corner store, recounting the splendid details of their latest voyage down the mighty Mississippi. To their fellow villagers, many of whom had never traveled anywhere in their lives, these veterans of the river must have seemed heroic.[11]

The curious blend of myth and reality in the boatmen's self-perceptions is fascinating. As shown in Chapter 6, it was the rivermen of the Steamboat Age who first began to cultivate a self-image and to grasp the romantic aspects of their trade. At the same time, these men were daily confronted with the difficult, boring, and utterly unromantic aspects of real river life. This paradox made for some interesting

---

Waters, 253. Taliaferro quoted in Dickson A. Bruce, *Violence and Culture in the Antebellum South* (Austin, Tex., 1979), 228–29. For thorough discussions of American violence see Bruce, *Violence and Culture*, 89–113; W. Eugene Hollon, *Frontier Violence: Another Look* (New York, 1974); and Richard Maxwell Brown, *Strain of Violence: Historical Studies of American Violence and Vigilantism* (New York, 1975). D. H. Lawrence used the term *wish-fulfillment* to describe a less sordid western hero, Leatherstocking, in *Studies in Classic American Literature* (1923; rpr., New York, 1977), 54.

11. Archibald Shaw (ed.), *History of Dearborn County, Indiana* (Indianapolis, 1915), 448.

cognitive dissonance. A Terre Haute, Indiana, flatboatman, for instance, wavered between myth and reality in an elaborate travel journal he wrote in 1845. He was delighted to see "a very pretty girl . . . gaz[ing] at us for some time with such earnestness as though she wanted to know something about Flatboating," and he also wrote at length of sleeping under the stars and floating serenely through a verdant green landscape. "There is something more romantic than you can imagine," he gushed, "in breakfasting on the deck of a broadhorn on a fine morning floating down the river." After ten days afloat, however, this Hoosier's enthusiasm began to wane. Soon he was complaining continually of the hard work, heat, and mosquitoes. Arriving at last in Memphis, the erstwhile romantic "put on a coat and hat in a most outrageous hurry," ascended the bluff "to the Exchange Hotel, and got a Room to myself [with] a Musquitoe Bar. . . . Oh Heavens what luxury. The Pleasure was indescribable." [12]

Riverman George Forman's memoirs demonstrate the same split personality, but in a more subtle manner. Forman's reminiscence, written many years after his stint as a riverman, is an honest depiction of the rigors of boating, and at times paints quite a grim picture of life on the western rivers in the years 1849–1851. At one point Forman describes in minute detail a spring lumber-rafting trip from the St. Croix River in Wisconsin to St. Louis. On the way, his crew suffered many hardships. For example, because their raft kept breaking up and running aground, Forman and his fellow raftsmen spent much of the trip neck-deep in the ice-cold water of the Upper Mississippi River. This depiction of river life is anything but romantic, yet only a few pages earlier Forman had described rafting as "a pleasant and easy life floating down the stream looking like a floating village, not working half the time, swimming and boating. . . . And when off watch we would go ashore on the Islands and gather grapes or rob the farmers of Green Corn, Watermelons, Shoats (Young Pigs), or rob hen roosts. So that the Jolly raftsmen were the terror of the river. . . . We generally had some fiddlers aboard, and altogether we had good times." The abrupt change in Forman's tone is fascinating, as is his use of the phrase "Jolly raftsmen" and his reference to fiddlers. Was Forman,

12. "The Beauties of Flatboating; or, Journal of a Trip to New Orleans," in "Atalantian" (MS in Indiana Historical Society, Indianapolis), II, entry for August 4, 1845.

who wrote his memoirs twenty-five years after his boating days, describing a George Caleb Bingham scene because he knew his readers expected it? Was he trying to appear literary and romantic? Or was he in fact a true romantic who imagined himself a "jolly raftsman"?[13]

In fairness to Forman and other rivermen who evinced this split personality, it must again be said that boating was itself a two-sided proposition. River work could prove arduous and even deadly, but it also entailed long periods of idleness and leisure. In any case, one does not have to be an incurable romantic to see that embarking on a 1,500-mile voyage down the Ohio and Mississippi valleys to St. Louis or New Orleans must have seemed a grand adventure. Professional rivermen embraced these romantic aspects of their calling, but they simultaneously knew all too well its hardships and drawbacks. They wrestled with this contradiction on a daily basis, and many left the river forever because of it. The romance won out for those who stayed, and perhaps a strong dose of romance was a prerequisite for any professional riverman. As T. C. Collins wrote:

> There is not one man out of twenty, who makes anything flat boating, but there was a charm about it I could not resist until I had given [twenty-four] years of my life experimenting, and I was not sorry. Flat boating is like a great many other occupations, it has its ups and downs. Sometimes they have it rough and hard, then again it is comparatively easy. There is a charm about it that one can hardly account for, unless it's because one is on the move nearly all the time. Almost every trip I took, I would say: "This is my last," but, soon as I got home and rested a few days, I wanted to go again, and so it was with most of those who tried it.[14]

Unlike the western boatmen, most Americans of the pre–Civil War days did not have to wrestle with the realities of flatboating on a daily basis. To their minds there was no conflict at all between the Alligator Horse and the actual Ohio and Mississippi rivermen. All boatmen became Alligator Horses, and this case of mistaken identity has

13. George Forman, "Biographical Sketch of Life and Ancestry of Geo. Forman of Stratford-Ontario, Canada Written in 1875 and 1883 by Himself," ed. E. Luella Galliver (Typescript in Western History Research Center, University of Wyoming, Laramie), 112, 119–22.

14. Herbert L. Roush, Sr. (ed.), *The Adventures of T. C. Collins—Boatman: Twenty-Four Years on the Western Waters, 1849–1873,* (Baltimore, 1985), 66.

provided us with a rich folklore and several clues to the psyche of Jacksonian America. In the process, the real Ohio and Mississippi river boatmen have been obscured completely, but that probably does not matter. In studying history, perhaps one should always ask: What is more important—the way things were, or the way people *thought* they were? Is myth any less real than reality? In the case of the Alligator Horse, the mythology assumed a life of its own.

Last of the Boatmen

My first hand knowledge of flatboating was just an afterglow of a factor that had been vital to our family and our town for a long time. How eagerly I listened each year for the throaty whistle of steam boats which meant the return of family members who had taken a flatboat "down the river." And we were sure that in addition to a returning brother there would be a bunch of bananas—a luxury in that day. Too, I enjoyed the annual September exploration of flatboats, the loading, and the smell of new lumber. So you see I had a bit of flatboating. And long afterward, at a New York art exhibition, I found a picture of a flatboat painted by an early American artist. I wonder if any others who viewed that painting had ever heard of a flatboat?

—Abby May Warren

It is ironic that two of the "last of the boatmen" were women. Actually, they were little girls, for in the 1880s, Abby May Warren and Lucie Rieman each accompanied her merchant navigator father on a flatboat trip from Indiana. "The entire trip from Natchez to New Orleans seemed indescribably lovely," Mrs. Warren reminisced more than fifty years later, adding that New Orleans was "over-whelming to a little girl from Rising Sun [Indiana]." Ten-year-old Lucie Rieman in fact made two trips during the course of 1884 and 1885, "attended the wonderful Cotton Exposition" in New Orleans, and later saw "the Mardi Gras, which so impressed me that I am thrilled [today] at the memory of that gorgeous parade." Writing in 1944, Mrs. Rieman noted that "the last trips from Aurora [Indiana] were made in 1893 when flatboating ceased to be a profitable business." Like "all 'old flatboaters' I would like to make the trip again," she concluded. "But now few remain of the men who owned and operated flatboats."[1]

Flatboating died slowly. Even before the Civil War ended, flatboatmen resumed shipments south and hoped to pick up where they had left off during the heyday of the late 1840s and early 1850s. This was not to be. The forces inimical to flatboat commerce continued to

1. Abby May Warren to T. W. Records, July 20, October 12, 1944, in T. W. Records (ed.), "Flatboats," *Indiana Magazine of History,* XLII (December, 1946), 336–37; Lucie Rieman to Records, September 9, 24, 1944, *ibid.,* 332–33.

grow. Shippers continued to shift their business to steamboats, canal boats, and, ultimately, railroads. Indeed, the flatboatmen's plight foreshadowed a general post–Civil War collapse of *all* river commerce, steamboats included. Railroads proved to be the wave of the future, and by 1865 products that formerly had floated south on the Ohio and Mississippi now rolled east on the tracks of a mammoth national rail network.[2]

Steamboatmen struggled to hold onto at least a portion of the trade. They lobbied for federally funded river improvements, and the government responded with millions of dollars in aid. More money was appropriated for river improvements during the 1880s than in the entire history of improvements prior to that time. On the Ohio River the army engineers removed snags, dredged sandbars, constructed wing dams and, starting in 1879, built a series of locks and dams that would one day ensure year-round navigation. In 1879 also, Congress created the Mississippi River Commission to deepen the Mississippi's channel, build levees, and install beacon lights and buoys to aid steamboatmen. Yet even this massive aid could not resurrect the moribund steamboat economy.[3]

The efforts to deepen channels and facilitate navigation with wing dams and locks and dams, which helped steamboatmen, proved utterly devastating to flatboatmen and lumber and log raftsmen. These unmechanized rivermen lacked the sophisticated steering apparatus and backing-up capability absolutely necessary to steer clear of a wing dam or negotiate a lock. Flatboatmen and raftsmen vehemently opposed this latest round of improvements, but no one listened. Their difficulties further escalated a trend that already was revolutionizing

2. For river commerce during the war, see Ellis M. Coulter, "Commercial Intercourse with the Confederacy in the Mississippi Valley, 1861–1865," *Mississippi Valley Historical Review,* V (March, 1919), 377–95; New Orleans *Tribune,* January 11, 1865. For the demise of postbellum river commerce, see Erik F. Haites and James Mak, "Ohio and Mississippi River Transportation, 1810–1860," *Explorations in Economic History,* VIII (Winter, 1970), 175–77; Harry N. Scheiber, "The Ohio-Mississippi Flatboat Trade: Some Reconsiderations," in David M. Ellis (ed.), *The Frontier in American Development: Essays in Honor of Paul Wallace Gates* (Ithaca, 1970), 286, 290; R. B. Way, "Commerce on the Lower Mississippi in the Period 1830–1860," *Proceedings of the Mississippi Valley Historical Association,* X (1919–21), 59–65.

3. Issac Lippincott, "A History of River Improvement," *Journal of Political Economy,* XXII (July, 1914), 649–60; Louis C. Hunter, *Steamboats on Western Rivers: An Economic and Technological History* (Cambridge, Mass., 1949), 209–15.

the boating trade: the towing of log and lumber rafts and flatboats or, as they soon began to be called, "barges." There are instances of raft and flatboat tows prior to the Civil War, but it was during the postwar years that towing became the dominant mode of transport on the western rivers.[4]

As their trade declined, ambitious flatboatmen became involved in towing schemes. The most common system was to float south, sell out, then reload a new cargo, hire a steamer to tow the flatboat north, sell out again, and repeat the process over and over. Lucie Rieman's father engaged in this endeavor on a regular basis during the 1880s, as did a great many other flatboatmen. The natural next step for the flatboatman was to hire his flat towed in *both* directions. This was safer, easier, and ultimately less expensive. When steamboat entrepreneurs began to build their own flatboats for this purpose, the middleman (flatboatman) was eliminated. During the post–Civil War years, Ohio and Mississippi valley shipyards began to construct thousands of flatboats without living quarters, calling these craft, in the new terminology, "barges." Thus, in a newspaper article entitled "Flatboats Are Played Out," a New Orleans writer informed his readership: "Barges seem to have superseded flatboats. Workmen are at this time picking away at the . . . flatboat landing. . . . Probably we will never again see the old days of the flatboats revived, they being at best a barbarous Noah's Ark sort of an institution, not equal in their monthly voyages to the urgent demands of the age."[5]

A few flatboatmen continued to ply their trade until the turn of the century. Along shallow, isolated tributary streams such as the Upper Cumberland and Tennessee rivers, where steamers could not always navigate, flatboats, keels, and lumber and log rafts continued to prove useful. Some flatboatmen, too, found work transporting oil and coal on the Allegheny and Upper Ohio throughout the postwar years. These rivermen must have appeared rather odd as they floated down the western rivers, weaving in and out of the paths of steamboats, in

4. Hunter, *Steamboats on Western Rivers,* 209, 567–84; Walter A. Blair, *A Raft Pilot's Log* (Cleveland, 1930).

5. Records (ed.), "Flatboats," 333–36; Herbert L. Roush, Sr. (ed.), *The Adventures of T. C. Collins—Boatman: Twenty-Four Years on the Western Waters, 1849–1873* (Baltimore, 1985), 155–219; New Orleans *Times,* November 23, 1866. For the development of barge commerce in general, see Hunter, *Steamboats on Western Rivers,* 567–84. The term *barge* was earlier used to describe a preindustrial, keelboatlike craft.

view of the railroads, factories, and cities springing up along the banks. Surely these boatmen appeared anachronistic: preindustrial men in an industrial age.[6]

There are a number of firsthand accounts of these flatboatmen of the 1870s, 1880s, and 1890s, but a brief look at the extensive correspondence of Ohioan William E. Devol provides a composite picture. Devol, a descendant of a long line of Marietta, Ohio, flatboatmen, worked as a merchant navigator from 1867 to 1873, coasting apples, potatoes, and hardy produce from Marietta to the Lower Mississippi. Many of Devol's activities were typical of the boatmen of the 1823–1861 era. He hired mostly teenaged farm boys as deckhands, while his pilots were middle-aged, professional rivermen. He complained constantly of money matters and fretted over commodity prices, insurance coverage, and wharf taxes. Devol and his flatboat crews enjoyed an improved and comfortable lifestyle. They received mail on a regular basis and were able to send telegraph messages home to loved ones. They had their laundry done and ate elaborate, nutritious meals, including a Christmas dinner of roast goose and oyster pie. Flatboatmen before the war returned home on the deck of a steamboat; Devol and his crew took the train. Revealingly, William Devol's last flatboating trip, in 1873, was not really a flatboat trip at all: he lashed several of his boats together and hired a steamboat to tow them south.[7]

Even this improved, modern lifestyle could not induce William Devol to continue flatboating. As competition from steamers and railroads stiffened, he found it increasingly difficult to turn a profit. During the particularly bad winter season of 1872–1873, he wrote his wife, Bitha, complaining, "I am now taking the bitterest pill in the way of flatboating that I have ever swallowed and it is not sugar coated either." The economic depression that soon followed ended Devol's boating career, but his decision to quit was motivated personally as

6. Hunter, *Steamboats on Western Rivers*, 52–60; Steven A. Schulman, "Rafting Logs on the Upper Cumberland River," *Pioneer America*, VI (1974), 14–24; Charles Henry Ambler, *A History of Transportation in the Ohio Valley* (Glendale, Calif., 1932), 300; New Orleans *Times*, November 23, 1866.

7. For postbellum flatboating, see H. A. Trotter to John [?], December 15, 1870, in John Brandenburg Collection, Indiana Historical Society, Indianapolis; Arkansas City (Kans.) *Traveller* August 21, 1878; Louisville *City Courier*, April 9, 1939; Records (ed.), "Flatboats," 323–42; Roush (ed.), *T. C. Collins—Boatman*, 155–219; Robert Leslie Jones (ed.), "Flatboating Down the Ohio and the Mississippi, 1867–1873: Correspondence and Diaries of the William Devol Family of Marietta, Ohio," *Ohio State Archeological and Historical Quarterly*, LIX (July and October, 1950), 287–309, 385–418.

well as financially: Bitha was dead-set against his flatboating. "I am completely out of patience with flatboating," she wrote him, imploring, "Don't ask me to agree to your going again, for I can't do it." In January of 1873, Devol assured his wife that she would "be enabled to keep me at home here after." He had taken his last flatboat trip.[8]

Like Devol, thousands of diehard flatboatmen gave up the profession during the 1870s, 1880s, and 1890s. Captain Miles Stacy, who had returned briefly to the river after serving in the Civil War, soon gave up boating because, as he wrote later, it was not as profitable "as it had been before the War." Hurt by economic depression in 1873, T. C. Collins also sold his boats. Years later he reminisced: "Times got hard on the river and I concluded that I would get out of it by degrees and perhaps quit altogether. The dear old river that I had become so well acquainted with I hated to abandon, notwithstanding [the hardships] I had seen on it. It seems like home to me but—it seemed I was to drift into a new business." The remaining flatboatmen slowly followed suit. As Lucie Rieman recalled, Aurora, Indiana, saw its last flat depart in 1893, and by 1900 flatboating was, for all practical purposes, gone forever.[9]

In the meantime, our old friend the Alligator Horse was himself undergoing quite a transformation. Although remaining a jaunty Lower Mississippi Valley folk type, he was developing a personality as two-sided as that of flatboating itself. Around the turn of the century, the Alligator part of him became associated with the burgeoning black jazz scene in New Orleans, where musicians and aficionados of their work began to refer to one another as "alligators." In jazz parlance, an "alligator" was a hipster musician and, later, a jitterbug enthusiast. Thus, this side of the Alligator Horse lost his penchant for violence, but remained an individualistic folk idol. He is enshrined in the jazzy folk expression "See you later, Alligator!"[10]

As for the Horse, he took up with a rather different crowd—the

8. Jones (ed.), "Flatboating Down the Ohio and Mississippi, 1867–1873," 306, 403, 408.

9. Miles A. Stacy, "Flatboating Down Old Man River, 1849–1869: Reminiscences of Captain Miles A. Stacy as Related to His Daughter Adelaide Frost Stacy, February, 1913. Rearranged and Typed by Her, April, 1945" (Typescript in Ohio Historical Society, Campus Martius, the Museum of the Northwest Territory, Marietta, Ohio), 18; Roush (ed.), *T. C. Collins—Boatman,* 219; Records (ed.), "Flatboats," 332.

10. Stuart Berg Flexner, *Listening to America: An Illustrated History of Words and Phrases from Our Lively and Splendid Past* (New York, 1982), 23.

white farmers, ranchers, and workingmen of the South and South-west, especially Texas. To this day, many such men greet casual acquaintances with a friendly but not overly committal, "Hey, hoss!" This chopped form of "horse" also has surfaced in numerous country-and-western lyrics, but its most visible manifestation was the character of Hoss Cartwright in the TV series *Bonanza*. Although the Horse has mellowed in old age, he has not become quite as tame as the Alligator. Uttered in just the right tone and context, "hoss" can be a clear indication that the speaker does not much care for the person he is addressing. As such, "hoss" has been the prelude to more than one barroom scrap in which Mike Fink himself would have felt right at home.[11]

In 1903 the first screw-propellered steamboat journeyed up the Ohio River. Subsequent navigation improvements, the completion of locks and dams on the Ohio and Upper Mississippi, and the eventual conversion from steam to diesel-powered riverboats created the towboat technology and commerce with which modern Americans are familiar on the western rivers. Today, upon viewing a snub-nosed, 10,000-horsepower towboat pushing forty grain barges up the Lower Mississippi, one might well conclude that modern riverboating and rivermen share nothing in common with their flatboatmen ancestors of the nineteenth century.[12]

To the observant trained eye, however, there still appear some fascinating vestiges. Most obvious is the steel barge, which is simply a large, modern version of the flatboat—the shape is identical. Despite diesel engines, towboatmen today land barges and secure them with lines in a manner strikingly similar to that of the preindustrial boatmen. Modern boatmen "building tow" (connecting a "string" of barges together with steel cables and ratchets) are performing with steel and iron the same task that nineteenth-century raftsmen did with rope, leather, and sapling strips connecting "stringers" of logs or lumber for a downstream journey. And modern rivermen still adhere

---

11. Many thanks to Gerry Anders of Baton Rouge, Louisiana, for his thoughts on this subject.

12. Michael Allen, "Life on the Mississippi—Towboat-Style," *The Lookout*, LXXIV (June–July, 1982), 13–16; George P. Parkinson, Jr., and Brooks F. McCabe, Jr., "Charles Ward and the *James Rumsey*: Regional Innovation in Steam Technology on the Western Rivers," *West Virginia History*, XXXIX (January–April, 1978), 143–80.

to the antiquated flatboat (and steamboat) watch system—six hours on duty, six hours off—eight-hour-day laws notwithstanding.[13]

Like their flatboatmen predecessors, modern towboat deckhands are usually teenagers or young men, while pilots, mates, and engineers are older professional rivermen. Ohio and Mississippi river pilots are licensed nowadays, but their licenses are called, anachronistically, "western rivers licenses," despite the fact that the Mississippi Valley has not been called "the West" since the 1840s. Modern rivermen work in spurts, just like the flatboatmen, with periods of intense work followed by long rest periods. When a flatboat crew finished supper, the men would relax and lounge by the steersman's post—on the "lazy board," as it was called. Today, towboatmen eat supper and retire to the wheelhouse (where a much more complicated version of steering is conducted) to sit on a small couch—the modern "lazy board"—and swap stories before retiring for the evening.

What of the character of modern boatmen as compared with their ancestors? When asked what "sort of persons" worked on the river, one modern riverman answered quite succinctly: "The river people . . . they're just all stripes, from the sublime to the ridiculous. I've known some of them . . . [who] could quote Robert Burns by the yard . . . [while] the next one was dumb as an ox, would reach in the plate to get his mashed potatoes with his hand." Surely this description would apply to the early boatmen as well. Like their river ancestors, modern towboatmen share a great pride in their status as professional rivermen. They know their lifestyle is often lonely and filled with drudgery, yet they also know it is the only possible life for them. Modern towboatmen scorn the forty-hour week, rush-hour traffic, and many other tedious aspects of life on "the bank," as they disdainfully refer to the rest of the world. Like flatboatmen, they tend to romanticize their calling. Despite all of its drawbacks, the towboatman's job has retained a mystique. Towboatmen know very well the envious look in the landsman's eye as a crowd of awed spectators watches them "lock through" at Al-

13. This paragraph and most of the remainder of the Epilogue is based on my personal recollection of three years as a towboat deckhand and cook on the Upper and Lower Mississippi, Arkansas, Ouachita, St. Croix, and Illinois rivers and the Gulf of Mexico. I also have consulted Edwin and Louise Rosskam's *Towboat River* (New York, 1948) and Jane M. Curry, *The River's in My Blood: Riverboat Pilots Tell Their Stories* (Lincoln, Neb., 1983).

ton, Illinois, on a Sunday afternoon on their way to Pittsburgh, Minneapolis, or New Orleans. A towboat mate once said to me: "You tell someone that you work in a grocery store, or that you're a mechanic or a plumber, and they'll just look at you, 'cause that's nothing special. But you tell them you're a *towboatman* and . . . well, that's got a ring to it."[14]

14. Captain Fred Way, Jr., quoted in Curry, *The River's in My Blood,* 264; Jimmy Dale Berryhill quoted in Allen, "Life on the Mississippi—Towboat-Style," 16.

Two Songs and a Poem

The Boatmen's Dance (De Boatmen's Dance)

The following version of "The Boatmen's Dance" is the original, written by American minstrel Dan Emmett as "De Boatmen's Dance" and published by C. H. Keith of Boston in 1843. There are many different versions. The song has been attributed to steamboatmen and flatboatmen alike, but it reached the common workingmen via professional entertainers, not oral tradition. The tune paints an image of the archetypal Alligator Horse.

> High row, de boatmen row,
> Floatin' down de river de Ohio.
> De boatmen dance, de boatmen sing,
> De boatmen up to ebry ting;
> An when de boatman gets on shore,
> He spends his cash an works for more.
>
> Den dance de boatmen dance,
> O dance de boatmen dance,
> O dance all night till broad daylight,
> An go home wid de gals in de morning.
>
> De oyster boat should keep to de shore,
> De fishin smack should venture more;
> De schooner sails before de wind,
> De steamboat leaves a streak behind.
> O dance, etc.
>
> I went on board de odder day,
> To see what de boatmen had to say;
> Dar I let my passion loose,
> An dey cram me in de callaboose.
> O dance, etc.
>
> I've come dis time, I'll come no more,
> Let me loose, I'll go on shore;

For dey whole hoss, an dey a bully crew,
Wid a hoosier mate an a captin too.
O dance, etc.

When you go to de boatmen's ball,
Dance wid my wife, or dont dance at all;
Sky blue jacket an tarpaulin hat,
Look out my boys for de nine tail cat.
O dance, etc.

De boatman is a thrifty man,
Dars none can do as de boatman can;
I neber see a putty gal in my life,
But dat she was a boatman's wife.
O dance, etc.

When de boatman blows his horn,
Look out old man your hog is gone;
He cotch my sheep, he cotch my shoat,
Den put em in a bag an toat em to de boat.
O dance, etc.

French-Canadian Boatmen's Rowing Song

In 1810 traveler John Bradbury recorded the words to this rowing song he heard sung in call-and-response pattern by his French-Canadian keelboat crew. The translation into English below is also Bradbury's. See John Bradbury, *Travels in the Interior of America, 1809–1811,* in Reuben Gold Thwaites (ed.), *Early Western Travels, 1748–1846* (32 vols.; Cleveland, 1904–1907), V, 39–40 n. 10.

Derrière chez nous, il y a un etang,
    Ye, ye ment.
Trois canards s'en vont baignans,
Tous du long de la rivière,
Légèrement ma bergère,
    Légèrement, yet ment.

Trois canards s'en vont baignans,
    Ye, ye ment.
Le fils du roi s'en va chassant,
Tous du long de la rivière,

Légèrement ma bergère,
  Légèrement, yet ment.

Le fils du roi s'en va chassant,
  Ye, ye ment.
Avec son grand fusil d'argent,
Tous du long de la rivière,
Légèrement ma bergère,
  Légèrement, yet ment.—&c. &c.

Behind our house there is a pond,
  Fal lal de ra.
There came three ducks to swim thereon,
All along the river clear,
Lightly my shepherdess dear,
  Lightly, fal de ra.

There came three ducks to swim thereon,
  Fal lal de ra.
The prince to chase them he did run,
All along the river clear,
Lightly my shepherdess dear,
  Lightly, fal de ra.

The prince to chase them he did run,
  Fal lal de ra.
And he had his great silver gun,
All along the river clear,
Lightly my shepherdess dear,
  Lightly, fal de ra.—&c. &c.

The Boatman's Horn

"The Boatman's Horn," by General William O. Butler, was originally published in the *Western Review* (Lexington, Ky.) in 1821. The poem paints an idyllic portrait of the western boatmen and is reprinted from the *Western Pennsylvania Historical Magazine,* I (1918), 26.

O, boatman! wind that horn again,
  For never did the listening air,
Upon its lambent bosom bear
  So wild, so soft, so sweet a strain!

What, though thy notes are sad and few,
    By every simple boatman blown,
Yet is each pulse to nature true,
    And melody in every tone.
How oft in boyhood's joyous days,
    Unmindful of the lapsing hours,
I've loitered on my homeward way
    By wild Ohio's bank of flowers;
While some lone boatman from the deck
    Poured his soft numbers to the tide,
As if to charm from storm and wreck
    The boat where all his fortunes ride!
Delighted Nature drank the sound,
    Enchanted echo bore it round
In whispers soft and softer still,
    From hill to plain and plain to hill,
Till e'en the thoughtless, frolic boy,
    Elate with hope and wild with joy,
Who gamboled by the river side,
    And sported with the fretting tide,
Feels something new pervade his breast,
    Change his light step, repress his jest,
Bends o'er the flood his eager ear
    To catch the sounds far off, yet dear—
Drinks the sweet draft, but knows not why
    The tear of rapture fills his eye.

Glossary

ARK. Same as FLATBOAT.

BAR. An underwater sandhill, its top near the surface of the water.

BARGE. Originally a larger version of the KEELBOAT. After the Civil War the term was appropriated to describe flatboats in tow and, eventually, the steel barges that towboats push today.

BATTEAU. French for *boat*. Also, a flat-bottomed rowboat built out of planks.

BOW. The forward portion ("front") of a boat.

BROADHORN. Same as FLATBOAT.

BUSHWACKING. A physically arduous method of moving a keelboat upstream by pulling on nearby bushes and branches.

CAPSTAN. A preindustrial version of today's power-winch capstan. Located on the bow of a boat, the capstan was used to tightly reel in lines attached to trees, docks, or other boats. This was done either to secure the boat or, occasionally, to draw it upstream (*see* WARPING).

CAPTAIN. The man in charge of a boat. Also called *patroon, master,* or *supercargo*.

CAULKING. A sealant pounded in between the boards of a boat to prevent leakage. Rope, hemp, and tar-soaked rags served this purpose.

CHECK POST. In addition to the capstan, each flatboat possessed several sturdy check posts at every corner, to which lines could be secured when landing. Also called *snubbing post*.

CHUTE. A navigable but often narrow, fast-flowing, and dangerous opening in a RAPIDS or FALLS.

COALBOAT. A large flatboat used exclusively for transporting coal during the industrial age. Eventually became the *coal barge*.

COAST. The noun describes the "German Coast," a section along the Mississippi River above New Orleans. The verb *to coast* refers to the activities of a class of flatboatmen who regularly supplied the needs of the residents of the German Coast.

CORDELLING. A method of moving a keelboat upstream. A line was attached to the bow and the crew sent ashore with the other end of the line, whereupon they literally pulled the boat upstream.

DOG WATCH. A derisive term used by rivermen to describe a work system in which they were always "on call" and had no guaranteed rest period. Thus, they were called to work "like dogs."

EDDY. A whirlpool. Boats sometimes became trapped in eddies.

FALLS. Another name for RAPIDS, especially on the Ohio and Upper Mississippi rivers.

FLATBOAT. A clumsy but functional large, rectangular, flat-bottomed boat. Flatboats constituted 90 percent of nonsteam riverboats throughout the early history of boating. Pre-1823 flatboats averaged sixty feet in length and fifteen in width and carried a crew of five. Later flatboats nearly doubled in size and crew. Flatboats usually were sided up about six feet above the water. Flatboatmen steered their craft with four long (thirty- to fifty-five-foot) oars or SWEEPS, one on each side of the boat. Also called *Flat, Ark, Kentucky Boat,* or *Broadhorn.*

FLEET. Two or more flatboats tied together in transit or secured together to the bank.

GOUGER. A short steering oar on the bow of a flatboat or raft.

GREENHORN. A boatman making his first downriver trip. Also *Greenie.*

GUNBOAT. A floating house of prostitution.

HAND. A common boatman; "deckhand."

HAWSERS. Strong ropes carried aboard all boats and used in landing and securing the craft. Also called *lines.*

KEELBOAT. The most sophisticated of presteam riverboats. Built on a keel-and-ribs frame with pointed bow, a keelboat floated downstream and could, with considerable effort, be navigated upstream by means of poling, cordelling, bushwacking, rowing, and (rarely) sailing. Keelboats averaged sixty feet in length and eight feet in width, and never flourished in great number. On the western rivers, the steamboat began to replace the keelboat as the sole upstream craft in 1811 and fairly quickly rendered the older craft extinct. Also called simply *keel.*

KENTUCKIAN. A westerner (trans-Appalachian West), especially a western boatman. Also *Kaintock* (French).

KENTUCKY BOAT. Same as FLATBOAT.

LIGHTER. A flatboat or keelboat used to temporarily take cargo off a steamer so as to "lighten" that vessel enough to enable navigation of shallow stretches of river (*see* SHOALS). Some steamers always carried a lighter in tow, and this, combined with other factors, eventually led to barge towing.

LINES. Same as HAWSERS.

LOCK AND DAM. Often simply "lock." A radical river improvement that reached the western rivers mainly in the post–Civil War years, the lock and dam backed up river water, thus insuring year-round navigation depths. Boats could "lock through" a dam by entering a lock chamber, in which the water level was raised or lowered to correspond to the depth into which the boat was heading. Unlike steamboats, flatboats and rafts lacked the navigational equipment necessary to safely negotiate a lock and dam.

MIXED LOAD. A flatboat carrying a variety of produce and goods was said to be carrying a *mixed load*. *See also* STRAIGHT LOAD.

OAR. A long pole with a plank on the end, used to steer a flatboat or raft. Flatboats had four oars—one large STEERING OAR on the stern, one starboard and one port oar, and a GOUGER on the bow. Lumber and log rafts could possess as many as forty oars. Flatboat and raft oars, also called *sweeps,* were used for navigation, not locomotion. Thus, they should not be confused with the much shorter oars used to row a skiff, batteau, or keelboat.

PATROON. From the French *patron.* Same as CAPTAIN.

PILOT. Same as STEERSMAN.

PIROGUE. A small dugout canoe.

PLANTER. A fallen tree with one end secured firmly in the river bottom and the other floating visibly above the water's surface. A hazard for boatmen. *See also* SAWYER, SNAG.

PORT. The left-hand side of a boat for an observer facing forward from the stern. Also called *larboard.*

RAFT. There were two kinds of rafts. The first were minor rivercraft made by lashing small logs together, as in Huck and Jim's raft in *Huckleberry Finn.* The second and more important kind were the much larger lumber and log rafts used throughout the nineteenth century to transport timber to and down the Upper and Lower Mississippi and Ohio rivers from their tributaries. Log rafts were constructed by roping or chaining a log perimeter around hundreds of free-floating logs. Lumber rafts were built by stacking sawed lumber several layers high and securing the boards together with sapling strips, wooden pins, leather thongs, ropes, or chain links. Rafts were built in sections called "stringers," which could be combined or separated as navigation required. Some Mississippi rafts measured 100 yards in length and 25 yards in width.

RAFTSMAN. A special type of boatman who navigated log and lumber rafts. As many as forty raftsmen were employed on a single raft.

RAPIDS. A rough, rocky, sharply-descending stretch of river, usually difficult to navigate or unnavigable, especially in times of low water.

ROW. To steer or propel a flatboat, raft, or keelboat. In flatboating and rafting, rowing was used for steering (*i.e.,* navigation), whereas in keelboating it was used for propulsion.

RUN. To move goods to market on a boat. Used as a verb or noun.

SAWYER. A fallen tree with one end secured in the river bottom and the other bobbing spasmodically above and below the surface of the water. The difference between a sawyer and a PLANTER is that a sawyer was periodically out of view, thus rendering it extremely dangerous to unsuspecting pilots. *See also* SNAG.

SCOTCH-IRISH ITCH. Any bite caused by vermin such as lice, fleas, etc. Common aboard boats. Also called *Scotch fiddle*.

SHOAL. A shallow stretch of river. Potentially dangerous because of the possibility of running a boat aground.

SHIP. Verb meaning "to secure employment on a boat"; *e.g.,* "I shipped on a southbound flat."

SKIFF. A small rowboat. Most flatboats, keels, and rafts carried a skiff on board to use for quick trips to the shore and to assist in landing operations.

SNAG. A general term for any log, stump, or "trash wood" obstruction in the river. Includes PLANTERS and SAWYERS. Also called a *Mississippi produce buyer*.

SNAG BOAT. A steamboat equipped for removing snags. Invented by Henry Miller Shreve.

SNUBBING. The means by which a flatboatman used a line ("hawser") to land a boat. A line was secured to a check post and a stationary object ashore. Then the boatman pulled in line and wrapped it around the post or released line ("paid it out") until the boat was safely ashore. Snubbing could also be used to maneuver a boat in a fleet.

SNUBBING POST. Same as CHECK POST.

STARBOARD. The right-hand side of a boat for an observer facing forward from the stern.

STEERING OAR. Located on the stern, this huge (sometimes fifty-five feet in length) oar was the most important means of guiding a flat, keel, or raft.

STEERSMAN. The boatman who manned the stern steering oar. Also called the *pilot*. Note that the steersman or pilot was not necessarily the captain of a boat.

STERN. The tail end of a boat.

STICK. To run aground on a BAR or SHOAL.

STOVE-IN. A boat that was punctured by a rock or snag was said to be *stove-in* or simply *stove*.

STRAIGHT LOAD. A flatboat carrying only one kind of produce or good was said to be carrying a *straight load*. *See also* MIXED LOAD.

SUPERCARGO. Same as CAPTAIN.

WARPING. A method of moving a keelboat upstream that was the reverse of cordelling. A rope was taken upstream and attached to a stout tree. Then the men on the boat proceeded to pull the craft toward the tree, usually with the aid of the capstan.

WING DAM. A mid-nineteenth century river improvement initiated by the Army Engineers. Made of piled rocks, wing dams jutted out from the bank and forced water toward the middle of the river, thus deepening the channel for navigational purposes. Flatboatmen and raftsmen benefited very little from wing dams because flats and rafts lacked the sophisticated steering technology necessary to avoid these structures.

WOODBOAT. A flatboat, skiff, or batteau loaded with cordwood to be sold to passing steamboats. Woodboats docked at "woodyards" and were manned by "woodboatmen." Some steamers bought the entire outfit, lashed the boat alongside, and burned the contents for fuel en route.

Bibliographical Essay

Researching the western boatmen, like sailing a flatboat from the Upper Mississippi to New Orleans, can prove an arduous yet rewarding endeavor. The following essay provides a general survey of the primary and secondary literature of riverboating. Researchers should also consult the bibliography of my "Alligator Horses: Ohio and Mississippi River Flatboatmen, Keelboatmen, and Raftsmen, 1763–1860" (Ph.D. dissertation, University of Washington, 1985) as a navigational guide before shoving off into the currents of river research.

Manuscripts and Published Boatmen's Accounts

The headwaters of river studies are the historical archives of the Ohio and Mississippi valleys. In my research, I visited most of the major depositories and found at least one firsthand reminiscence by an actual riverman everywhere I went. Of course, the stores of some archives are richer than others, and richest of all is the Indiana Historical Society's collection in Indianapolis. There one can work with twenty sets of flatboating papers, including the Atalantian journals and the papers of rivermen William Palmer Dole, Samuel Chew Madden, Manasseh Barney Slawson, and Peter W. Williams. Downstairs in the same building, the Indiana Division of the Indiana State Library also possesses several firsthand river accounts in the Dyar Cobb and Archibald Shaw collections and the Flatboat Letters of Switzerland County, Indiana.

Other libraries contain less abundant but essential manuscript sources on early American riverboating. In Marietta, Ohio, the Campus Martius Museum of the Northwest Territory holds a typescript of Miles Stacy's flatboating memoir, which proved extremely helpful. Across the river in Parkersburg, West Virginia, I found the extensive writings of merchant navigator T. C. Collins. The Ohio Historical

Society in Columbus provided keelboatman William Adams' journal and other sources, and the Fountain and Roderick Perry Papers, which include everything from diaries to bills of lading, fill two boxes in the Special Collections and Archives at the University of Kentucky Library in Lexington.

There are many lumber and log rafting materials in the Mississippi Valley, most notably at the Minnesota Historical Society in St. Paul and the State Historical Society of Wisconsin in Madison. Researchers in Madison should work with the memoirs of raftsman Stephen R. Bentley, keelboatman Thomas Forsyth, merchant James Wier, and the numerous river materials in the Draper Collection.

Far to the south, in Vicksburg, Mississippi, the Old Courthouse Museum houses merchant Ephraim Forman's papers, typescripts of the 1850 census (which included many raftsmen), and valuable city codes and wharf regulations. In Louisiana, I spent weeks gathering manuscript source materials at Louisiana State University, the New Orleans Public Library, Louisiana Historical Center (associated with the Louisiana State Museum), and Tulane University. Researchers at LSU should examine the James Earl Bradley Papers and Thomas Bolling Robertson's river travel journal. In New Orleans, a photocopy of flatboatman Henry Troth's journal is stored at the Louisiana Historical Center (the original MS is in possession of Tyrrell W. Brooke, Vienna, Virginia). The papers of Shepherd Brown and Company, which conducted much business on the Lower Mississippi, fill several boxes at the New Orleans Public Library. Finally, I made good use of river merchant John McDonogh's Papers at Tulane University.

Happily, several boatmen's reminiscences have been edited and published. I list here only those that contain substantial information about river life and commerce and that were, therefore, of great use in this work. Researchers must read Robert Leslie Jones (ed.), "Flatboating Down the Ohio and Mississippi, 1867–1873: Correspondence and Diaries of the William Devol Family of Marietta, Ohio," *Ohio State Archaeological and Historical Quarterly,* LIX (July and October, 1950), 287–309, 385–418; Donald F. Carmony (ed.), "William P. Dole: Wabash Valley Merchant and Flatboatman," *Indiana Magazine of History,* LXVII (December, 1971), 335–63; Herbert L. Roush, Sr. (ed.), *The Adventures of T. C. Collins—Boatman: Twenty-Four Years on the Western Waters, 1849–1873* (Baltimore, 1985); and John G. Stuart, "A

Journal: Remarks or Observations in a Voyage Down the Kentucky, Ohio, Mississippi Rivers etc.," *Register of the Kentucky Historical Society,* L (January, 1952), 5–25. My edition of George Forman's mid-nineteenth-century experiences as a flatboatman, raftsman, and steamboat deckhand appears as "Reminiscences of a Common Boatman," *Gateway Heritage,* V (Fall, 1984), 36–49.

Finally, researchers of lumber and log raftsmen should consult two excellent published accounts. Henry Baxter, "Rafting on the Allegheny and Ohio, 1844," *Pennsylvania Magazine of History and Biography,* LI (1927), 27–78, 143–71, 207–43, provides an all-encompassing view of antebellum lumber rafting. John Hebron Moore, "Simon Gray, Riverman: A Slave Who Was Almost Free," *Mississippi Valley Historical Review,* LIX (December, 1962), 472–84, draws on business records to depict a Natchez, Mississippi, raftsman who was also a black slave.

Published Firsthand Accounts by Nonboatmen

Having navigated the pools of archival research and the eddies of boatmen's unpublished and published memoirs, the researcher will find himself facing the broad but often shoal waters of published travelers' accounts. This body of literature constitutes both a blessing and a curse; its overly abundant writings must be weighed most carefully against one another and against other sources of information concerning rivermen. Eventually, I consulted scores of published eighteenth- and nineteenth-century travel accounts, of which the half-dozen listed here are among the most fundamental.

Because of its immense scope and excellent index, I started with Reuben Gold Thwaites (ed.), *Early Western Travels, 1748–1846* (32 vols.; Cleveland, 1904–1907). Francis Bailey, *Journal of a Tour in Unsettled Parts of North America in 1796 and 1797,* ed. Sir Jack D. L. Holmes (London, 1969) is a lucid early account by an Englishman who retained the services of two farmer flatboatmen. M. Perrin du Lac, *Travels Through the Two Louisianas and Among the Savage Nations of the Missouri . . . 1801, 1802, and 1803* (London, 1807) chronicles a Frenchman's odyssey to the frontiers of river society. Christian Schultz, an American traveler, wrote a great deal about keelboatmen in his *Travels on an*

Inland Voyage . . . in the Years 1807 and 1808 (2 vols.; 1810; rpr. Ridge-wood, N.J., 1968). The American travel writer the Reverend Timothy Flint and naturalist John James Audubon both penned works relevant to river studies. Flint's *A Condensed Geography and History of the Western States, or the Mississippi Valley* (1828; rpr. Gainesville, Fla., 1970) and Audubon's *Journal of John James Audubon Made During His Trip to New Orleans in 1820–1821,* ed. Howard Corning (Boston, 1929) contain vital observations about rivermen and their role in early American commerce and society.

Other important sources of information are the published reminiscences of those I call "river-town observers"—men and women who lived for years along the shores of the Ohio and Mississippi and who discussed riverboating in their memoirs and other published works. Included in this group are Cincinnatians Dr. Daniel Drake and James Hall, both of whom authored numerous volumes during their lifetimes. Drake's *Notices Concerning Cincinnati* (Cincinnati, 1810) and Hall's *Letters from the West* (1828; rpr. Gainesville, Fla., 1967) contain many discussions of river life. Another river-town observer was Zadok Cramer, whose river guidebooks *The Ohio and Mississippi Navigator* (Pittsburgh, 1802) and *The Navigator* (1814; rpr. Ann Arbor, 1966) were issued in many editions and constitute a treasure trove for the river historian. River scenes of a later period were painted boldly (albeit romantically) by Memphian James Dick Davis in *The History of the City of Memphis . . . [and] the "Old Times Papers"* (Memphis, 1873).

Many accounts by travelers and river-town observers exist as rare volumes in the collections of the Newberry Library in Chicago and the Huntington Library in San Marino.

Newspapers and Government Documents

Newspaper and government document collections provide profitable ports of call for any river researcher. I worked with newspapers representing all major towns that flourished on the Ohio-Mississippi trunk line during the 1763–1861 period. These publications included the Pittsburgh *Gazette, Centinel of the Northwest Territory* (Cincinnati), Louisville *Public Advertiser,* St. Paul *Daily Minnesotan,* St. Louis *Missouri Republican,* Memphis *Daily Appeal,* Vicksburg *Register,* Natchez

Daily Courier, New Orleans *Louisiana Gazette,* and *New Orleans Prices-Current and Commercial Intelligencer,* all of which are on film in their respective city and state archives. Researchers should consult helpful newspaper indexes in the libraries of the Western Pennsylvania Historical Society (Pittsburgh), Cincinnati Historical Society, State Historical Society of Missouri (Columbia), and the New Orleans Public Library. In the Minnesota Historical Society Archives, St. Paul, one can find the Works Progress Administration's "Transcripts of Minnesota Newspaper Articles, 1849–1887: Transportation Articles."

State and local court records hold much information about boatmen. A good place to start is the index to the Ste. Genevieve, Missouri, Municipal Archives, 1756–1930, on microfilm in the Joint Collection, State Historical Society of Missouri, Columbia. I also consulted criminal court records, police department reports, and police codes in the collections of Tulane University and the New Orleans Public Library. May Wilson McBee (ed.), *The Natchez Court Records, 1767–1805* (2 vols.; Greenwood, Miss., 1953) contains synopses of all early cases in the Natchez Chancery Court Archives.

City government wharf records provide another source of information. Tulane University and the New Orleans Public Library both possess nearly complete records of the New Orleans wharfmasters' "Wharfinger Reports," containing itemized lists of flatboat cargoes, crews, and tax information. The Louisiana State University Libraries possess the Works Progress Administration typescript edition of "Flatboats on the Mississippi in 1807: A Compilation of Craft Names, Marine Hospital Tax, and Cargoes Carried on Flat and Keelboats Down the Mississippi River During One Month, May 1 to May 29, in the Year 1807." Similar information can be gleaned from the WPA's edition of "Returns of Seamen for Marine Hospital Tax, Port of New Orleans, 1805 to 1833" at the Louisiana Historical Center in New Orleans.

Spain controlled Lower Mississippi commerce from 1763–1803, and Spanish government records are essential to an understanding of this subject. A good deal of material has been translated, such as the WPA's typescripts of "Dispatches of the Spanish Governors of Louisiana" in the Louisiana Historical Center. Researchers also should read the pioneering translations of the first generation of borderlands scholars: Louis Houck (ed.), *The Spanish Regime in Missouri* (New York, 1971); Lawrence Kinnaird (ed.), *Spain in the Mississippi Valley, 1765–*

1794: Translations of Materials from the Spanish Archives in the Bancroft Library (4 vols.; Washington, D.C., 1946; part of the American Historical Association's *Annual Report,* 1945); and Abraham P. Nasatir (ed.), *Before Lewis and Clark: Documents Illustrating the History of Missouri, 1785–1804* (St. Louis, 1952). Sources describing the important French role in Louisiana are interwoven with these collections as well as with the materials in the Ste. Genevieve, Missouri, Municipal Archives cited above.

Standard Secondary Works

For charting the bends and channels of broader stretches of river history, a few secondary works will prove quite valuable. My short article "Historical Works on Early American Rivermen," *Bookman's Weekly,* LXXVIII (November 24, 1986), 2141–43, serves as an introduction to this small but sturdy body of literature.

The study of nonsteam river transport began with Archer B. Hulbert's *Waterways of Westward Expansion: The Ohio River and Its Tributaries* (Cleveland, 1903) and *The Paths of Inland Commerce* (New Haven, 1921). These pioneering works, however, lack the kind of primary documentation necessary for a definitive study of American rivermen. Leland D. Baldwin's classic *The Keelboat Age on Western Waters* (Pittsburgh, 1941) filled many voids by treating for the first time the subjects of keelboat and flatboat construction, navigation techniques, and commercial patterns. Baldwin's only weakness was his chapter on the boatmen themselves, for he lacked the sources to draw a social portrait of western boatmen.

A handful of diplomatic and economic works, although not focused directly on nonsteam rivermen, are nevertheless essential for an understanding of the subject. Arthur Preston Whitaker's *The Spanish-American Frontier, 1783–1795: The Westward Movement and the Spanish Retreat in the Mississippi Valley* (1927; rpr. Lincoln, Neb., 1969) and *The Mississippi Question, 1795–1803: A Study of Trade, Politics, and Diplomacy* (1934; rpr. Gloucester, Mass., 1962) accurately depict the economic and diplomatic milieu of early flatboat and keelboat commerce. Louis C. Hunter, *Steamboats on Western Rivers: An Economic and Tech-*

nological History (Cambridge, Mass., 1949) remains a bible for any student of nineteenth-century river life.

Hunter's work has been complemented (but not supplanted) in recent years by economic historians who, among many other accomplishments, have succeeded in drawing a broad portrait of flatboat and keelboat economics based on quantitative evidence. I have relied heavily on Erik F. Haites, James Mak, and Gary M. Walton, *Western River Transportation* (Baltimore, 1975); Haites and Mak, "Ohio and Mississippi River Transportation, 1810–1860," *Explorations in Economic History,* VIII (Winter, 1970), 153–80; and Harry N. Scheiber, "The Ohio-Mississippi Flatboat Trade: Some Reconsiderations," in David M. Ellis (ed.), *The Frontier in American Development: Essays in Honor of Paul Wallace Gates* (Ithaca, 1970).

Literature and Folklore

The end of the journey is almost in sight, but the researcher of rivermen must negotiate a rugged detour down an old "false river" before sailing at last into port. No study of western boatmen can neglect the literature of the mythological boatman—the Alligator Horse.

The Mike Fink legend is the logical place to start. The literature in this field is near-complete. All of the important tales are gathered and interpreted in Walter Blair and Franklin J. Meine (eds.), *Half-Horse, Half-Alligator: The Growth of the Mike Fink Legend* (Chicago, 1956). Their *Mike Fink, King of the Mississippi Keelboatmen* (1933; rpr. Westport, Conn., 1971) is a folkloric biography with a bibliography citing original sources. I have related and interpreted the major tales in my "Sired by a Hurricane: Mike Fink, Western Boatmen, and the Myth of the Alligator Horse," *Arizona and the West,* XXVII (Autumn, 1985), 237–52.

The problems inherent in gathering and interpreting literary and folkloric accounts of rivermen can be minimized by following a well-founded methodology. Students should read Richard M. Dorson (ed.), *Handbook of American Folklore* (Bloomington, 1983), *American Folklore and the Historian* (Chicago, 1971), and *America in Legend: Folklore from the Colonial Period to the Present* (New York, 1973) to learn how printed tales, superstitions, speech, songs, and other folkways fit into the historical milieu. Older but still solid studies of the Alligator Horse in literature are Bernard DeVoto, *Mark Twain's America* (1932; rpr. Boston, 1967) and Constance Rourke, *American Humor: A Study of the National Character* (1931; rpr. New York, 1959).

Although they do not focus on rivermen per se, several other works have shaped my attitudes and perceptions of the mythological dimensions of western folk heroes. Most important is Henry Nash Smith's classic *Virgin Land: The American West as Symbol and Myth* (New York, 1950). Arthur K. Moore investigates the Alligator Horse at great length in *The Frontier Mind* (New York, 1963), and John William Ward and Marvin Meyers interpret the problem in the Jacksonian context in, respectively, *Andrew Jackson, Symbol For An Age* (1955; rpr. New York, 1968) and *The Jacksonian Persuasion: Politics and Belief* (Stanford, 1957), books that remain giants in the field. Finally, I have read and reread a fine little essay by Richard E. Oglesby, "The Western Boatman: Half Horse, Half Myth," in John Francis McDermott (ed.), *Travelers on Western Waters* (Urbana, 1970), 252–66.

Putting behind him the shadowy backwaters where the Alligator Horse lives, the river researcher can return to the main channel under the steady hand of Frederick Jackson Turner. Turner's essay "The Significance of the Frontier in American History," ed. Harold P. Simonson (New York, 1966), was first published nearly a hundred years ago and continues to influence historical writing. There can be no better companion, over the last few miles to port, for the weary navigator who wishes to lean back on the "lazy board" and contemplate the meaning of all that he has seen.

Index